Workbook

American Red Cross
Child Care Course
Health and Safety Units

Produced in cooperation with

American Academy
of Pediatrics

ISBN: 0-86536-183-5

Acknowledgments

This 1992 edition of the *American Red Cross Child Care Course Health and Safety Units* workbook includes the information formerly found in the First Aid Cards, which were originally a separate item. The information is now at the back of this book in the section called First Aid Guides. Also, the Infant and Child First Aid Unit in this edition was revised to make the information more consistent with other Red Cross first aid courses.

Members of the 1990 American Red Cross Child Care Course instructional design and development team included Jessica Bernstein, M.P.H.; Robert Dirmeyer: Iris Graham; Alexandra G. Greeley; Cindy Green, M.P.H.; Carol Hunter-Geboy, Ph.D.; Alice D. Lowe; Pamela B. Mangu, M.A.; Lynda Ramsey; and Bruce Spitz. Assistance was provided by Jeanne P. Luschin, M.B.A.; Lawrence D. Newell, Ed.D.; Cynthia Vlasich, R.N.; S. Elizabeth White, M.A.Ed.; and the Office of Health and Safety Operations.

Special technical assistance was provided by Susan Aronson, M.D., F.A.A.P., Hahnemann University.

Technical advice was provided by:

Jeanie Snodgrass Almo, R.N., M.S.N.

Robert G. Bruce, Ph.D.

Valerie Williams Drake, M.A.

Patricia D. Fosarelli, M.D., The Johns Hopkins Children's Center

Andrea Carlson Gielen, Sc.D., The Johns Hopkins University School of Hygiene and Public Health

Murray L. Katcher, M.D., Ph.D., State of Wisconsin Division of Health

Janet Brown McCracken, M.Ed.

Andrew McGuire, The Trauma Foundation at San Francisco General Hospital

Suzanne M. Randolph, Ph.D., University of Maryland

Patricia Riley, C.N.M., M.P.H., U.S. Public Health Service

Frederick Rivara, M.D., University of Washington

Anita Sandretto, M.P.H., The University of Michigan School of Public Health

RoseAnn Soloway, R.N., M.S.Ed., C.S.P.I., National Capital Poison Center, Georgetown University Hospital

John A. Steward, R.S., M.P.H., Centers for Disease Control

Stephen Teret, J.D., M.P.H., The Johns Hopkins University School of Hygiene and Public Health

Daniel W. Webster, M.P.H., The Johns Hopkins University School of Hygiene and Public Health

Mark D. Widome, M.D., M.P.H., Pennsylvania State University College of Medicine

Thanks to the National Association for the Education of Young Children, Washington, D.C., for the use of their materials.

Thanks to SCIPP (Statewide Comprehensive Injury Prevention Program), Massachusetts Department of Public Health, for the use of their materials.

Special thanks to selected members of the American Academy of Pediatrics for reviewing and refining the materials.

These manuscripts were reviewed by the National Academy of Sciences Institute of Medicine, Committee to Advise the American National Red Cross.

Funding for this project was provided in part by the U.S. Department of the Army, contract number MDA903-87-C-0736.

Field representatives providing advice and guidance through the American Red Cross Child Care Course Advisory Committee included:

Lin Arnette, Virginia Capital Chapter, Richmond, Va.

Carolyn Branson, R.N., Eastern Operations Headquarters, Alexandria, Va.

William Calhoun, M.A., Field Service Manager, Midwestern Operations Headquarters

Julianne Crevatin, M.P.H., Seattle-King County Chapter, Seattle, Wash.

Carolyn Elliott, Bluegrass Area Chapter, Lexington, Ky.

Angie Turner-Elliott, R.N., Hawkeye Chapter, Waterloo, Iowa

Deborah MacSwain, American Red Cross, Air Force Academy Station, Peterson Air Force Base, Colorado Springs, Colo.

C. Ray McLain, R.N., M.S.N., Assistant Professor, Auburn University at Montgomery, Montgomery, Ala.

Joan Manning, M.P.H., Heartland Chapter, Omaha, Nebr.

Sandra Nation, M.Ed., U.S. Department of the Army Child Development Services, Washington, D.C.

Josephine Otis, R.N., B.S.N., Metropolitan Atlanta Chapter, Atlanta, Ga.

Carol Weis, M.S., Nashville Area Chapter, Nashville, Tenn.

Acknowledgments

Red Cross chapters that participated in field tests included:

East Bay Chapter
Oakland, Calif.

Hawkeye Chapter
Waterloo, Iowa

Metropolitan Atlanta Chapter
Atlanta, Ga.

American Red Cross of Massachusetts Bay
Boston, Mass.

Nashville Area Chapter
Nashville, Tenn.

Seattle-King County Chapter
Seattle, Wash.

American Red Cross, Fort Lewis, Wash.

American Red Cross, Fort Carson, Colo.

American Red Cross, Letterman Army Medical Center,
Presidio of San Francisco, Calif.

Contents

First Aid Guides

About the American Red Cross Child Care Course

The American Red Cross has developed the Child Care Course to improve the quality of child care nationwide by training caregivers in health, safety, and child development. Because more women with children have entered the paid labor force, the population of children requiring child care has expanded rapidly and will continue to expand. This has created a critical shortage of high-quality child care in the United States. The quality is directly affected both by the training and by the relevant experience of the child care staff. Millions of child care workers are employed in the United States, but many of these caregivers have received little or no training. The American Red Cross Child Care Course is being delivered through the Red Cross chapters to train all caregivers, whether they are based in centers or in homes.

The American Red Cross Child Care Course consists of the following 7 units:

Health and Safety Units
A. Preventing Childhood Injuries
B. Infant and Child First Aid
C. Preventing Infectious Diseases
D. Caring for Ill Children

Child Development Units
E. Learning About Child Development
F. Communicating With Children and Parents
G. Recognizing and Reporting Child Abuse

The Health and Safety Units are included in this workbook. In addition to the 7 units of the Child Care Course, the Red Cross encourages all caregivers to take the American Red Cross CPR: Infant and Child course.

American Red Cross Child Care Course: Preventing Childhood Injuries

Contents

About the Preventing Childhood Injuries Unit

Injuries are the number one killer of children over 9 months old in the United States. Each year thousands of children in the United States are killed and tens of thousands more are seriously hurt by injuries. Some of these injuries happen because adults do not take preventive steps to protect youngsters. Infants and young children, in particular, need special protection.

This unit will teach you how to be a role model for safety, to protect children by removing dangers, and to teach parents and children safety habits and rules. You can prevent injuries by making your child care setting a safer place for children.

What You Will Learn

This unit will teach you—
1. The connection between a child's age and the kinds of injuries he or she may have.
2. How to use the General Safety Rules for the child care setting.
3. How to act as role model, protector, and teacher at all times.
4. How to use a Safety Checklist to identify hazards.
5. How to develop a Plans for Change sheet for correcting hazards in the child care setting.
6. How to reduce the risk of injuries to infants and children in the child care setting, in vehicles, and at playgrounds.

Further Information

For further information about preventing childhood injuries, write the American Academy of Pediatrics, P.O. Box 927, Elk Grove Village, IL 60009-0927; the Center for Environmental Health and Injury Control, Centers for Disease Control, 1600 Clifton Rd., NE, Atlanta, GA 30333; the National Center for Education in Maternal and Child Health, 38th & R Sts., NW, Washington, DC 20057; the American Public Health Association, Child Care Project, 1015 15th St., NW, Washington, DC 20005; or the Consumer Product Safety Commission, Washington, DC 20207.

Activity 1
Orientation

Objective

After you have finished this activity, you will be able to do the following:

1. Tell the unit requirements

Lessons

- Your instructor will discuss the unit with you and what you must do to pass it. The unit requirements are—
  - Satisfactory performance on the test—80 percent or higher (or 20 correct answers).
  - Attendance of the class for the entire unit.
- You will review the contents of the workbook.

Preventing Childhood Injuries Unit Agenda

Activity	Topic
1	Orientation
2	Introductions
3	The Caregiver as Role Model, Protector, and Teacher
4	Child Age and Injury
5	*Preventing Childhood Injuries* Video
6	General Safety Rules
Break	
7	Acting as Role Model, Protector, and Teacher
8	Checking Safety
9	Hazard Hunt
10	Plans for Change
11	Test and Unit Evaluation

Activity 2
Introductions

Objectives

After you have finished this activity, you will be able to do the following:

1. Use the All About You sheet to tell the group about yourself
2. Tell why you are taking this unit
3. Tell about any previous training you have had in preventing injuries

Lesson

- Fill out the All About You sheet. The sheet is on the next page.

All About You

Fill in the blanks.

1. What is your name? _____

2. Where do you work? _____

3. What is your job there? _____

4. How old are the children in your group? _____

5. Why are you taking this unit? _____

6. What do you hope to learn? _____

_____

_____

Activity 3
The Caregiver as Role Model, Protector, and Teacher

Learning Objectives

After you have finished this activity, you will be able to do the following:
1. Name 3 roles you can play to make your child care setting safer for children
2. Use the Plans for Change sheet during the rest of the class
3. Put your Plans for Change into practice in the child care setting

Role model

Protector

Lessons

- As a caregiver, you must learn to act as role model, protector, and teacher. This helps you make any child care setting safer.
  - As a role model, you set a good example for children by practicing safety.
  - As a protector, you perform a daily check to remove hazards from the child care setting to prevent burns, choking, poisoning, and other types of injuries. As a protector, you should always keep an Emergency Telephone Guide by your telephone. Turn to and read Appendix A, Emergency Telephone Guide.
  - As a teacher, you teach parents, children, and other caregivers about safety practices.
- You will see a Plans for Change sheet on page A-9. Remove the sheet from the book. When you think of a way to make your child care setting safer, write your idea on this sheet. You will talk about your ideas with the other participants in a later activity.

Teacher

Plans for Change

When making Plans for Change, think about how you can be role
model, protector, and teacher. Remove this sheet from your
workbook.

-1 Cover the outlet on all electrical

Activity 4
Child Age and Injury

Learning Objective

After you have finished this activity, you will be able to do the following:

1. State the connection between a child's age and the kinds of injuries he or she may have

Lessons

- The age of a child tells you what type of injury the child may have. For example, a 9-month-old baby may put small toys in her mouth, and the toys could choke her. A 2-year-old is more likely than an infant to eat a poisonous plant. A 5-year-old child can get hurt while riding a bicycle or tricycle.
- Car-related injuries are the most common in all age groups. *Car-related injuries* means those injuries that happen to children when they are riding in a car (passenger injuries) or when they are walking, or riding bikes, and get hit by a car (pedestrian injuries). Other frequent childhood injuries include falls, poisoning, burns, choking, and drowning.
- Knowing which injuries are most common in children of different ages will help you make your child care setting safer.

Activity 5
Preventing Childhood Injuries Video

Lesson

- Watch the video.

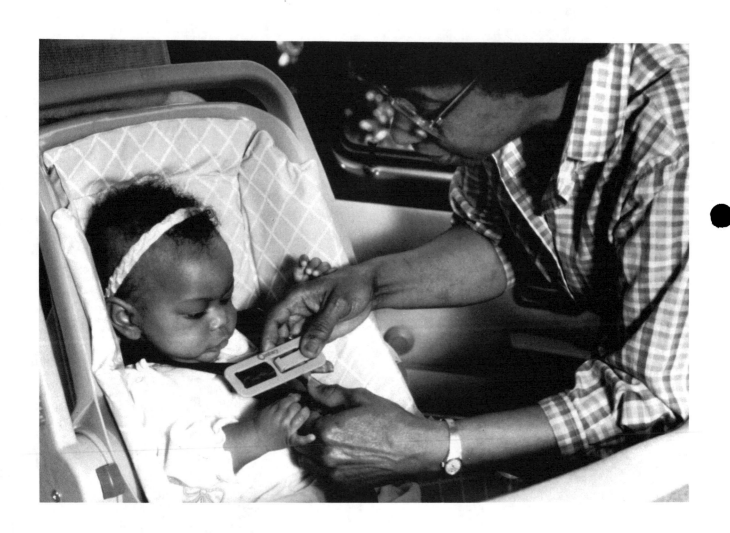

Activity 6
General Safety Rules

Learning Objectives

After you have finished this activity, you will be able to do the following:
1. Discuss the General Safety Rules
2. Pick out hazards that you will correct in your child care setting
3. Use your Plans for Change sheet

Lesson

• Read the General Safety Rules below. For each rule, think about what you can change in your child care setting to follow that rule. Add your ideas to your Plans for Change sheet.

General Safety Rules
Follow these General Safety Rules to protect the children you care for:
1. Use safe playgrounds.

2. Use gates on stairs.

3. Supervise children in or near water, *always*.

4. Check for fire and burn dangers.

5. Buckle up.

6. Stop children from darting into the street.

7. Keep plastic bags, cords, and small objects away from young children.

8. Never keep guns in any child care setting.

9. Call the Poison Control Center if you think a child has been poisoned.

10. Post emergency numbers next to your telephone.

Take a closer look at these rules to see what they mean.

1. **Use safe playgrounds.**

    Most playground injuries happen when children fall off equipment. To help prevent injuries, use playgrounds where the surface under the play equipment is covered with soft, loose materials that cushion children when they fall. Sand, wood chips, and pea gravel are the most common cushioning materials; sand probably absorbs impact the best. These materials must be properly maintained—debris must be removed and surfaces must be raked to keep them loose. (Manufactured energy-absorptive surfaces, which resemble large cushioned mats, are also good and are being used in some new playgrounds. These new playground surfaces must meet standards set by an organization called ASTM.) Make sure the play equipment is age appropriate and in good shape. Teach children how to use equipment safely.

2. Use gates on stairs.

Put gates on the tops and bottoms of stairs. Keep gates closed to help prevent injuries from falls. Make sure that the holes in the gates are small enough so a child's head can't fit through. Do not use accordian-type gates.

3. Supervise children in or near water, *always.*

Children can drown in very small amounts of water. An adult must always supervise young children in or near a bathtub or pool or near a toilet. Check with your Red Cross chapter for information on water safety courses for children.

4. **Check for fire and burn dangers.**
   The skin of an infant or child is much thinner than an adult's and can be burned very easily. Prevent severe hot water burns by setting your hot water heater so that the water is between 120 degrees and 130 degrees Fahrenheit or lower. The lower the water temperature, the safer it is for young children. Review Appendix F for other ways to prevent burns from hot liquids.

   - Develop a fire escape plan and practice it often. Your local fire department can help you develop the plan.
   - Keep a fire extinguisher in your child care setting. Check the label to make sure that you have an ABC-type extinguisher. This works on any kind of fire. In the kitchen, mount it securely on a wall near the stove.
   - Make sure you have smoke detectors in your child care setting. Check with your local fire department to see exactly how many you must have and where you should put them. Replace the batteries at least once a year. See Appendix E for more information on smoke detectors.

5. Buckle up.

Infants and young children must always be buckled up when riding in any car, bus, or van. Choose a federally approved car seat. There are many types of car seats. You must use them according to the manufacturer's instructions. Know how to buckle the seat into the car and how to buckle the child into the seat. In many communities, car seats can be borrowed through loaner programs. Most states have "buckle-up" laws. Know and follow the law.

6. Stop children from darting into the street.

Teach children that they must always hold hands while crossing the street. Use lights and crosswalks if possible. Teach young children never to dart out between parked cars. Teach children to cross streets only with an adult. Begin to teach them to look left-right-left before crossing.

7. Keep plastic bags, cords, and small objects away from young children.

Children can choke on small objects that can fit all the way into their mouth. Small pieces of food, such as nuts, raw vegetables, hard candies, hot dogs, popcorn, and grapes, can also cause choking. Keep all toys with small removable parts, or parts that can easily break off, away from young children. Balloons and hanging cords from curtains or blinds are also dangerous.

8. **Never keep guns in any child care setting.**
   Every day at least one child is killed by a gun in the United States, and many other children are seriously hurt. Guns are dangerous and must not be kept in the child care setting.

9. **Call the Poison Control Center if you think a child has been poisoned.**
   Children can be poisoned by many things, such as medicines, cleaning products, and plants. Store all poisons in a locked place out of the reach of children. If you think a child has been poisoned, call the Poison Control Center right away. Follow their directions exactly. If your child care setting's policy permits, keep an unexpired bottle of syrup of ipecac in a locked place. Use it only if the Poison Control Center tells you to use it to make a child vomit.

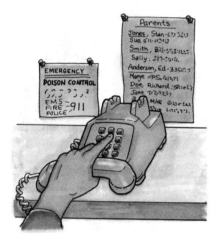

10. **Post emergency numbers next to your telephone.**
    This list should include the following numbers:
    - Emergency medical services (EMS) system
    - Fire department
    - Police department
    - Poison Control Center

    In addition, keep an *updated* list of the following numbers for each child by each telephone:
    - Numbers where each parent can be reached during the hours the child is in your care
    - The child's doctor or clinic
    - A close neighbor of the child
    - For additional safety information, turn to the following:
      - Appendix B, Dangerous Art Materials and Their Substitutes
      - Appendix C, About Poisonous Plants
      - Appendix D, Toy Safety
      - Appendix E, Smoke Detectors
      - Appendix F, Preventing Hot-Liquid Burns
      - Appendix G, Fires

Activity 7
Acting as Role Model, Protector, and Teacher

Learning Objective

After you have finished this activity, you will be able to do the following:

1. Reduce the risk of injuries in the child care setting

Lessons

- The instructor will ask you to join a group, and then will assign each group a Safety Problem to read and to discuss. The problem is a realistic situation in which you would have to act as role model, protector, and teacher to prevent injuries. Your group will develop safety solutions using some of the ideas you have learned in this course and other ideas that you or your group may have. A note taker from your group will write the group's ideas on the flip chart. Then your group will discuss the problem and your safety ideas with the rest of the group.
- Add new ideas to your Plans for Change sheet.

Safety Problems

Problem 1—Buckle Up

A mother drives up to the child care setting to pick up her 2-year-old. The car seat is on the floor of the back seat. The parent says she is in a hurry to pick up her older children at the gym. She says that it is only a short distance away. As she gets ready to drive off, you notice that she has not put the young child in the car seat and that she has not buckled her own seat belt.

Problem 2—Darting

The caregiver takes a group of 4 children on a walking field trip to the park. The oldest, a 5-year-old boy, is bouncing a ball that rolls into the street between 2 parked cars. A 2-year-old boy starts to chase after the ball and is stopped by the caregiver and the 5-year-old just before darting into the street to get the ball.

Problem 3—Burns

One evening a parent stops by to pick up her infant from the caregiver. She decides to drink a cup of coffee and pours a cup from the coffeepot, which is on the back of the stove, out of the reach of children. She is holding her infant while drinking the coffee. A toddler runs into the kitchen and nearly bumps into her.

Problem 4—Playground

The caregiver has taken 4 children to a different playground because their regular one has been closed for repairs. This is the only other playground within walking distance of the child care setting. The children rush onto the climbers before the caregiver notices that the playground covering under the climbers is exposed concrete. All the wood chips have been kicked away.

Activity 8
Checking Safety

Learning Objectives

After you have finished this activity, you will be able to do the
following:
1. Use the Safety Checklist and the Fix-It-Quick Sheet
2. Fill out an injury report form and an injury log

Lessons

- The instructor will show you how to use the sample of the
  Safety Checklist and the Fix-It-Quick Sheet. Turn to Appendix
  H, the Safety Checklist and the Fix-It-Quick Sheet. Use this
  longer version to perform a safety check at your child care
  setting.
- You must fill out an injury report form and place it in the file
  of the injured person when an injury occurs in the child care
  setting. You must also get the signature of an injured child's
  parent and give the parent a copy of the form. Please turn to
  and read the Injury Report Form on page A-23. You should use
  one like this in your child care setting.
- You must also fill out an injury log as a record when an injury
  occurs in the child care setting. Please turn to and read the
  Injury Log on page A-24. You should use one like this in your
  child care setting.

(Sample)
Safety Checklist
and Fix-It-Quick Sheet

General Indoor Areas

Yes **No**

☒ ☐ Windows cannot be opened more than 6 inches from
       the bottom.

☒ ☐ Safety covers are on all electrical outlets. —

Fix-It-Quick Sheet

Name of Safety Checker: _____

Date of Safety Check: _____/_____/_____/

1 Area Observed	**2** Risky Behavior, Hazard, or Comments	**3** Correction and Date Made

Injury Report Form

Complete within 24 hours of injury. For an injured child, obtain the signature of a parent or legal guardian. File the completed form in the injured child's (or injured adult's) record. Give a copy (or a carbon copy) of the child's form to the parent.

Name of injured _____ Age _____

Date of injury_____ Time of injury_____a.m./p.m.

Witness(es) _____

_____

Where injury happened _____

_____

Any equipment or products involved _____

_____

_____

Name of parent notified_____

Time notified _____a.m./p.m.   Notified by _____

Description of injury and how it happened _____

_____

_____

_____

_____

Who gave first aid and what did they do _____

_____

_____

_____

First aid given by medical personnel, telling who, what, when, and where_____

_____

_____

_____

Follow-up plan for the injured _____

_____

_____

_____

Injury prevention steps taken _____

_____

_____

Caregiver completing form _____

Date form completed _____ Parent's signature _____

This page may be duplicated by individuals and entities for noncommercial purposes.

Injury Log

When did the injury happen?		Staff member reporting the injury.	Name of the injured child.	How old is the injured child?
Date	Time			
What happened to cause the injury?		Where did it happen?	What needs to be done so it won't happen again?	When was this done?
				Date

When did the injury happen?		Staff member reporting the injury.	Name of the injured child.	How old is the injured child?
Date	Time			
What happened to cause the injury?		Where did it happen?	What needs to be done so it won't happen again?	When was this done?
				Date

When did the injury happen?		Staff member reporting the injury.	Name of the injured child.	How old is the injured child?
Date	Time			
What happened to cause the injury?		Where did it happen?	What needs to be done so it won't happen again?	When was this done?
				Date

Activity 9
Hazard Hunt

Learning Objectives

After you have finished this lesson, you will be able to do the following:
1. Find at least 2 hazards in each video scene
2. Tell how to correct hazards to help prevent injuries

Lessons

- Watch the video. For each scene, you will have time to find the hazards and to write down your answers. You will have time for discussion when the instructor replays the video. You will score your sheet. Tell the instructor your score. The 2 highest scores win.
- Add your ideas to your Plans for Change sheet.

Hazard Hunt Answers

Scene 1 _____   Scene 6 _____

_____   _____

_____   _____

_____   _____

Scene 2 _____   Scene 7 _____

_____   _____

_____   _____

_____   _____

Scene 3 _____   Scene 8 _____

_____   _____

_____   _____

_____   _____

Scene 4 _____   Scene 9 _____

_____   _____

_____   _____

_____   _____

Scene 5 _____   Scene 10 _____

_____   _____

_____   _____

_____   _____

Total Score _____

Activity 10
Plans for Change

Learning Objectives

After you have finished this activity, you will be able to do the following:
1. Share your Plans for Change with the other participants
2. Discuss Appendix I, Safety Calendar

Lessons

- You will tell the group about one idea from your Plans for Change sheet. The instructor will add your idea to the flip chart.
- Turn to Appendix I, Safety Calendar. This will help you make plans to change and improve the safety rules you already follow. It will also remind you of safety habits you can practice all year long to protect children from injuries. Your instructor will go over the Safety Calendar with you.

Activity 11
Test and Unit Evaluation

Objective

After you have finished this activity, you will be able to do the following:
1. Complete the test

Lessons

- The test that the instructor will give you has 25 questions about what you learned in this class. Answer the questions on the answer sheet. You must score 80 percent or higher (or answer 20 or more questions correctly) to pass this unit.
- Your instructor will also give you a unit evaluation sheet. Please tell us what you thought of this unit by filling out this sheet and returning it to the instructor.
- Thank you for your participation in the American Red Cross Child Care Course. By taking all of the units of the Child Care Course, you are showing your commitment to giving the best possible child care. Now that you understand the information and skills presented, you will be able to put your caring and concern for children into action.

Appendixes

Emergency Telephone Guide

Keep a copy of this list in your first aid kit and posted by every phone.

Emergency Telephone Numbers

Date completed _____

Emergency medical services (EMS) system _____

Fire _____   Police _____

Poison Control Center _____   Ambulance _____

Name, address, and phone number of nearest medical facility _____

_____

_____

Taxi _____

Other important numbers _____

_____

Health consultant's name and number _____

Be ready to provide the following information:

1. Location of child—

   Street address and apt. or room number _____

   City _____

   Directions (cross streets, landmarks, etc.) _____

   _____

2. Telephone number you are calling from _____

3. Caller's name _____

4. What happened _____

5. Number and ages of children injured _____

6. Condition of child (children) _____

7. Help (first aid) given _____

Note: Let the EMS dispatcher hang up before you do.

Dangerous Art Materials and Their Substitutes

Dangerous Art Materials

Substitutes

Clay in dry form. Powdered clay, which is easily inhaled, contains free silica and possibly asbestos. Do not sand dry clay pieces or do other dust-producing activities.

Order talc-free, premixed clay (for example, an approved white clay). Wet mop or sponge surfaces thoroughly after using clay.

Cold water, fiber-reactive dyes, or other commercial dyes

Use vegetable and plant dyes (for example, onionskins, tea, flowers), and food dyes.

Instant papier-mâchés (create inhalable dust and some may contain asbestos fibers, lead from pigments in colored printing inks, etc.)

Make papier-mâché from black and white newspaper and library or white paste, or use approved papier-mâchés.

Powdered tempera colors create inhalable dust

Use approved liquid paints or paints the teacher mixes ahead of time.

Pastels, chalks, or dry markers that create dust

Use crayons, oil pastels, or approved dustless chalks.

Solvents (for example, turpentine, shellac, toluene, rubber cement thinner) and solvent-containing materials (solvent-based inks, alkyd paints, rubber cement)

Use water-based products only.

Aerosol sprays

Use water-based paints with brushes or spatter techniques.

Epoxy, instant glue, airplane glue, or other solvent-based adhesives

Use white glue, school paste, and preservative-free wheat paste.

Permanent felt-tip markers, which may contain toluene or other toxic solvents

Use only water-based markers.

Casting plaster (creates dust, and casting hands and body parts has resulted in serious burns)

Caregiver can mix plaster in a separate ventilated area or outdoors for plaster casting. Never cast hands or other body parts in plaster.

Scented felt-tip markers. These teach children bad habits about eating and sniffing art materials.

Use unscented markers.

Some art and craft projects are not suitable for the child care setting. These include airbrushing, ceramic glazing, silk screening or other similar printing techniques, stained glass projects, metal casting or filing, acid etching, enameling, photo developing, soldering, and wood burning.

Adapted from *Data Sheet—Art Materials: Recommendations for Children Under 12,* Center for Safety in the Arts, New York, New York, 1990. Used with permission.

About Poisonous Plants

Tips About Poisonous Plants

- Keep **all** plants away from small children. Teach children never to eat unknown plants.
- Different parts of plants are poisonous. Phone the Poison Control Center before treating a child who has eaten a plant. Follow their directions. Keep an unexpired bottle of syrup of ipecac in a locked place if your policy allows. Use it only if the Poison Control Center tells you to make a child vomit.

Poisonous Plants (not a complete list)

Flower Garden Plants

Autumn Crocus
Bleeding Heart
Chrysanthemum
Daffodil
Foxglove
Hyacinth
Iris
Jonquil
Lily of the Valley
Morning Glory
Narcissus

House Plants

Bird of Paradise
Castor Bean
Dumbcane (Dieffenbachia)
English Ivy
Holly
Jequirty Bean (Rosary Pea)
Jerusalem Cherry
Mistletoe
Mother-in-Law
Oleander
Philodendron
Rhododendron

Trees and Shrubs

Black Locust
Boxwood
Elderberry
English Yew
Horse Chestnut
Oak Tree

Vegetable Garden Plants

Sprouts and green parts of potato
Rhubarb leaves
Green parts of tomato

Wild Plants

Bittersweet
Buttercups
Jack-in-the-Pulpit
Jimson Weed
Mushroom (certain ones)
Nightshade
Poison Hemlock
Poison Ivy, Oak, Sumac
Skunk Cabbage

Toy Safety

Toys should be fun and also should help children learn. But some toys can harm children, such as toys that are poorly designed, toys that are not age-appropriate, toys that are used incorrectly, or toys that are broken or worn out. Follow these rules to keep children playing safely and happily:

1. **Give children age-appropriate toys.** For example, if a toy is labeled "for children ages 3 and older," never give it to a child under age 3. It could have small parts or sharp pieces that are dangerous to younger children.

2. **Children who ride bicycles or who are passengers on a bicycle should wear helmets.**

3. **Keep any toy with small parts** (parts that can fit completely into the mouth) **away from children** under age 3 and away from older children who still put toys in their mouths. Children might choke on such toys.

4. **Keep toys made with glass or breakable plastic away from children.**

5. **Deflated or broken balloons are dangerous.** They can suffocate children. Keep balloons away from young children.

6. **If a child uses a riding toy, keep him or her away from stairs, porches, cars, and pools.**

7. **Make sure toy chests have air holes and a lid support or have no lid.** A lid that slams shut could cause head injuries or suffocation.

8. **Check children's toys for the following hazards:**
   - Sharp points, jagged edges, and rough surfaces
   - Small, detachable parts that can be swallowed or stuck in the throat, nose, or ears
   - Cords or strings longer than 12 inches on pull toys
   - Nuts, bolts, and clamps that are loose
   - Very loud noises that can damage hearing
   - Parts that can fly off and harm eyes or hurt others
   - Battery toys with frayed or loose wires. Any electrical wiring should be labeled "UL approved"

Smoke Detectors

A smoke detector in working condition will give you enough warning time to escape a burning building.

In centers, smoke detectors should be placed according to recommendations made by the fire department.

In the family day care home, smoke detectors should be placed on the ceiling outside the sleeping areas, at the top of stairs on floors where bedrooms are located, and at the top of basement stairs. You may want to ask a representative of your local fire department to recommend where to place smoke detectors.

Smoke detectors can save lives only if they are working properly. Be sure to replace batteries at least once a year. Choose a day that's easy to remember, such as your birthday or a special holiday. Never remove smoke detector batteries to use in toys, radios, etc. A smoke detector will not protect you if the batteries are removed.

Note: If a smoke detector goes off from cooking fumes, move it to a better spot and reconnect it right away.

Preventing Hot-Liquid Burns

Scald burns from hot liquids, grease, and bathwater can be painful and very serious. Many scalds happen to toddlers who are beginning to walk, climb, and reach.

To prevent burns in the kitchen—

1. Keep hot foods and drinks away from the edge of tables and counters. Don't leave them on a tablecloth that a child can grab.
2. Put an infant in a safe place before you pick up something hot. You can't hold both safely.
3. Keep children in a safe place while you are cooking. Teach them to keep away from the "danger zone" in front of the stove. Turn pot handles toward the back of the stove where a child can't reach easily.
4. Test hot food, especially bottles, before feeding children. Do not use a microwave oven to heat infant foods and bottles.

To prevent burns in the bathroom—

1. Measure the temperature of your hot tap water (let it run for 3 minutes) with a meat, candy, or microwave thermometer. For safety, set your hot water heater so that the temperature is between 120 degrees and 130 degrees Fahrenheit or lower. The lower the water temperature, the safer it is for young children.
2. Check the water before placing any child in the tub. A child's skin is more tender than an adult's and burns more easily in hot water.
3. Watch a child during bath time. Don't leave a child alone ever, not even to answer the phone or the door. Children like the fun of running water and may be burned if they turn on the faucet themselves. Adult supervision also helps prevent drowning.

Fires

Stop, Drop, Roll, and Cool

Young children can save their own lives by dropping and rolling when their clothes catch fire. Teach children age 3 or older to Stop, Drop, Roll, and Cool.

1. **Stop.** Stop where you are—do not run.

2. **Drop.** Drop to the ground or to the floor and cover your face with your hands.

3. **Roll.** Roll to put out the flames.

4. **Cool.** Cool the burn right away with water only.

5. **Phone EMS.**

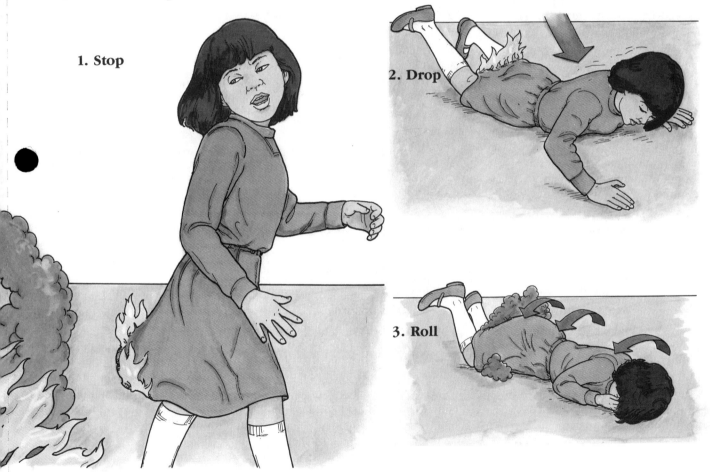

1. Stop

2. Drop

3. Roll

Space Heaters

Heating devices that are incorrectly placed or poorly maintained can cause serious fires, injuries, and deaths. All heaters must have a screen or other barrier around them. Do not use free-standing space heaters.

Safety Checklist and Fix-It-Quick Sheet

Safety Checks

1. Inspect the child care setting, including outdoor play areas, for each item on the following Safety Checklist. If you cannot find each item, ask the person in charge to help you.
2. If you find a risky behavior or hazard, note the area where you observed it in column 1 of the Fix-It-Quick Sheet at the end of the Safety Checklist.
3. Write down in Column 2 the hazard or risky behavior and any added comments.
4. Place the Fix-It-Quick Sheet in a place to remind you to correct hazards and risky behaviors, or give it to the person in charge.
5. In Column 3, write down the correction and the date when it was made.

General Indoor Areas

Yes	No	
☑	☐	Guns are not kept in the child care setting.
☐	☐	Floors are smooth and have nonskid surfaces. Rugs are skid-proof.
☐	☐	Doors to places that children can enter, such as bathrooms, can be easily opened from the outside by a child or by an adult.
☐	☐	Doors in children's areas have see-through panes so children are visible to anyone opening the door.
☐	☐	Doors have slow closing devices and/or rubber gaskets on the edges to prevent finger pinching.
☐	☐	Glass doors and full-length windows have decals on them that are at the eye levels of both children and adults.
☐	☐	Windows cannot be opened more than 6 inches from the bottom.
☐	☐	All windows have closed, permanent screens.
☐	☐	Bottom windows are lockable.
☐	☐	Walls and ceilings have no peeling paint and no cracked or falling plaster.
☐	☐	The child care setting is free of toxic or lead paint and of crumbly asbestos.
☐	☐	Safety covers are on all electrical outlets.
☐	☐	Electrical cords are out of children's reach. Electrical cords are placed away from doorways and traffic paths.
☐	☐	Covers or guards for fans have openings small enough to keep fingers out.
☐	☐	Free-standing space heaters are not used.
☐	☐	Pipes, radiators, fireplaces, wood burning stoves, and other hot surfaces cannot be reached by children or are covered to prevent burns.
☐	☐	Nobody smokes or has lighted cigarettes, matches, or lighters around children.
☐	☐	Tap water temperature is 120 degrees to 130 degrees Fahrenheit or lower.

Adapted from *Healthy Young Children: A Manual for Programs,* with the permission of the National Association for the Education of Young People, Washington, D.C.

General Indoor Areas (continued)

☐ ☐ Trash is covered at all times and is stored away from heaters or other heat sources.

☐ ☐ Drawers are closed to prevent tripping or bumps.

☐ ☐ Sharp furniture edges are cushioned with cotton and masking tape or with commercial corner guards.

☐ ☐ Emergency lighting equipment works.

☐ ☐ Regular lighting is bright enough for good visibility in each room.

☐ ☐ Enough staff members are always present to exit with children safely and quickly in an emergency.

☐ ☐ All adults can easily view all areas used by children.

☐ ☐ Pets are free from disease, are immunized as appropriate, and are maintained in a sanitary manner.

☐ ☐ Poisonous plants are not present either indoors or outdoors in the child care areas.

☐ ☐ All adult handbags are stored out of children's reach.

☐ ☐ All poisons and other dangerous items are stored in locked cabinets out of children's reach. This includes medicines, paints, cleansers, mothballs, etc.

☐ ☐ Pesticides are applied only to surfaces that children cannot reach and surfaces not in direct contact with food.

☐ ☐ A certified pest control operator applies pesticides while observed by a caregiver.

☐ ☐ Cots are placed in such a way that walkways are clear for emergencies.

☐ ☐ Children are never left alone in infant seats on tables or other high surfaces.

☐ ☐ Teaching aids such as projectors are put away when not in use.

Toys and Equipment

Yes No

☐ ☐ Toys and play equipment have no sharp edges or points, small parts, pinch points, chipped paint, splinters, or loose nuts or bolts.

☐ ☐ All toys are painted with lead-free paint.

☐ ☐ Toys are put away when not in use.

☐ ☐ Toys that are mouthed are washed after use.

☐ ☐ Children are not permitted to play with any type of plastic bag or balloon.

☐ ☐ Toys are too large to fit completely into a child's mouth and have no small, detachable parts to cause choking.

☐ ☐ Infants and toddlers are not permitted to eat small objects and foods that may easily cause choking, such as hot dogs, hard candy, seeds, nuts, popcorn, and uncut round foods such as whole grapes and olives.

☐ ☐ Toy chests have air holes and a lid support or have no lid. A lid that slams shut can cause head injuries or suffocation.

☐ ☐ Shooting or projectile toys are not present.

☐ ☐ Commercial art materials are stored in their original containers out of children's reach. The word *nontoxic* appears on the manufacturer's label.

☐ ☐ Rugs, curtains, pillows, blankets, and cloth toys are flame-resistant.

Toys and Equipment (continued)

☐ ☐ Hinges and joints are covered to prevent small fingers from being pinched or caught.

☐ ☐ Cribs, playpens, and highchairs are away from drapery cords and electrical cords.

☐ ☐ Cribs, playpens, and highchairs are used properly and according to the manufacturer's recommendations for age and weight.

☐ ☐ Cribs have slats placed $2^3/_8$ inches apart or less and have snug-fitting mattresses. Mattresses are set at their lowest settings and sides are locked at their highest settings.

☐ ☐ Toys are not hung across the cribs of infants who can sit up.

☐ ☐ Rattles, pacifiers, or other objects are never hung around an infant's neck.

Hallways and Stairs

Yes No

☐ ☐ Handrails are securely mounted at child height.

☐ ☐ Handrails are attached to walls for right-hand descent, but preferably are attached to the walls on both right and left sides.

☐ ☐ Stairway gates are locked in place when infants or toddlers are nearby. Gates should have openings small enough to prevent a child's head from fitting through. No accordion-type gates are used.

☐ ☐ Doorways to unsupervised or unsafe areas are closed and locked unless the doors are used for emergency exits.

☐ ☐ Emergency exit doors have easy-open latches.

☐ ☐ Safety glass is used in all areas of potential impact.

☐ ☐ Caregivers can easily monitor all entrances and exits to keep out strangers.

☐ ☐ Stairways and hallways are clear of objects that can cause a fall.

Kitchen and Food Preparation and Storage Areas

Yes No

☐ ☐ Caregivers always wash hands before handling food.

☐ ☐ Caregivers always wash children's hands before mealtimes.

☐ ☐ Trash is always stored away from food preparation and storage areas.

☐ ☐ Refrigerator temperature is monitored by thermometer and is kept at or below 40 degrees Fahrenheit.

☐ ☐ All perishable foods are stored in covered containers at 40 degrees Fahrenheit or lower.

☐ ☐ Hot foods are kept at 140 degrees Fahrenheit or higher until ready to be eaten.

☐ ☐ Pest strips are not used.

☐ ☐ Cleansers and other poisonous products are stored in their original containers, away from food, and out of children's reach.

☐ ☐ Nonperishable food is stored in labeled, insect-resistant metal or plastic containers with tight lids.

☐ ☐ Refrigerated medicines are kept in closed containers to prevent spills that would contaminate food.

Kitchen and Food Preparation and Storage Areas (continued)

- ☐ ☐ Food preparation surfaces are clean and are free of cracks and chips.
- ☐ ☐ Eating utensils and dishes are clean and are free of cracks and chips.
- ☐ ☐ Appliances and sharp or hazardous cooking utensils are stored out of children's reach.
- ☐ ☐ Pot handles are always turned towards the back of the stove.
- ☐ ☐ An ABC-type fire extinguisher is securely mounted on the wall near the stove.
- ☐ ☐ All caregivers know how to use the fire extinguisher correctly and have seen a demonstration by members of the fire department.
- ☐ ☐ There is a "danger zone" in front of the stove where the children are not allowed to go.
- ☐ ☐ A sanitarian has inspected food preparation and service equipment and procedures within the past year.
- ☐ ☐ Children are taught the meaning of "hot."
- ☐ ☐ Trash is stored away from the furnace, stove, and hot water heater.
- ☐ ☐ Kitchen area is not accessible to children without constant adult supervision.
- ☐ ☐ Caregivers do not cook while holding a child.
- ☐ ☐ Hot foods and liquids are kept out of children's reach.
- ☐ ☐ Stable step stools are used to reach high places.

Bathrooms

Yes No

- ☐ ☐ Stable step stools are available where needed.
- ☐ ☐ Electrical outlets have safety covers or are modified to prevent shock.
- ☐ ☐ Electrical equipment is stored away from water.
- ☐ ☐ Cleaning products and disinfectants are locked in a cabinet out of children's reach.
- ☐ ☐ Toilet paper is located where children can reach it without having to get up from the toilet.
- ☐ ☐ If potty chairs are used, they are easy to clean with a bleach solution in a utility sink used only for that purpose, if possible.
- ☐ ☐ Potty chairs are not used in the food preparation or dining areas, and potty chairs cannot be reached by children when they are not in use.
- ☐ ☐ There are enough toilets so children do not have to stand in line.
- ☐ ☐ Caregivers and children always wash hands after toileting and diaper changing.
- ☐ ☐ The changing of diapers or soiled underwear is done in a special, separate area away from food and play.
- ☐ ☐ The diapering or changing table has rails to keep the child from rolling off.
- ☐ ☐ Trash cans for diapers, tissues, and other materials that come in contact with body fluids can be opened with a step pedal and are lined with a plastic bag, emptied daily, and kept clean.
- ☐ ☐ Paper towels and liquid soap are readily available at the sink.
- ☐ ☐ Thermometers are used to check that water temperatures are between 120 degrees and 130 degrees Fahrenheit or lower. The lower the water temperature, the safer it is for young children.
- ☐ ☐ Cosmetics are stored out of children's reach.

Bathrooms (continued)

☐ ☐ Bathtubs have skid-proof mats or stickers.

☐ ☐ Children take baths only when adults can supervise.

☐ ☐ Children are never left alone on a changing table, bed, or any other elevated surface.

☐ ☐ Children are never left unsupervised in or near water.

Playground

Yes No

☐ ☐ The playground is designed for safety. Caregivers regularly remind children of playground safety rules and give specific instructions for specific pieces of equipment or as otherwise needed.

☐ ☐ Caregivers can easily view and supervise the entire play area.

☐ ☐ The playground offers a wide range of parallel and interactive activities.

☐ ☐ The play area is clear of trash, tools, litter, debris, and animal feces.

☐ ☐ The play area is free of standing water and has no drainage problems.

☐ ☐ The play area is free of poisonous plants.

☐ ☐ Playground features do not have sharp points, corners, edges, or protrusions that could pierce or otherwise injure a child or entangle his or her clothing.

☐ ☐ Playground features have no openings that could cause head entrapment. (A head entrapment space is an opening that measures greater than 3 1/2 inches and less than 9 inches.)

☐ ☐ A statement is on file from the manufacturer of your play equipment stating that the equipment is appropriately scaled to the age of the children using the playground according to the *U.S. Consumer Products Safety Commission Handbook for Public Playground Safety.*

☐ ☐ Written documentation is on file that the equipment meets ASTM/USCPSC guidelines or, if not, documentation states what is not in compliance.

☐ ☐ Equipment or other playground features do not have missing or broken components, such as handrails, guardrails, protective barriers, or steps or rungs.

☐ ☐ The play equipment has no cracked, splintered, or rotting wood.

☐ ☐ The play equipment has no exposed concrete footings or other hard anchoring material.

☐ ☐ The play equipment is not corroded where it comes in contact with the ground.

☐ ☐ Any broken or partly broken structure is put off limits until it is repaired or removed.

☐ ☐ Any large unanchored piece of play equipment is removed from the playground until it can be anchored.

☐ ☐ No wooden, heavy solid rubber, metal, or otherwise heavy swing seats are in the play area.

☐ ☐ Six (6) feet of space exists between any piece of play equipment and another obstruction.

☐ ☐ Most pieces of play equipment are 12 feet apart.

☐ ☐ No obstacles exist in the equipment zones, which include the fall zone, the area under and around the equipment where protective surfacing is required, (6 feet in all directions from the perimeter of the equipment) and the no-encroachment zone, the area beyond the fall zone in which children using the equipment are moving about (specific dimensions vary for each piece of equipment according to type and orientation).

☐ ☐ Play areas have clean drinking water and lots of shade.

Playground (continued)

- ☐ ☐ Areas are set aside for running, organized games, and biking, separate from the play equipment areas.
- ☐ ☐ Children 2–5 years of age and children 5–12 years of age have separate play areas.
- ☐ ☐ The play space is laid out in such a way that a caregiver or caregivers can easily supervise the entire space.
- ☐ ☐ Safety surfacing is in place under all pieces of indoor and outdoor play equipment.
- ☐ ☐ The safety surfacing extends beyond the play equipment into the fall zone of each piece of equipment.
- ☐ ☐ Any loose-fill surfacing is installed and maintained at a depth that will protect children who fall on it from serious injury. For example: sand—10 inches, wood chips—12 inches, rubber outdoor matting—follow manufacturer's recommendations.
- ☐ ☐ Any loose-fill surfacing with a diameter of less than 1 1/4 inches is separated from children 3 years of age and younger who could potentially choke on this material.
- ☐ ☐ Loose surfacing material contains no foreign objects or debris.
- ☐ ☐ Loose surfacing material is not compacted or reduced in depth.
- ☐ ☐ Manufactured safety surfacing meets ASTM standards.
- ☐ ☐ The safety surface is free from tripping hazards.
- ☐ ☐ The maximum height of equipment for children up to the age of 6 years is 5 1/2 feet and no higher than 3 feet for children up to the age of 3 years.
- ☐ ☐ Swing sets are placed 9 feet or more from other equipment and at least 8 feet from walls, fences, walkways, and other play areas.
- ☐ ☐ A clear space two times the height of the swing beam is in front and behind the swing set.
- ☐ ☐ On swings using S-hooks, the S-hooks are completely closed.
- ☐ ☐ Swings are hung at least 24 inches apart from each other.
- ☐ ☐ The points at which swing seats and chains meet are enclosed in plastic tubing.
- ☐ ☐ Hanging rings are less than 5 inches or more than 20 inches in diameter (smaller or larger than a child's head).
- ☐ ☐ The run-out space at the base of the slides measures 4 feet plus the height of the slide.
- ☐ ☐ Slides have an enclosed "transition" platform at the top for children to rest on and get into position.
- ☐ ☐ Metal slides are placed in the shade.
- ☐ ☐ Slide ladders have flat steps and a handrail on each side.
- ☐ ☐ The slide incline is equal to or less than a 30-degree angle.
- ☐ ☐ Slides have a flat surface at the bottom to slow children down.
- ☐ ☐ Steps and rungs are 9–11 inches apart and are evenly spaced for easy climbing.
- ☐ ☐ Climbing or swinging bars stay in place when grasped.
- ☐ ☐ Climbers have regularly spaced footholds from top to bottom.
- ☐ ☐ Rungs on climbers are painted in bright or contrasting colors for easy visibility.
- ☐ ☐ Merry-go-rounds are installed so that a child cannot fit head or body beneath the turning platform.
- ☐ ☐ The tops of climbers have a safe way out for children.
- ☐ ☐ Sandbox sand is raked at least every 2 weeks to remove debris.

Playground (continued)

☐	☐	Sandboxes are located in the shade, have smooth frames, and are covered when not in use.
☐	☐	Pools are fenced in and closed to trespassers. They have been inspected and their safety equipment, sanitation, procedures, and supervision have been approved.
☐	☐	Children learn how to use sports equipment and how to use the proper safety equipment for each sport.
☐	☐	Children learn water safety and are always watched by adults when they are in or near the water.

Vehicles

Yes No

☐	☐	All vehicles work well.
☐	☐	Everyone, during every ride, uses age-appropriate safety restraints.
☐	☐	Staff helps to unbuckle and buckle-up children at drop-off and pickup.
☐	☐	Drivers use child-resistant door locks when the vehicle is in motion.
☐	☐	All vehicles are locked when not in use.
☐	☐	A well-stocked first aid kit is in the vehicle for every ride.
☐	☐	The caregiver has on hand current emergency contact information when driving children.
☐	☐	Trip plans include how to manage emergencies.
☐	☐	Children wear identification when transported.
☐	☐	Pickup and drop-off points are safe from traffic.
☐	☐	Infant seats are installed correctly, with seats facing the rear of the car until the child weighs 20 pounds.
☐	☐	Driver knows where children are before putting vehicle in reverse.
☐	☐	Bicycles and other riding toys are stable, well-balanced, and of the appropriate size. They do not have broken parts.
☐	☐	Children use helmets approved by ANSI (American National Standards Institute) or Snell Memorial Foundation when riding bikes.
☐	☐	Young bikers know traffic rules.
☐	☐	Children do not horse around while riding bikes and do not ride in the street.
☐	☐	Young children never cross the street without an adult. Children should know rules for crossing the street.

Emergency Preparedness

Yes No

☐	☐	All caregivers have roles and responsibilities in case of fires, injury, or other disasters.
☐	☐	One or more caregivers certified in first aid and in infant and child CPR are always present.
☐	☐	All first aid kits have the required supplies. The kits are stored where caregivers can easily reach them in an emergency.
☐	☐	Caregivers always take a first aid kit on trips.
☐	☐	Smoke detectors and other alarms work.

☐ ☐   Each room and hallway has a fire escape route clearly posted.

☐ ☐   Emergency procedures and telephone numbers are clearly posted near each phone.

☐ ☐   Children's emergency phone numbers are posted near the phone and can be easily taken along in case of an emergency evacuation.

☐ ☐   Emergency procedures include the following:

- How to phone emergency medical services (EMS) system
- Transportation to an emergency facility
- Notification of parents
- Where to meet if the child care setting is evacuated
- Plans for an adult to care for the children while a caregiver stays with injured children. This includes escorting children to emergency medical care.

☐ ☐   All exits are clearly marked and free of clutter.

☐ ☐   Doors and gates all open out for easy exit.

☐ ☐   Children are taught to tell if they or anyone else is hurt.

☐ ☐   Children are taught the words *stop* and *no*. Caregivers avoid using those words unless there is danger.

☐ ☐   Children are taught their own telephone number, address, and parent's work numbers.

☐ ☐   Children are taught how to phone EMS (9–1–1).

☐ ☐   Children are taught how to Stop, Drop, Roll, Cool in case their clothes catch fire.

☐ ☐   Children are taught to turn in any matches they find to an adult.

☐ ☐   _____

☐ ☐   _____

☐ ☐   _____

☐ ☐   _____

☐ ☐   _____

☐ ☐   _____

☐ ☐   _____

☐ ☐   _____

☐ ☐   _____

☐ ☐   _____

☐ ☐   _____

☐ ☐   _____

☐ ☐   _____

☐ ☐   _____

☐ ☐   _____

☐ ☐   _____

☐ ☐   _____

☐ ☐   _____

Fix-It-Quick Sheet

Name of Safety Checker: _____

Date of Safety Check: _____/_____/_____/

1 Area Observed	**2** Risky Behavior, Hazard, or Comments	**3** Correction and Date Made

Safety Calendar

August

Safety Checklist performed by program director.

Review and plan the safety education program for September.

Review special precautions for children with disabilities, allergies, or other special health problems.

Review safety materials on hand to plan year of safety education in the curriculum.

Hold an evacuation drill early in the morning.

Send for new materials for safety education curriculum.

September

Safety Checklist performed by a caregiver.

Review and plan the safety education program for October.

National Farm Safety Week. Teach children, staff, and parents about safety around farm equipment. (Write National Safety Council, 444 N. Michigan Ave., Chicago, IL 60611, or call 800-621-7619.)

Hold an evacuation drill during midmorning.

October

Safety Checklist performed by parent.

Review and plan the safety education program for November.

Teach Halloween safety.

Fire Prevention Week. (Second week. Write National Fire Protection Association, One Batterymarch Park, Quincy, MA 02269-9109.)

Hold an evacuation drill just before lunchtime and have it observed by a local fire department representative.

National School Bus Safety Week. (Second full week. Write National School Bus Safety Week Committee, P.O. Box 2639, Springfield, VA 22152.)

Safety Calendar

November

Safety Checklist
performed by food service staff.

Review and plan the safety education program for December.

Hold an evacuation drill during lunchtime.

Child Safety and Protection Month.
(Write National PTA, 700 N. Rush St., Chicago, IL 60611-2571.)

Holiday Toy Safety.
(Thanksgiving until Christmas. Write U.S. Consumer Product Safety Commission, Washington, D.C. 20207, or call 800-638-2772.)

December

Safety Checklist
performed by director or supervisor.

Review and plan the safety education program for January.

Hold an evacuation drill just before children are due to get up from their naps.

National Drunk and Drugged Driving Awareness Week.
Teach how to prevent "driving under the influence" to staff and parents. (Second week. Write National Highway Traffic Safety Administration, NTS-13, 400 7th St., S.W., Washington, DC 20590.)

January

Safety Checklist
performed by a parent.

Review and plan the safety education program for February.

Hold an evacuation drill right after nap time.

Safety Calendar

February

Safety Checklist
performed by a caregiver.

Review and plan the safety education program for March.

National Child Passenger Safety Week. (Week of Valentine's Day. Write National Highway Traffic Safety Administration, NTS-13, 400 7th St., S.W., Washington, DC 20590.)

Hold an evacuation drill during the afternoon activity period.

National Safety Sabbath. Teach children their responsibility not to harm others. (Second weekend. Write National Safety Council, 444 N. Michigan Ave., Chicago, IL 60611, or call 800-621-7619.)

March

Safety Checklist
performed by director or supervisor.
Inspect and arrange for the repair of playground equipment and surfaces.
Review with staff the procedures for maintaining a safe playground.

Review and plan the safety education program for April.

Hold an evacuation drill at the end of the day, just before the peak period when children are picked up.

National Poison Prevention Week. (Third full week. Write Poison Prevention Week Council, P.O. Box 1543, Washington, DC 20013.)

Red Cross Month. Contact your Red Cross chapter for information about CPR courses. Encourage parents and other caregivers to become certified.

April

Safety Checklist
performed by one or more volunteers and/or community safety experts (for example, sanitarian, building inspector, police officer, etc.).

Review and plan the safety education program for May.

Teach playground safety curriculum to children.

Teach children first aid for bumps, cuts, scrapes, splinters, and falls.

Hold an evacuation drill just before closing time.

National Volunteer Week. Hold a recognition ceremony for volunteers who help keep children safe. (Last full week. Write the National Center, 1111 N. 19th St., Suite 500, Arlington, VA 22209.)

Safety Calendar

May

Safety Checklist performed by maintenance staff.

Review and plan the safety education program for June.

National Electrical Safety Month. Teach children how to prevent injuries from electrical wires and appliances. (Write U.S. Consumer Product Safety Commission, Washington, DC 20207, or call 800-638-2772.)

Hold an evacuation drill on a day when some of the staff are scheduled to be out of the building.

Safe Kids Week (Third week. Write National Safe Kids Campaign, Washington, DC 20010.)

Buckle-Up America Week. (Week before and including Memorial Day weekend. Write National Highway Traffic Safety Administration, NTS-13, 400 7th St., S.W., Washington, DC 20590.)

June

Safety Checklist performed by a caregiver or parent.

Review and plan the safety education program for July.

National Safety Week (Last week. Write American Society of Safety Engineers, 1800 E. Oakton, Des Plaines, IL 60018-2187.)

National Safe Boating Week. Teach water safety curriculum to parents. (First full week. Write National Safety Council, 444 N. Michigan Ave., Chicago, IL 60611, or call 800-621-7619.)

Encourage certification of all caregivers in infant and child CPR and adult CPR.

Hold an evacuation drill unannounced.

July

Safety Checklist performed by a caregiver or parent.

Review and plan the safety education program for August.

Check certification for first aid training for all staff, volunteers, and parents.

Teach July 4th safety precautions.

Hold an evacuation drill just after the first children arrive.

Send for materials for next year's safety curriculum.

**American Red Cross
Child Care Course:
Infant and Child
First Aid**

Contents

About the Infant and Child First Aid Unit

Injuries are the number one killer of children over 9 months old in the United States. Each year tens of thousands of children are seriously hurt or die from injuries. Because children can be injured in the child care setting, you, the caregiver, should be able to give first aid.

This unit teaches you a plan to follow when a child is injured. The plan includes the emergency action principles—steps you follow to stay calm during an emergency and to give first aid. You will also learn steps to follow once the emergency is over. You will practice first aid for injuries that are common among children from birth to the age of 5. The skills you will learn include rescue breathing, first aid for a child or infant who is choking, controlling bleeding, and splinting a suspected fracture.

Further Information

For further information about first aid for infants and children, write the American Academy of Pediatrics, P.O. Box 927, Elk Grove Village, IL 60009-0927.

What You Will Learn

This unit will teach you—
1. What the first aid action plan is and how to follow it.
2. How to use the contents of a first aid kit.
3. What the 4 emergency action principles are and why they must be followed in order.
4. How to position a child or infant for rescue breathing.
5. How to give rescue breathing to a child and an infant.
6. How to give first aid for choking to a conscious and an unconscious child and infant.
7. When and how to notify a parent that a child is injured.
8. How to meet the needs of the other children in the group when an injury occurs.
9. How to complete an injury report form.
10. How to use an injury log to monitor and correct possible dangers.
11. When and how to give first aid for common childhood injuries.
12. How to use the first aid guides.

When a child or infant gets injured in the child care setting, you must follow the first aid action plan and its specific first aid guidelines—the emergency action principles. The emergency action principles may help you save the life of the injured child by taking several important steps—to decide how serious the situation is, to phone the emergency medical services (EMS) system for help, to find the injuries, and to take care of the most serious injuries first.

The skills you practice and the techniques you learn in this unit will prepare you to—
- Stay calm in emergencies because you know what to do.
- Make decisions about appropriate steps to take to keep a child alive and as comfortable as possible until medical help arrives.

First Aid and the Law

Legally, a victim must give consent to an offer to help before a person trained in first aid begins to help him or her. The law assumes that an unconscious person would give consent. If a victim is conscious, ask permission before helping him or her.

You should also make a reasonable attempt to get consent from the parent or guardian when the victim is an infant or child or a person who is mentally or emotionally disturbed. If a parent or guardian is not available, you may give first aid without consent. That is known as *implied consent* because the law assumes the parent would have given consent. Consent is also implied for a person who is unconscious, or who is so badly injured or ill that he or she cannot respond.

State "Good Samaritan" laws give legal protection to rescuers who act in good faith and are not guilty of gross negligence or willful misconduct. The type of rescuer covered and the scope of protection vary from state to state. Know your state's laws.

Activities and Materials

The unit and its materials will teach you the concepts and skills you need to give first aid to an injured child. Each activity has been designed to involve you in the learning process. You will watch videos and participate in class discussions and practice sessions.

The workbook is designed for you to use both during the unit and afterwards as a reference. Each activity in the workbook starts with a list of learning objectives that tell what you will learn in that activity. The lessons in each activity present the information you need to know. The videos show situations that teach you how to use the first aid action plan and how to give first aid. You will follow along in the workbook while the instructor teaches. You will also receive a set of first aid guides that explain what to do for an injured child. You will use these guides in class and in your child care setting.

Practice Sessions

After you watch a video, the instructor will help you practice the following skills:
- How to identify a life-threatening condition.
- How to give first aid when a child or an infant stops breathing.
- How to give first aid for choking to a child or to an infant.
- How to check for injuries.
- How to control bleeding and splint a suspected fracture.

You will work with a partner to practice the skills. You will practice some of the skills on a manikin and some on your partner. You will use the first aid guides when you practice.

Health Precautions and Guidelines

Infection and Disease
Since the beginning of citizen training in first aid, the American Red Cross and the American Heart Association have trained more than 50 million people in lifesaving skills. According to the Centers for Disease Control (CDC), there has never been a documented case of any infectious disease transmitted through the use of manikins.

The Red Cross follows widely accepted guidelines for the cleaning and decontamination of training manikins. **If these guidelines are consistently followed, and basic personal hygiene (for example, frequent handwashing) is practiced, the risk of any kind of disease transmission during first aid training is extremely low.**

There are some **health precautions** and guidelines that you should know. You should take these precautions if you have an acute or chronic infection, or have a condition that would increase your risk or the other participants' risk of exposure to infections. Most acute infections or conditions, such as a cold, a cut on the hand, or breaks in the skin in or around the mouth, are short-lived. The safest and most practical thing to do if you have an acute infection or condition is to postpone training until, for instance, your cut or abrasion heals, or your cold or influenza is over.

Other infections and conditions may be chronic or require a longer recovery period, making it impractical to postpone training. In this instance, for your safety and the safety of others, you should use a separate manikin for training, after you have discussed your participation with your private physician.

You should **postpone** participation in training if you—

- Have a respiratory infection, such as a cold or a sore throat.
- Believe or know you have recently been exposed to any infection to which you may be susceptible.
- Are showing any signs and symptoms of any infectious disease such as a cold, chicken pox, or mumps, or if you have a fever.
- Have any cuts or sores on your hands, or in or around your mouth (for example, cold sores or a recent tooth extraction).
- Know you are seropositive (have had a positive blood test) for hepatitis B surface antigen (HBsAg), indicating that you are currently infected with hepatitis B virus.*

You should request a **separate manikin** if you—

- Know you have any chronic infection such as indicated by long-term seropositivity (long-term positive blood tests) for hepatitis B surface antigen (HBsAg)* or a positive test for anti-HIV (that is, a positive test for antibodies to HIV, the virus that causes AIDS).

---

*A person with hepatitis B infection will test positive for the hepatitis B surface antigen (HBsAg). Most persons infected with hepatitis B will get better within a period of time. However, some hepatitis B infections will become chronic and will linger for much longer. These persons will continue to test positive for HBsAg, and their decision to participate in training should be guided by their physician.

After a person has had an acute hepatitis B infection, he or she will no longer test positive for the surface antigen but will test positive for the hepatitis B antibody (anti-HBs). Persons who have been vaccinated for hepatitis B will also test positive for the hepatitis antibody. A positive test for the hepatitis B antibody (anti-HBs) should not be confused with a positive test for the hepatitis B surface antigen (HBsAg).

- Have an acute infection or condition but are unable to postpone training.
- Have a type of condition that makes you unusually susceptible to infection.

If, after you read and consider the above information, you decide that you need to have your own training manikin, ask your instructor if one can be made available for your use. If you qualify under the above conditions for the use of a separate manikin, you should discuss this with your instructor, but you will not be required to provide details in your request. The manikin will not be used by anyone else until it has been cleaned according to the recommended end-of-class decontamination procedures. The Red Cross will do its best to provide you with a separate manikin. However, please understand that it may be impossible to do so, especially on short notice, because of a limited number of manikins for class use. In this instance, you may wish to reschedule training for a later date. The more advance notice you provide, the more likely it is that the Red Cross will be able to accommodate your request.

Guidelines to Follow During Training

To protect yourself and other participants from infection, you should do the following:

- Wash your hands thoroughly before working with the manikin and repeat handwashing as often as is necessary or appropriate.
- Do not eat, drink, use tobacco products, or chew gum immediately before or during manikin use.
- Dry the manikin's face with a clean gauze pad before using it. Next, vigorously wipe the manikin's face and the inside of its mouth with a clean gauze pad soaked with either a solution of liquid chlorine bleach and water (sodium hypochlorite and water) or rubbing alcohol. Place this wet pad over the manikin's mouth and nose and wait at least 30 seconds. Then wipe the face dry with a clean gauze pad.
- Simulate (pretend to do) the finger sweep when you practice first aid for an obstructed airway.

Physical Stress and Injury

The practice sessions require active participation. If you have a medical condition or disability that will prevent you from taking part in the practice sessions, please let your instructor know.

Damage to Manikins

In order to protect the manikins from damage, you should do the following before you begin practice:

- Remove pens and pencils from your pockets.
- Remove all jewelry.
- Remove lipstick and excess makeup.
- Remove chewing gum, candy, and tobacco from your mouth.

Activity 1
Orientation

Objective

After you have finished this activity, you will be able to do the following:

1. Tell the unit requirements

Lessons

- Your instructor will discuss the unit with you and what you must do to pass it. The unit requirements are—
  - Satisfactory performance of the skills.
  - Satisfactory performance on the test—80 percent or higher (or 20 correct answers).
  - Attendance of the class for the entire unit.
- You will review the contents of the workbook.

Infant and Child First Aid Unit Agenda

Activity	Topic
1	Orientation
2	Introductions
3	About the First Aid Action Plan
4	Overview of Emergency Action Principles
Break	
5	Primary Survey, Rescue Breathing, and Choking
Break	
6	Secondary Survey
7	First Aid Self-Test
8	Practicing First Aid Skills
9	Test and Unit Evaluation

Activity 2
Introductions

Objectives

After you have finished this activity, you will be able to do the following:

1. Use the All About You sheet to tell the group about yourself
2. Tell why you are taking this unit

Lesson

• Fill out the All About You sheet. The sheet is on the next page.

All About You

Fill in the blanks.

1. What is your name? _____

2. Where do you work? _____

3. What is your job there? _____

4. How old are the children in your group? _____

5. Why are you taking this unit? _____

6. What do you hope to learn? _____

_____

_____

Activity 3
About the First Aid Action Plan

Learning Objectives

After you have finished this activity, you will be able to do the following:
1. Define first aid
2. Identify the parts of the first aid action plan and tell why it is needed
3. Tell how to meet the needs of the other children in an emergency
4. Identify the common injuries that usually occur in the child care setting
5. Tell how and when to use the Injury Report Form and the Injury Log

Lessons

• First aid is the *immediate care given to help the victim of an injury or illness until the child receives professional medical help.*

   Injuries can happen in the child care setting, so you need to know what to do in an emergency. You need to know how to give first aid to an injured child.
• You will watch the video.
• The first aid action plan gives you a step-by-step way to handle an emergency involving a child. The 4 points of the first aid action plan are listed below.

1. Help the injured child.
It is important to follow the emergency action principles to guide you as you give first aid. You must take charge of an emergency situation in a calm and orderly way. If you remain calm and follow the first aid action plan, you can help the injured child and protect the other children from danger and injury. You must follow the 4 *emergency action principles* in order. You will learn about the emergency action principles in the next activity.

2. Tell the parent.
Contact the injured child's parent or guardian as soon as possible. Speak to the parent in a calm, reassuring voice. Tell the parent the child is hurt. Describe the injury and the help that is being given to the child.

You should be familiar with your policy about emergency situations and contacting parents. The person contacting the parent may not be the person caring for the child. For example, in a center, the center director or the room supervisor may call the parent. In a family day care home, the caregiver will call the parent.

At the time a parent or guardian registers a child for a child care program, the parent should be—
• Told about the program's policy on first aid.
• Asked to complete a Consent and Contact Form.

Read Appendix A, Consent and Contact Form. Use this form or a similar one to record the emergency contact information. This information should be checked and updated every 6 months, or when there is a change in the parent's home or work telephone number. You must have the current telephone number to reach the parent in an emergency.

You should carry the information from the Consent and Contact Form with you when you take the children away from the child care setting. You may want to write the emergency contact numbers on index cards and keep these cards in the first aid kit for trips.

You must always be able to contact the parent. If a child has a life-threatening injury and is taken to a medical facility, the child will be treated. But if a child has an injury that is not life-threatening but needs medical treatment, the parent must give informed consent to the medical personnel before they treat the child. The consent may be given by a witnessed phone call between the parent and the medical personnel.

3. Talk with the children.
It is important for you to meet the needs of the other children. You can do this if you supervise, reassure, explain, and teach.
• *Supervise*—You can ask another adult to take charge of the children and to protect them and keep them safe.
• *Reassure*—You can reassure the children that first aid is being given to the injured child and that emergency help is on the way.
• *Explain* and *teach*—You can tell the children that you will talk to them about what has happened as soon as possible. Later, you can answer their questions and comfort them by using one of the following activities: Story-telling, reading books, circle time, puppet play, songs, and craft projects as gifts for the injured child. You can also help children understand what happened by asking EMS personnel to visit the child care setting and talk to the children.

4. Complete the Injury Report Form and the Injury Log.

Use these 2 forms to write down what happened. You must complete the Injury Report Form when a child or an adult is injured and receives first aid. You must keep one copy for the child's record for legal and insurance review, and you must also give one copy to the parent. Ask the parent to sign your file copy.

You must also enter injury data on the Injury Log after the emergency is over. The log will help you keep a record of injuries. You can use the log to correct problems to help prevent other injuries from happening.

Read the Injury Report Form and the Injury Log on the next 2 pages.

Injury Report Form

Complete within 24 hours of injury. For an injured child, obtain the signature of a parent or legal guardian. File the completed form in the injured child's (or injured adult's) record. Give a copy (or a carbon copy) of the child's form to the parent.

Name of injured _____ Age _____

Date of injury_____ Time of injury_____a.m./p.m.

Witness(es) _____
_____

Where injury happened _____
_____

Any equipment or products involved _____
_____
_____

Name of parent notified _____

Time notified _____a.m./p.m.   Notified by _____

Description of injury and how it happened _____
_____
_____
_____
_____

Who gave first aid and what did they do _____
_____
_____
_____
_____

First aid given by medical personnel, telling who, what, when, and where_____
_____
_____
_____
_____

Follow-up plan for the injured _____
_____
_____
_____

Injury prevention steps taken _____
_____
_____

Caregiver completing form _____

Date form completed _____ Parent's signature _____

This page may be duplicated by individuals and entities for noncommercial purposes.

Injury Log

When did the injury happen?	Staff member reporting the injury.	Name of the injured child.	How old is the injured child?
Date / **Time**			
What happened to cause the injury?	Where did it happen?	What needs to be done so it won't happen again?	When was this done? **Date**

When did the injury happen?	Staff member reporting the injury.	Name of the injured child.	How old is the injured child?
Date / **Time**			
What happened to cause the injury?	Where did it happen?	What needs to be done so it won't happen again?	When was this done? **Date**

When did the injury happen?	Staff member reporting the injury.	Name of the injured child.	How old is the injured child?
Date / **Time**			
What happened to cause the injury?	Where did it happen?	What needs to be done so it won't happen again?	When was this done? **Date**

Activity 4
Overview of Emergency Action Principles

Learning Objectives

After you have finished this activity, you will be able to do the following:

1. List the 4 emergency action principles and tell why they must be followed in order
2. Tell how and when to contact the emergency medical services (EMS) system or other emergency services groups in your community
3. List the necessary emergency numbers to post by every telephone in the child care setting
4. Name the conditions that threaten a child's life

Lessons

- You will watch the video.
- The emergency action principles are the basic steps you must follow when you take care of an injured child. You must remain calm and follow the steps in their exact order. When you do, you will not forget anything that affects your personal safety. You will not forget anything that affects the safety and survival of the injured child.

  Look at the first aid guides that shows the 4 emergency action principles. These include the following:

Emergency Action Principle 1—Survey the scene.

When you arrive at the scene of an emergency, you should look at the whole scene, not just at the injured child. This survey should take only a few seconds, and it should answer the following questions:

- *Is the scene safe?* Is it safe for you to go to the injured person? For example, what if a child falls off a tricycle into the street? You should look for signs of danger, such as passing cars. Once you reach the child, you should quickly decide if it is safe for you and the child to stay where you are. Unless the child faces real danger—for example, if the child and the tricycle are in the middle of a street with heavy traffic—you should not move the child. Are the other children safe?
- *What happened?* Look for clues that tell what might have happened to the child. The scene itself often gives the answers. For example, if you found an unconscious child lying on the ground next to a tricycle, you might think that the child fell off the tricycle and has head, arm, or back injuries. What the scene tells is important, particularly if the child is unconscious and cannot speak, and no one else is present.
- *How many children are injured?* Look beyond the victim you see first. Maybe only one child fell off a tricycle, but more than one child may be injured. For example, you may see one injured child in the street near the tricycle, but you may not notice another child with more serious injuries because that child is unconscious and out of sight behind a parked car.
- *Are there bystanders who can help?* Look for bystanders—adults or children who are nearby and who can give you information. Ask them what happened. Bystanders can also phone the EMS system and help you care for other children.

  If you ever have to deal with an injured child whom you don't know, you should identify yourself as someone trained in first aid. This reassures people that a trained person is handling the situation. It will also help you to take charge of the situation, make decisions quickly, and tell other people what they can do to help, such as phoning the EMS system for help or caring for other children. If a parent is with the injured child, ask what happened. You should try to find out if the child has any medical problems. This information can help you figure out what is wrong with the child.

If the parent or legal guardian of a child under the age of 18 is there, you should get their permission before giving first aid. Whether a child or an infant is conscious or unconscious, if he or she needs first aid right away and the parent or guardian is not there, you should give first aid. You do not need to wait for permission before helping the child and giving first aid. The parent's or guardian's consent is implied. This means that the law assumes that the parent or guardian would have given permission for you to give first aid if they had been present. You should always tell the parent as soon as possible about the child's injury and any first aid given.

Emergency Action Principle 2—Do a primary survey for life-threatening conditions.

The purpose of the primary survey is to check for conditions that threaten a child's life and to make decisions about what first aid is needed. A child has a life-threatening condition if the airway is blocked, if the child is not breathing, or if there is a problem with circulation (the child has no pulse or is bleeding severely).

A primary survey involves checking the airway, breathing, and circulation. This is known as checking the ABCs:
- A = Open the airway
- B = Check for breathing
- C = Check circulation (check for pulse and severe bleeding)

First, you should check for unresponsiveness. Tap the injured child on the shoulder or gently shake the child's shoulder. Ask, "Are you OK?" If the child does not respond, you know you must check the ABCs. If the child is coughing, crying, or talking, you know that the child has an open airway, can breathe, and has a pulse.

Later in this unit you will learn how to check the ABCs. You will learn how to open the airway and check breathing and circulation. You will learn to help a child who is not breathing. You will also learn how to give first aid to a child whose airway is blocked.

Emergency Action Principle 3—Phone the emergency medical services (EMS) system for help.

When a call is made to the EMS system, a dispatcher answers. The information you learn from the primary survey should be given to the EMS dispatcher. This information will help the dispatcher send the right kind of help.

Try to get someone else to make the call. Send one or 2 bystanders, if possible. You must be sure the callers are prepared to give the following information:

- Where the emergency is located. The caller must give the exact street address or location, name of the building, apartment or room number, the name of the city or town, the nearby cross streets and landmarks.
- The telephone number from which the call is made.
- The caller's name.
- What happened—car crash, burns, child fell off tricycle, etc.
- Number of children injured and their ages.
- Condition of the child or children.
- Help (first aid) given.

Read Appendix B, Emergency Telephone Guide (page B-59). Post a completed copy of this form by each telephone in your child care setting.

The caller must not hang up until the EMS dispatcher hangs up. This ensures that the caller has given all the information the dispatcher needs to send the right help to the scene. The caller should report back to you to tell you the call has been made and that help is on its way. If possible, the caller should then wait at the street to guide the ambulance to you and the injured child.

If you are alone and no one answers your shouts for help, you may have to phone the EMS system yourself. Use your common sense to get help as fast as possible. If you do not suspect the child has a back or neck injury, you may carry the child to the phone. Give the dispatcher the information listed above.

When help arrives, you or another caregiver should go with the injured child to the emergency medical facility. Another caregiver or responsible adult should care for other children.

You may feel uneasy or unsure about phoning the EMS system for help, but it is better to phone the EMS system in an emergency than to risk a child's life. Always phone the EMS system for help if you have any question about whether the child's condition is serious or life-threatening. Always phone the EMS system if the child—

- Is unconscious, semiconscious, or unusually confused.
- Is not breathing.
- Is having difficulty breathing (if the child is breathing so hard or fast that he or she cannot talk, cry, play, or drink).
- Has pain in the chest or abdomen that does not go away.

- Has no pulse.
- Is bleeding severely.
- Is vomiting blood or passing blood (if the child's stools are black or have blood mixed in them).
- Has been poisoned.
- Has a severe headache, stiff neck, or neck pain when the head is moved or touched, or slurred speech.
- Has a seizure for the first time or if a seizure lasts more than 15 minutes.
- Has injuries to the head, neck, or back.
- May have broken bones.

Emergency Action Principle 4—Do a secondary survey for specific injuries.

Once you are certain the child has no life-threatening conditions, you can begin the secondary survey. The secondary survey is a way of finding other injuries or conditions that may need care. They may not be an immediate threat to the child's life, but could become life-threatening if not cared for. For example, you might find possible broken bones. You will learn more about the secondary survey in Activity 6.

If the child has a life-threatening condition, for example, if the child is unconcious or is not breathing, do not do a secondary survey. Instead, phone the EMS system and care for the life-threatening condition.

Activity 5
Primary Survey, Rescue Breathing, and Choking

Learning Objectives

After you have finished this activity, you will be able to do the following:
1. Describe why breathing is critical for life
2. Describe the ABCs and tell when rescue breathing is needed
3. Position a child or infant for rescue breathing
4. Give rescue breathing to a child and an infant
5. List 2 reasons why infants and children choke
6. List the signals of choking in a conscious child or infant
7. Give first aid to a conscious child who is choking
8. Give first aid to a conscious infant who is choking
9. Describe how you would find out that an unconscious child or infant has a blocked airway
10. Give first aid to an unconscious child who has a blocked airway
11. Give first aid to an unconscious infant who has a blocked airway
12. Describe how to give first aid to both a conscious child and a conscious infant who becomes unconscious while choking

Lessons

Primary Survey

• When you do the primary survey, you are checking for life-threatening conditions. First, check to find out if the child is conscious. Then check the child's airway, breathing, and circulation. This is sometimes called "checking the ABCs."

  If the child is conscious and is able to talk or is crying, the child has an open airway, is breathing, and has a pulse. You should check for severe bleeding. If there is no severe bleeding, then do a secondary survey.

Checking the ABCs
A—Airway
Does the child have an open airway (the passage through which the child breathes)? Open the child's airway by tilting the head gently back and lifting the chin. This lifts the tongue away from the back of the throat and opens the airway.

B—Breathing

Is the child breathing? Look for the chest to rise and fall, listen for breathing, and feel for air coming out of the child's mouth and nose. Chest movement alone does not mean that the child is breathing.

C—Circulation

1. Is the child's heart beating? If the child is breathing, the child's heart is beating. If the child is not breathing, you must find out if the child's heart is beating. You do this by checking the child's pulse.

   If the child is one year of age or older, feel for the pulse at the side of the neck. This pulse is called the carotid pulse. If the child is less than a year old, feel for the pulse in the upper arm. This pulse is called the brachial pulse.

2. Is the child bleeding severely? Check by looking over the child's body quickly for wet, blood-soaked clothing. Bleeding is severe when blood spurts from the wound or if you cannot control it. First check the pulse, then control any severe bleeding.

   Do not give any first aid until you have checked the child's airway, breathing, and circulation. By checking them first, you will be able to identify conditions that you should care for first. If there is a problem with the child's airway, breathing, or circulation, you must give first aid at once.

Breathing Emergencies

- Breathing emergencies are common in children. If a child or infant is having difficulty breathing or is not breathing, this is a breathing emergency. A breathing emergency is life-threatening.

  A breathing emergency can be caused by serious injuries such as electric shock, near-drowning, and injuries from a motor vehicle crash. An illness or medical condition can also cause a breathing emergency.

- You must know the early warning signs of a breathing emergency. These include the following:
  - The child is agitated or excited.
  - The child seems drowsy.
  - The child's skin color changes (to pale or blue).
  - The child is having difficulty breathing.
  - The child is breathing faster.
  - The child's heart is beating faster.
  - The child is making unusual noises, such as wheezing, gurgling, or crowing.
  - The child feels dizzy.

Rescue Breathing

- The first aid for a breathing emergency is called *rescue breathing*. To do rescue breathing, you breathe air from your own lungs into the child's lungs. This air contains more than enough oxygen to keep the child alive.
- You will watch the video. After the video, you are going to practice the rescue breathing skills that follow. You will work with a partner. Then your instructor will check your skills.

Instructions:

Rescue Breathing

1. **Check for Unresponsiveness**
   Check to see if the child is conscious. Tap or gently shake the child's shoulder to see if he or she responds *(Fig. 1)*. Shout, "Are you OK?" Does the child move or make a noise?

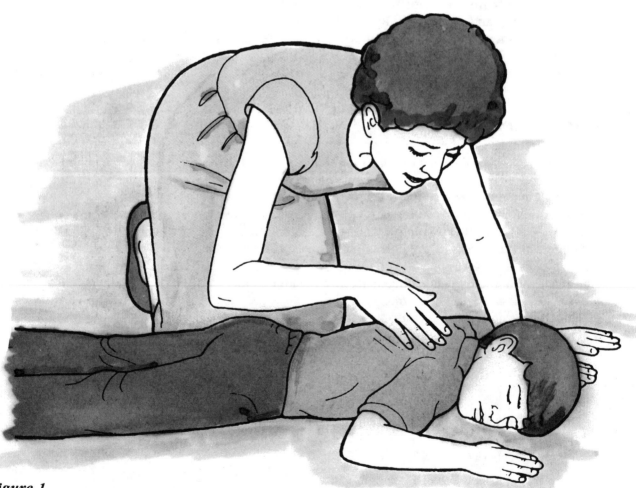

Figure 1
Check for Unresponsiveness

2. Shout for Help

If the child does not move or make a noise, he or she may be unconscious. Shout for help (*Fig. 2*) to attract the attention of someone who can phone the EMS system for help after you do the primary survey.

Figure 2
Shout for Help

3. Position the Child

Move the child onto his or her back. Do this by rolling the child as a unit (*Fig. 3*). This will help you avoid twisting the body and making any injuries worse. To position the child—

- Kneel facing the child, midway between the child's hips and shoulders. (For infants, stand or kneel facing the infant.)
- Straighten the child's legs, if necessary.
- Move the child's arm—the one closer to you—so that the arm is stretched out above the child's head.
- Lean over the child and place one hand on the child's shoulder. Put your other hand on the child's hip.
- Roll the child towards you as a unit by pulling slowly and evenly. Don't let the child's head and body twist.
- As you roll the child onto his or her back, move your hand from the shoulder to support the back of the head and neck.
- Place the child's arm—the one closer to you—beside the child's body. Position the child on his or her back as quickly as possible.

Figure 3
Position the Child

4. "A"—Open the Airway

This is the most important step you can take to help the child live. To open the airway—

- Put your hand—the one nearer the child's head—on the child's forehead.
- Place one or two fingers (not the thumb) of the other hand under the bony part of the child's lower jaw at the chin.
- Tilt the child's head gently back by applying pressure on the forehead and lifting the chin *(Fig. 4)*. Do not close the child's mouth completely. Do not push in on the soft parts under the chin.

For an infant—

Put one hand on the infant's forehead and one finger under the bony part of the lower jaw at the chin. Tilt the head gently back by applying pressure on the forehead and lifting the chin (*Fig. 5*). Do not close the infant's mouth completely. Do not push in on the soft parts under the chin.

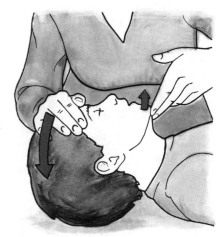

Figure 4
Open the Airway (Child)

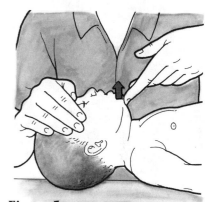

Figure 5
Open the Airway (Infant)

Figure 6
Check for Breathing

Figure 7
Give 2 Slow Breaths (Child)

5. **"B"—Check for Breathing** (Look, listen, and feel for breathing.)
   Check to see if the child is breathing (***Fig. 6***). Tilting the head and lifting the chin opens the airway. This may help the child start breathing again. To check the child's breathing—
   * Place your ear just over the child's mouth and nose and look at the child's chest and abdomen.
   * *Look, listen,* and *feel. Look* for the chest and abdomen to rise and fall. *Listen* for breathing. *Feel* for air coming out of the child's nose and mouth. Do this for 3 to 5 seconds. If the child is breathing, you will see the chest and abdomen move. You will hear and feel air coming out of the child's nose and mouth. Movement of the chest and abdomen does not always mean the child is breathing. The child may be trying unsuccessfully to breathe. Be sure to look, listen, and feel for breathing. No one sign is totally reliable.

6. **Give 2 Slow Breaths**
   If the child is not breathing, you must get air into the lungs at once (***Fig. 7***). To give breaths—
   * Keep the airway open. Gently pinch the child's nose shut with the thumb and index finger of your hand that is on the child's forehead.
   * Open your mouth wide and take a breath. Seal your lips tightly around the outside of the child's mouth. (For an infant, open your mouth wide and take a breath. Seal your lips tightly around the infant's mouth and nose.)
   * Give 2 slow breaths. Each breath should last 1 to 1½ seconds. Remove your mouth between breaths just long enough to take a breath. Watch for the chest to rise while you breathe into the child. Watch for the chest to fall after each breath. Listen and feel for air coming out of the nose and mouth.

   If air does not go in easily, you may not have opened the airway. Retilt the child's head and give 2 slow breaths. If air still does not go into the child's lungs, the airway may be blocked by something.

For an infant—

- Give 2 slow breaths *(Fig. 8)*. Each breath should last 1 to 1½ seconds. Remove your mouth between breaths just long enough for you to take a breath. Watch for the chest to rise while you breathe into the infant. Watch for the chest to fall after each breath. Listen and feel for air coming out of the nose and mouth.

    If air will not go into the infant's lungs easily, retilt the head and give 2 more breaths. If air still does not go into the infant's lungs, the airway may be blocked by food or some other material.

    Because an infant's airway is smaller than an adult's, it may be difficult to breathe air into the lungs. Be careful not to breathe too hard. If you blow too fast and too forcefully into the infant's airway, you can cause air to go into the stomach. On the other hand, if you blow too softly, you will not fill the infant's lungs with air. You should breathe slowly and watch for the chest to rise. When the chest rises, stop breathing into the infant.

Figure 8
Give 2 Slow Breaths (Infant)

7. **"C"—Check Circulation**

    Check to see if the child's heart is beating by feeling for a pulse at the side of the neck nearer to you. This pulse is called the *carotid pulse*. To check for a carotid pulse *(Fig. 9)*—

- Keep one hand on the child's forehead to keep the airway open. Use the other hand (the one nearer the child's feet) to find the pulse.
- Place your index and middle fingers on the child's Adam's apple. Then slide the fingers towards you, down into the groove between the windpipe and the muscle at the side of the neck.
- Press gently with your fingertips for 5 to 10 seconds to feel for the beat of the pulse. Do not use your thumb.

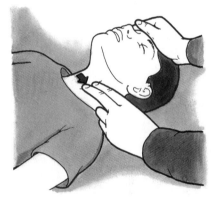

Figure 9
Check Circulation (Child)

For an infant—
Check to see if the infant's heart is beating by feeling for a pulse in the upper arm closer to you. This pulse is called the *brachial pulse* (*Fig. 10*). To check for a brachial pulse—
- Keep one hand on the infant's forehead to keep the airway open.
- Use your other hand to find the pulse in the infant's arm closer to you. Press gently with your index and middle fingers on the inside of the arm between the elbow and the shoulder.
- Feel for the brachial pulse with your fingers for 5 to 10 seconds.

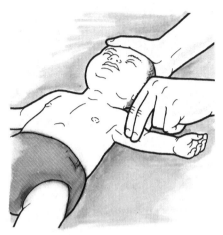

Figure 10
Check Circulation (Infant)

8. Phone EMS
After you have checked the pulse, you will have the information the EMS dispatcher needs—whether the child is conscious, breathing, and has a pulse. Tell the person who makes the call to give this information to the dispatcher *(Fig. 11)*.

Figure 11
Phone EMS

9. **Begin Rescue Breathing**

If you feel a pulse and the child is not breathing, then begin rescue breathing *(Fig. 12)*. (If you do not feel a pulse, the child's heart has stopped. You must start CPR, which is taught in the American Red Cross CPR: Infant and Child course.) To give rescue breathing—

- Keep the child's airway open.
- Pinch the nose shut.
- Seal your lips tightly around the child's mouth. Give one breath every 4 seconds. Each breath should last 1 to 1½ seconds. A good way to time the breaths is to count, "One one-thousand, two one-thousand, three one-thousand." Take a breath, and then breathe into the child. Look for the chest to rise as you breathe into the child.
- Remove your mouth from the child between breaths. Look for the chest to fall as you listen and feel at the child's mouth and nose for air to come out. Listen to hear if the child starts breathing again.

Figure 12
Rescue Breathing (Child)

For an infant—

If you feel a pulse and the infant is not breathing, begin rescue breathing *(Fig. 13)*. (If you do not feel a pulse, the infant's heart has stopped. You must start CPR, which is taught in the American Red Cross CPR: Infant and Child course.) To give rescue breathing—

- Keep the infant's airway open.
- Open your mouth wide and take a breath. Seal your lips tightly around the outside of the infant's mouth and nose. Give 1 breath every 3 seconds. Each breath should last for 1 to 1½ seconds. A good way to time the breaths is to count, "One one-thousand, two one-thousand." Take a breath, and then breathe into the infant. Watch for the chest to rise as you breathe into the infant.
- Between breaths, remove your mouth from the infant. Look for the chest to fall as you listen and feel at the infant's mouth and nose for air to come out. Listen to hear if the infant starts breathing again.

Figure 13
Rescue Breathing (Infant)

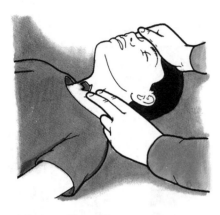

Figure 14
Recheck Pulse (Child)

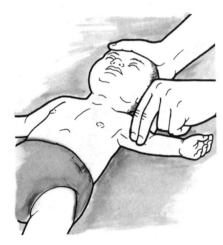

Figure 15
Recheck Pulse (Infant)

10. **Recheck Pulse**

After one minute of rescue breathing (for a child, about 15 breaths; for an infant, about 20 breaths), check the child's pulse. To check the pulse *(Figs. 14 and 15)*—

- Keep the airway open with the hand on the child's forehead.
- Feel for the carotid pulse (for an infant, brachial pulse) for 5 seconds with the other hand.

If the child has a pulse, then check for breathing for 3 to 5 seconds.

If the child is breathing, keep the airway open. Keep checking the breathing and pulse closely. This means that you should look, listen, and feel for breathing. Check the pulse once every minute. Cover the child. Keep the child warm and as quiet as possible.

If the child is not breathing, continue rescue breathing. Check the pulse once every minute. Continue giving rescue breathing until—

- The child begins breathing on his or her own.
- Another trained rescuer takes over for you.
- EMS personnel arrive and take over.
- You are too exhausted to continue.

Choking

- Choking is a common childhood injury that can kill infants and children. When a child is choking, the airway is partially or completely blocked. There are several ways the airway can become blocked.
    - **The back of the tongue may drop into the throat.** This often happens when an unconscious child is lying on his or her back.
    - **Tissues in the throat may swell and block the airway.** Swelling may be caused by injuries to the neck. Other causes are burns, allergies, insect stings and bites, and poison. Sometimes an illness may cause the tissues of the throat to swell.
    - **An object, such as a piece of food or toy, may block the airway.** The airway may also be blocked by fluids such as vomit or saliva.
- Choking may occur if a child or infant is—
    - Trying to swallow a piece of food that is poorly chewed.
    - Trying to swallow food that is too hard or too large to swallow.
    - Talking or laughing while eating or eating too fast.
    - Walking, running, or playing while eating.
    - Putting an object in the mouth to taste or explore it.

Signals of choking

A choking child or infant can quickly stop breathing, lose consciousness, and die. Therefore, it is very important to recognize when a child or infant needs first aid for choking. You must know the signals of choking. These include the following:

- The child or infant coughs weakly or makes a high-pitched sound while breathing. These signals mean the airway is partially blocked. The child or infant cannot breathe properly and needs first aid to clear the airway.

- The child cannot speak, cough, or breathe; the infant cannot cry, cough, or breathe. These signals mean that the airway is completely blocked. The child or infant needs first aid to clear the airway. The child may panic and clutch at his or her throat with one or both hands. This is the universal distress signal for choking (*Fig. 16*).

- If the child or infant can cough forcefully, this can be a signal that the airway is partially blocked. The child or infant is still able to breathe. Forceful coughing may clear the airway. Watch the child or infant carefully. Do not pat the child on the back. If the coughing does not stop soon, call the EMS system for help.

Watch the videos that show how to help a child who is choking. Then you will practice first aid for a child who is choking. Then, watch the videos that show you how to help an infant who is choking. After the videos, you will practice the first aid for an infant who is choking. The instructions for these skills are on pages B-32 through B-40. Then your instructor will check your skills.

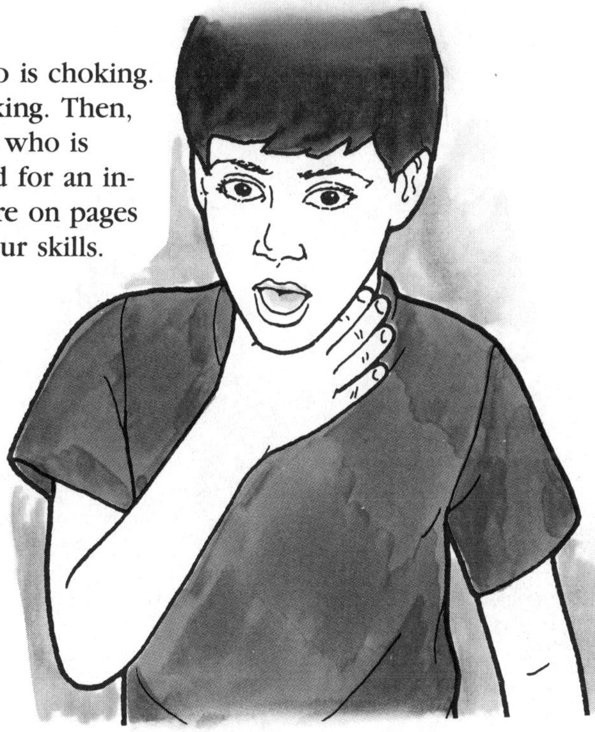

Figure 16
Universal Distress Signal for Choking

Instructions:

First Aid for Choking
(conscious child)

1. Begin a primary survey by asking, "Are you choking?"
2. If you are alone, shout for help.
3. Tell the child that you are trained in first aid and can help. Have someone phone the EMS system for help.
4. Do abdominal thrusts (also known as the Heimlich maneuver) as follows:
   - Stand or kneel behind the child. The child should be standing or sitting. Wrap your arms around his or her waist. Make a fist with one hand. Place the thumb side of your fist against the middle of the child's abdomen, just above the navel and well below the lower tip of the breastbone (*Fig. 17*).
   - Grasp your fist with your other hand. Keep your elbows out and away from the child. Press your fist into the child's abdomen with a quick, upward thrust (*Fig. 18*). Be sure that your fist is directly on the midline of the child's abdomen when you press. Do not direct the thrusts to the right or to the left. Think of each thrust as a separate and distinct attempt to dislodge the object.
   - Repeat the thrusts until the obstruction is cleared or the child becomes unconscious.

Figure 17
Giving Abdominal Thrusts

When to Stop
Immediately stop giving thrusts if the object is coughed up or the child starts to breathe or cough. Watch the child, and make sure that the child is breathing freely again. Even after the child coughs up the object, he or she may have breathing problems that will need a doctor's attention. You should also realize that abdominal thrusts may cause internal injuries. For these reasons, you should phone the EMS system. **The child should be taken to the hospital emergency department to be checked by a doctor even if he or she seems to be breathing well.**

Figure 18
Giving Abdominal Thrusts

Instructions:

First Aid for Choking
(unconscious child)

First aid for any unconscious child begins with a primary survey. While checking the ABCs, you may find that the child has a blocked airway. The procedure for finding out if an unconscious child has a blocked airway is given below. First, survey the scene. Then do a primary survey.

1. Check for unresponsiveness.
2. Shout for help.
3. Position the child on his or her back.
4. Open the airway.
5. Look, listen, and feel for breathing for 3 to 5 seconds.
6. If the child is not breathing, give 2 slow breaths.
7. If you are unable to breathe air into the child, retilt the head and give 2 more breaths. You may not have tilted the child's head into the correct position the first time.

   If you still cannot breathe air into the child, tell someone to phone the EMS system for help, and do the following:
8. Give 6 to 10 abdominal thrusts (as explained below).
9. Do a foreign-body check (as explained below).
10. Open the airway and give 2 slow breaths.
    Repeat steps 8, 9, and 10 until the airway is clear or EMS personnel arrive and take over.

Abdominal Thrusts
- Kneel at the child's feet. If the child is large, straddle the child's legs.
- Place the heel of one hand against the middle of the child's abdomen, just above the navel and well below the lower tip of the breastbone (*Fig. 19*). Put your other hand on top of your first hand, with the fingers of both hands pointed toward the child's head. Do not press your fingers on the child's ribs.
- Press into the abdomen with a quick upward thrust. Give 6 to 10 thrusts. Be sure that your hands are directly on the midline of the abdomen when you press. Do not thrust to the right or to the left. Each thrust should be a separate attempt to dislodge the object.

   After you have given 6 to 10 abdominal thrusts, do a foreign-body check to find out if the object has been dislodged.

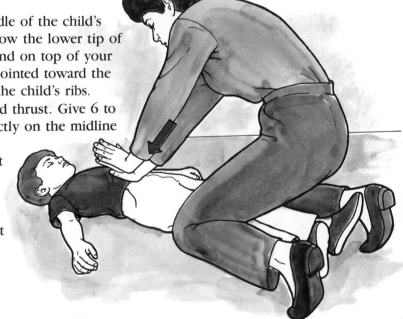

Figure 19
Abdominal Thrusts for Unconscious Child

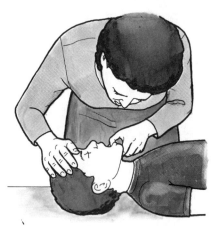

Figure 20
Foreign-Body Check

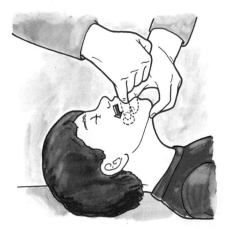

Figure 21
Finger Sweep for a Child

Foreign-Body Check
- Kneel beside the child's head.
- Open the child's mouth using the hand that is nearer the child's feet. Put your thumb into the mouth and grasp both the tongue and the lower jaw between your thumb and fingers. Lift the jaw upward (*Fig. 20*). This lifts the tongue away from the back of the throat and away from any object that may be lodged there.
- Look for the object. If you can see an object, try to remove it with the finger sweep (*Fig. 21*).

To do the finger sweep—
- Slide the little finger of your other hand into the child's mouth. Slide your finger down along the inside of the cheek to the base of the child's tongue. Be careful not to push the object deeper into the airway.
- Use a hooking action to sweep the object out of the throat.

Remember: Do the finger sweep only if you can see the object in the child's throat.

Give 2 Slow Breaths

After you do the foreign-body check, give 2 slow breaths, as follows:

- Open the airway. Tilt head gently back and lift chin (*Fig. 22*).
- Give 2 slow breaths (*Fig. 23*).

  Continue these 3 steps:

  1. Give 6 to 10 abdominal thrusts.

  2. Do a foreign-body check.

  3. Open the airway and give 2 slow breaths.

If your first attempts to clear the airway are unsuccessful, do not stop. The longer the child goes without oxygen, the more the muscles of the throat will relax. This will make it more likely that you will be able to remove the foreign body.

If you succeed in clearing the airway and are able to breathe air into the child, give 2 slow breaths, as you did for rescue breathing. Then check the child's pulse. If there is no pulse, begin CPR. If there is a pulse and the child is not breathing on his or her own, continue rescue breathing.

If the child starts breathing on his or her own, keep checking the child's breathing and pulse until EMS personnel arrive and take over. This means you should keep the airway open. Look, listen, and feel for breathing. Keep checking the pulse. Also, cover the child, and keep him or her warm and as quiet as possible.

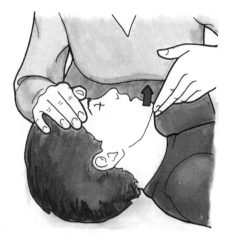

Figure 22
Open the Airway

Instructions:

First Aid for Choking When a Conscious Child Becomes Unconscious

Sometimes a child who is choking may lose consciousness and fall. If this happens, you should shout for help and slowly lower the child to the floor while supporting the child from behind. Support the child's head as you lower the child to the floor.

Once the child is on the floor, tell someone to phone the EMS system for help. Then kneel beside the child and do the following:

1. Do a foreign-body check.

2. Open the airway and give 2 slow breaths.

3. Give 6 to 10 abdominal thrusts if you are unable to breathe into the child's lungs. Repeat these 3 steps until the obstruction is cleared or EMS personnel arrive and take over.

Figure 23
Give 2 Slow Breaths

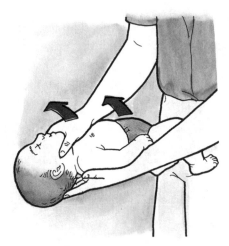

Figure 24
Hold Infant's Jaw

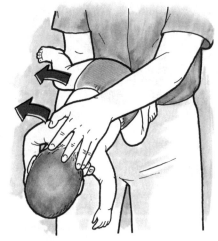

Figure 25
Turn Infant Over

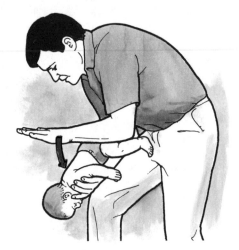

Figure 26
Give 4 Back Blows

Instructions:

First Aid for Choking (conscious infant)

If you suspect that an infant is choking, you should survey the scene as you approach the infant.

1. Begin a primary survey. Determine if the infant can cough, breathe, or cry.
2. If you are alone, shout for help.
3. Have someone phone the EMS system for help.
4. Give 4 back blows as follows:
   - Hold the infant's jaw between your thumb and fingers (**Fig. 24**).
   - Slide your other hand behind the infant's back so that your fingers support the back of the infant's head and neck.
   - Turn the infant over so that he or she is facedown on your forearm (**Fig. 25**).
   - Support the infant's head and neck with your hand by firmly holding the jaw between your thumb and fingers.
   - Lower your arm onto your thigh. The infant's head should be lower than his or her chest.
   - Give 4 back blows forcefully between the infant's shoulder blades with the heel of your hand (**Fig. 26**).

5. Then give 4 chest thrusts as follows:
   * Place your free hand and forearm along the infant's head and back so that the infant is sandwiched between your 2 hands and forearms.
   * Support the back of the infant's head and neck with your fingers.
   * Support the infant's neck, jaw, and chest from the front with one hand while you support the infant's back with your other hand and forearm.
   * Turn the infant faceup (*Fig. 27*).
   * Lower your arm that is supporting the infant's back onto your thigh. The infant's head should be lower than his or her chest. (If the infant is large or your hands are too small to support the infant, put the infant on your lap with his or her head lower than the chest.)
   * Use your hand that is on the infant's chest to locate the correct place to give chest thrusts. Imagine a line running across the infant's chest between the nipples. Place the pad of your ring finger on the breastbone just under this imaginary line. Then place the pads of 2 fingers next to your ring finger just under the nipple line. Raise your ring finger. If you feel the notch at the end of the infant's breastbone, move your fingers slightly toward the head. The pads of your fingers should lie in the same direction as the infant's breastbone.
   * Use these 2 fingers to compress the breastbone (*Fig. 28*). Compress the breastbone ½ to 1 inch (1.3 to 2.5 centimeters), and then let the breastbone return to its normal position. Keep your fingers in contact with the infant's breastbone. Compress 4 times.
6. Keep giving the infant back blows and chest thrusts until the object is coughed up or the infant loses consciousness.

When to Stop
Stop giving back blows and chest thrusts if the infant coughs up the object or starts to breathe or cough. Watch the infant, and make sure that the infant is breathing freely again. Even after the infant coughs up the object, he or she may have breathing and lung problems that will need a doctor's attention. You should also realize that chest thrusts may cause internal injuries. For these reasons, you should phone the EMS system for help. **The infant should be taken to the hospital emergency department to be checked by a doctor even if he or she seems to be breathing well.**

Figure 27
Turn Infant Faceup

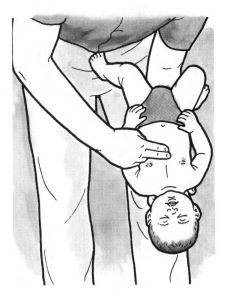

Figure 28
Position for Giving Chest Thrusts

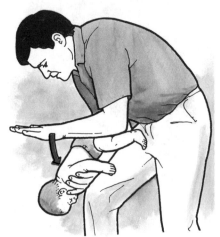

Figure 29
Give 4 Back Blows

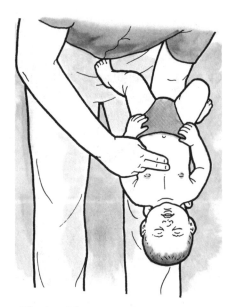

Figure 30
Give 4 Chest Thrusts

Instructions:

First Aid for Choking (unconscious infant)

First aid for any unconscious infant begins with surveying the scene. Then do a primary survey. While checking the ABCs, you may find that an infant has a blocked airway.

1. Check for unresponsiveness.
2. Shout for help.
3. Position the infant on his or her back on a firm, flat surface.
4. Open the airway.
5. Look, listen, and feel for breathing for 3 to 5 seconds.
6. Give 2 slow breaths.
7. If you are unable to breathe air into the infant, retilt the head and give 2 more breaths. You may not have tilted the infant's head into the correct position the first time.

If you still cannot breathe air into the infant, tell someone to phone the EMS system for help, and do the following:

8. Give 4 back blows (*Fig. 29*).
9. Give 4 chest thrusts (*Fig. 30*).
10. Do a foreign-body check.
11. Open the airway and give 2 slow breaths.

Repeat steps 8, 9, 10, and 11 until the airway is clear or EMS personnel arrive and take over.

Foreign-Body Check

To do a foreign-body check—

- Stand or kneel beside the infant's head.
- Open the infant's mouth using the hand that is nearer the infant's feet. Put your thumb into the infant's mouth and grasp both the tongue and the lower jaw between your thumb and fingers. Lift the jaw upward (*Fig. 31*). This lifts the tongue away from the back of the throat and away from any object that may be lodged there.
- Look for the object. If you can see an object, try to remove it with the finger sweep (*Fig. 32*).

  To do the finger sweep—
  - Slide the little finger of your other hand into the infant's mouth.
  - Slide your finger down along the inside of the cheek to the base of the tongue. Be careful not to push the object deeper into the airway.
  - Use a hooking action to loosen the object and move it into the mouth. If you can reach the object, take it out.

Remember: Do the finger sweep only if you can see the object in the infant's throat.

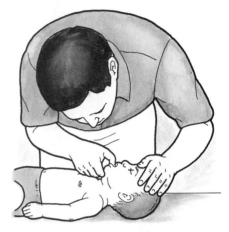

Figure 31
Foreign-Body Check

Give 2 Slow Breaths

After you do the foreign-body check, give 2 slow breaths, as follows:

- Open the airway. Tilt head gently back and lift chin.
- Give 2 slow breaths.

  Continue these 4 steps:
  1. Give 4 back blows.
  2. Give 4 chest thrusts.
  3. Do a foreign-body check.
  4. Open the airway and give 2 slow breaths.

If your first attempts to clear the airway are unsuccessful, do not stop. The longer the infant goes without oxygen, the more the muscles of the throat will relax. This will make it more likely that you will be able to remove the object.

If you are able to breathe air into the infant's lungs, give 2 slow breaths as you did for rescue breathing. Then check the infant's pulse. If there is no pulse, you must give CPR. If there is a pulse and the child is not breathing on his or her own, continue rescue breathing.

If the infant starts breathing on his or her own, keep checking breathing and pulse until EMS personnel arrive and take over. This means you should keep the airway open. Look, listen and feel for breathing. Keep checking the pulse. Cover the infant. Keep the infant warm and as quiet as possible.

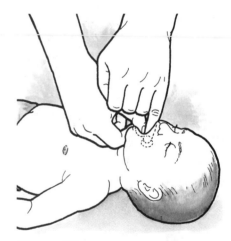

Figure 32
Finger Sweep for an Infant

Instructions:

First Aid for Choking When a Conscious Infant Becomes Unconscious

If an infant becomes unconscious while you are giving first aid for choking, you should shout for help. Have someone phone the EMS system for help. Place the infant on a firm, flat surface. Then—

1. Do a foreign-body check.
2. Open the airway and give 2 slow breaths.
3. Give 4 back blows.
4. Give 4 chest thrusts.

Repeat these 4 steps until the airway is clear or EMS personnel arrive and take over.

If you are able to breathe air into the infant's lungs, give 2 slow breaths as you did for rescue breathing. Then check the pulse. If the infant has no pulse, then you must begin CPR. If there is a pulse and the infant is not breathing on his or her own, continue rescue breathing.

If the infant starts breathing on his or her own, keep checking breathing and pulse until EMS personnel arrive and take over. This means you should keep the airway open. Look, listen, and feel for breathing. Keep checking the pulse. Cover the infant. Keep the infant warm and as quiet as possible.

Activity 6
Secondary Survey

Learning Objectives

After you have finished this activity, you will be able to do the following:

1. Do the steps of the secondary survey
2. Control bleeding
3. Recognize that a few teaspoonfuls of blood are not a significant blood loss
4. Recognize and care for shock

Lessons

Watch the video.

The steps of the secondary survey are—

- Talk with the child and/or bystanders. Find out what is wrong. An injured child or infant is usually frightened. You must stay calm and keep the child or infant calm, too. Use a friendly voice and say something like, "I'm going to help you." If you don't know the child you are going to help, introduce yourself. Then ask, "What happened? Where does it hurt?" Or say, "Point to where it hurts."

- Check the child's breathing, and skin appearance and temperature.

- Check the child from head to toe, looking for injuries. You should look for wounds; body fluids; deformities such as bumps, depressions, and body parts in unusual positions; and areas that are painful. If you find any injuries, give first aid and phone EMS for help, if necessary. (The first aid guides describe first aid for different injuries.)

Instructions:

Secondary Survey

Do a secondary survey only if the child is fully conscious. Watch the child's facial expressions and listen for changes in the tone of voice. If something hurts, the child's face or voice often reflects the pain. Ask the child to tell you or show you where it hurts. Do not apply pressure over any area the child says is painful. Do not apply pressure to the spine or any soft spots on the head. Check for a medical alert tag at the neck or wrist. If the child cannot or will not talk to you, this tag may provide some information about what might be wrong and how you should care for the child.

Talk with the child and/or bystanders.

- Ask what happened and what hurts, and note the child's answers *(Fig. 33)*.
- Tell the child that you are going to check for other injuries.
- As you talk to the child, check the child's breathing. Ask yourself if the child is gasping for air, breathing very fast or slow, seems to find breathing painful, or is breathing normally.

  Also check the child's skin color and skin temperature. Feel the child's forehead with the back of your hand. Ask yourself if the child's skin is cold or hot; unusually wet or dry; pale, bluish, ashen, or flushed.

Check all parts of the child's body.

If you think the child may have a serious head injury or a neck or back injury, ask the child to stay still. Do not move the child. Call EMS immediately.

While you are checking the child's body for injuries, ask simple questions, such as "Do you hurt anywhere?" "Can you wiggle your toes?" "Can you wiggle your fingers?" "Can you take a deep breath for me?" Do not ask the child to move any area that is painful.

Figure 33
Ask what happened and what hurts

- Look over the child's body. Look for bleeding, cuts, bruises, and obvious deformities.
- To check the arms, hands, and shoulders, ask if the child can bend his or her arms and wiggle the fingers. Check one arm at a time. Ask the child to shrug his or her shoulders.
- To check the feet, legs, and hips, ask if the child can move his or her legs and wiggle the toes. Check one leg at a time.
- To check the chest and abdomen, ask the child to take a deep breath and blow the air out.
- To check the neck, ask the child to move his or her head slowly from side to side.
- Check the child's scalp, face, ears, nose, and mouth. Look for blood or other fluid in the child's ears, nose, or mouth.

  Write down what you find so you can give the information to the parent or EMS personnel, or ask someone else to write it down.

Caring for shock

Shock occurs when the body cannot adjust to the stress placed on it by illness or injury, especially injury that causes severe bleeding. Shock is life-threatening. You should learn to recognize the signals of shock. These signals include—

- Being restless or irritable.
- Pale, bluish or ashen, cool, moist skin.
- Fast, weak pulse.
- Fast breathing.
- Strong thirst.
- Drowsiness or loss of consciousness.
- Nausea and vomiting.

Whenever you are dealing with a significant illness or injury, you should—

- Lay the child down.
- Control any external bleeding as soon as possible.
- Elevate the child's legs 8 to 12 inches above his or her body unless you suspect broken bones; a head, neck, or back injury; or the child is having difficulty breathing.
- Keep the child's body at a comfortable temperature.
- Reassure a conscious child.
- Keep checking the airway, breathing, and circulation, and care for any problems.
- Place the child on one side if the child vomits.
- Phone EMS immediately.
- Do not give the child anything to eat or drink.

Controlling bleeding

When a child is injured, you may have to control bleeding. Severe bleeding can lead to shock. Do not panic at the sight of blood. You will see a demonstration showing "blood loss" that proves that a small amount of bleeding can look like a lot. A small amount of blood loss may look serious although it often is not. Serious blood losses include—

- 24 teaspoonfuls (½ cup) for an infant from birth to one year of age.
- 72 teaspoonfuls (1½ cups) for a child from one to 5 years of age.

To control bleeding, you should—

- Apply direct pressure with a clean cloth.
- Elevate the wound unless you suspect a fracture or if elevating it hurts the child.
- Help keep pressure on the wound by snugly wrapping a bandage around the injured area.
- Maintain pressure and elevation until the bleeding stops.
- If the wound is large or deep or bleeding cannot be controlled, phone the EMS system or get medical help immediately.

Preventing Disease Transmission

To reduce the risk of disease transmission when controlling bleeding, you should—

- Place an effective barrier between you and the child's blood when you give first aid. Examples of such barriers are a piece of plastic wrap, rubber or disposable gloves, or even a clean, folded cloth.
- Wash your hands thoroughly with soap and water immediately after providing care, even if you wore gloves or used another barrier. Use a utility or rest room sink, not one in a food preparation area.
- Avoid eating, drinking, and touching your mouth, nose, or eyes while providing care or before washing your hands.

Activity 7
First Aid Self-Test

Learning Objective

After you have finished this activity, you will be able to do the following:
1. Tell how to give basic first aid for specific injuries
2. Put into correct order a set of pictures that show the first aid steps for 10 injuries

Lesson

- You are going to use the first aid guides to take the self-test on pages B-46 through B-50.

Bites, Animal or Human

Number the 3 pictures in the correct order.

3

2

1

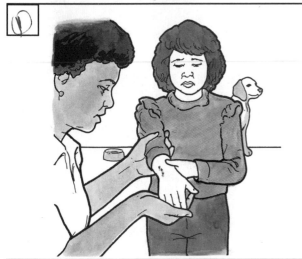

Bleeding, Scrapes

Number the 2 pictures in the correct order.

2

1

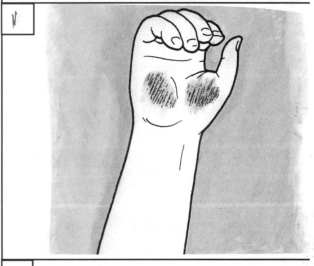

Burns, Chemical

Number the 3 pictures in the correct order.

3

2

1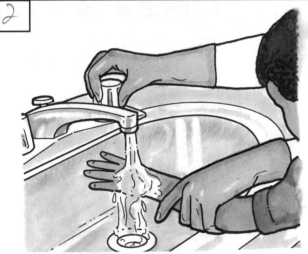

Burns, Electrical

Number the 3 pictures in the correct order.

2

3

1

Burns, Heat

Number the 3 pictures in the correct order.

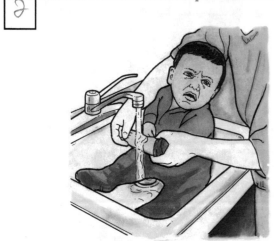

Cold Emergencies: Frostbite

Number the 3 pictures in the correct order.

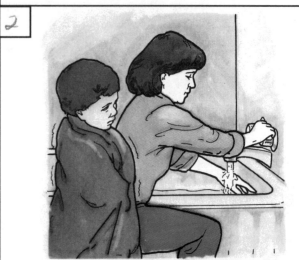

Head and Spine Injuries

Number the 3 pictures in the correct order.

2

3

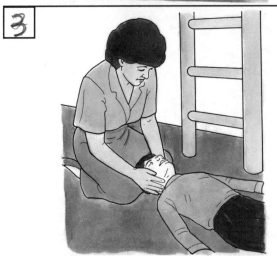

1

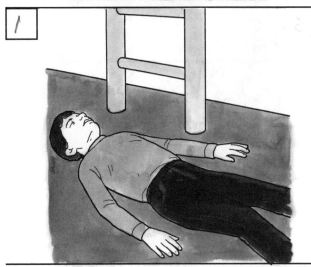

Heat Emergencies: Exhaustion

Number the 3 pictures in the correct order.

3

2

1

Poisoning: Swallowed Poisons

Number the 2 pictures in the correct order.

2

1

Puncture Wounds

Number the 3 pictures in the correct order.

3

1

2

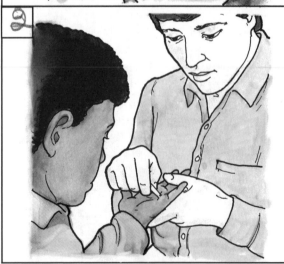

Activity 8
Practicing First Aid Skills

Learning Objectives

After you have finished this activity, you will be able to do the following:
1. Assemble the contents of a basic first aid kit
2. Know when and how to use the contents of a first aid kit
3. Care for an injured child by following the first aid action plan
4. Show how to control bleeding and how to splint a limb that may be fractured

Lessons

- You must know how to put together a first aid kit. Turn to Appendix C, Inventory for the First Aid Kit on page B-60. This lists the things you will need for your first aid kit and gives instructions for assembling it. You can get supplies at drug or department stores, or at hospital or medical supply stores.

  Store the first aid kit where you can easily reach it. Carry the kit and the emergency contact numbers with you whenever you leave the child care setting with the children. Be sure to replace any items that you use from the kit.
- You use the contents of a first aid kit to give first aid to an injured person in the following ways:
  - **To stop bleeding**—The first aid kit should contain sterile gauze pads in varying sizes, rolled flexible or stretch gauze or a clean cloth for applying pressure, roller bandages and tape to hold the bandage in place.
  - **To stop the spread of infections**—The first aid kit should contain soap and gauze pads to use to clean wounds. It should also contain cleansing wipes for cleaning injuries when running water is not available or for washing the rescuer's hands before and after giving first aid. (The first aid kit should contain disposable gloves that you can wear to keep hands free of germs and to prevent dirty hands from spreading germs to the child. Wearing disposable gloves also reduces the risk of disease transmission when controlling bleeding.)

- **To immobilize injured arms and legs**—The first aid kit should contain a large cloth or triangular bandage and rolled flexible or stretch gauze to help immobilize an injury. You can immobilize an injury by binding it to a rigid material or by binding it to the body. For example, an injured arm can be immobilized by binding it to a rolled-up magazine or by using safety pins to attach a child's long sleeve to the body of the shirt against the chest and supporting it with a triangular bandage.

- **To reduce swelling**—The first aid kit should also have space for a commercial cold pack or plastic bag for ice.

- **To call for help**—The first aid kit should contain coins for a pay telephone, phone numbers of parents or guardians, and the Emergency Telephone Guide. A pen or pencil and paper are handy, too.

- **To look at the eyes, or in the ear or mouth**—The first aid kit should contain a flashlight and fresh batteries.

- **To remove splinters or small objects**—The first aid kit should contain tweezers.

- **To rinse out eyes or wounds**—The first aid kit should contain a bulb syringe.

- **To take a child's temperature**—The first aid kit should contain a thermometer.

- **To remove poisons by vomiting**—The first aid kit should contain syrup of ipecac if the child care program policies allow it. You must always phone the EMS system or the Poison Control Center when you suspect a poisoning may have occurred and before giving a child syrup of ipecac. You must not give anything by mouth until advised by medical professionals. Some poisons will cause the least amount of damage if the child removes them from the body by vomiting. However, the rule does not apply to poisons that contain fumes or that can irritate tissues.

    You must **always** phone the Poison Control Center before giving syrup of ipecac.

- **For reminders about how to care for injuries**—The first aid kit should contain a copy of the first aid guides.

- **For children with special health problems**—The first aid kit should contain any special items, such as a bee sting kit or an inhaler for a child with asthma.

- You will join a group to role-play scenarios of injuries and how to give the right first aid care. Turn to the "Injured Child Scenarios" on page B-54. Your instructor will assign to you one (or more) of these scenarios. You will play the role of a caregiver or a child.

   Before your role-play, practice with your group. Use your first aid guides for instructions on giving first aid care. After each group's role-play, you will watch and discuss a video segment that shows the correct first aid for that injury. After you have finished all the scenarios, you will practice with a partner the first aid skills used to control bleeding and to splint fractures, dislocations, or sprains.

Injured Child Scenarios

1. Cuts

One of the caregivers asks a 4-year-old girl to help carry lunch outside, where another caregiver is watching the rest of the children play. After the girl leaves, the caregiver drops and breaks a glass on the floor. When the caregiver leaves the kitchen to get a broom to sweep up the glass, the girl returns to the kitchen. She picks up a piece of broken glass and cuts herself. (Roles: one caregiver, one child)

2. Knocked-out tooth

Two caregivers watch several children on the playground in back of the center. A little boy is kicking a ball. He trips and falls, knocking out one of his front teeth. He starts to cry. (Roles: 2 caregivers, at least one child)

3. Choking

Two caregivers are playing with the children. Some of the children are coloring with markers. One of the caregivers leaves to check on the infants napping in the next room. One of the children starts to choke on a marker top. (Roles: 2 caregivers, at least one child)

4. Burns

The caregiver works alone in her home. She cares for 5 children ranging from 9 months to 5 years of age. An infant knocks over a cup of hot coffee, and his forearm is burned. He screams in pain. (Roles: one caregiver, at least one child)

5. Fractures, dislocations, or sprains

Two caregivers and an aide are playing with a group of children on a playground away from the center. A public telephone is located nearby. One of the little girls falls off the slide. She sits up crying and holding her forearm. (Roles: at least 2 caregivers, at least one child)

Activity 9
Test and Unit Evaluation

Objective

After you have finished this activity, you will be able to do the following:

1. Complete the test

Lessons

- The test that the instructor will give you has 25 questions about what you learned in this class. Answer the questions on the answer sheet. You must score 80 percent or higher (or answer 20 or more questions correctly) to pass this unit.

- Your instructor will also give you a unit evaluation sheet. Please tell us what you thought of this unit by filling out this sheet and returning it to the instructor.

- Thank you for your participation in the American Red Cross Child Care Course. By taking all of the units of the Child Care Course, you are showing your commitment to giving the best possible child care. Now that you understand the information and skills presented, you will be able to put your caring and concern for children into action.

 **Appendixes**

Consent and Contact Form

This form is to be completed and signed by the child's parent or legal guardian.

Name of child _____

In the event the child named above is injured or ill, I understand that the caregiver will attempt to contact me, the other parent, or the legal guardian at the telephone number provided below.

Parent's (legal guardian's) name _____

    Telephone numbers _____ on _____ (hours/days)

    _____ on _____ (hours/days)

Parent's (legal guardian's) name _____

    Telephone numbers _____ on _____ (hours/days)

    _____ on _____ (hours/days)

In the event that I or the others listed are not available, I give my permission to the caregiver to provide first aid for the child named above and to take the appropriate measures including contacting the emergency medical services (EMS) system and arranging for transportation to _____

_____

or the nearest emergency medical facility. At no time will the caregiver drive an ill or injured child to an emergency medical facility unless accompanied by another adult.

Signature _____ Date _____

This page may be duplicated by individuals and entities for noncommercial purposes.

Emergency Telephone Guide

Keep a copy of this list in your first aid kit and posted by every phone.

Emergency Telephone Numbers

Date completed _____

Emergency medical services (EMS) system _____

Fire _____ Police _____

Poison Control Center _____ Ambulance _____

Name, address, and phone number of nearest medical facility _____

_____

_____

Taxi _____

Other important numbers _____

_____

Health consultant's name and number _____

Be ready to provide the following information:

1. Location of child—

   Street address and apt. or room number _____

   City _____

   Directions (cross streets, landmarks, etc.) _____

   _____

2. Telephone number you are calling from _____

3. Caller's name _____

4. What happened _____

5. Number and ages of children injured _____

6. Condition of child (children) _____

7. Help (first aid) given _____

Note: Let the EMS dispatcher hang up before you do.

Inventory for the First Aid Kit

Every child care setting should have a first aid kit stocked with items on the list below. You can buy the supplies for the first aid kit at drug stores or a hospital or medical supply stores.

Each first aid kit should be large enough to hold all the necessary supplies for first aid in the child care setting. Use a container that will close tightly. It should be stored where adults can reach it easily, but it must be stored out of the reach of children. You should arrange the contents so you can reach items easily without emptying the kit. You should be sure that the contents are wrapped tightly and are sanitary. You should restock the kit after each use.

A first aid kit should contain the following items:

- A copy of the first aid guides
- Adhesive strip bandages (½-inch, ¾-inch, 1-inch strips)
- Gauze bandages (4″×4″, nonstick, sterile)
- Rolled flexible or stretch gauze
- Roller bandages
- Bandage tape
- Nonstick, sterile pads (different sizes)
- Triangular bandages
- Small splints
- Eye dressing or pad
- Scissors
- Tweezers
- Safety pins
- Thermometer
- Flashlight with fresh batteries
- Disposable latex gloves

- Three-ounce rubber bulb syringe (to rinse out eyes, wounds, etc.)
- Special items for children with specific health problems (such as bee sting kit or an inhaler for a child with asthma)
- Emergency Telephone Guide
- Emergency contact information (phone numbers of the children's parents)
- Change for pay phone
- Pen or pencil and note pad
- Commercial cold pack or plastic bag for ice cubes
- Clean cloth
- Soap
- Small plastic cup
- Sealed packages of cleansing wipes
- Syrup of ipecac (1-ounce bottle)

**American Red Cross
Child Care Course:
Preventing Infectious
Diseases**

Contents

About the Preventing Infectious Diseases Unit

Every caregiver needs to know how to reduce the risk of infectious diseases and how to prevent illness in the child care setting. A child's surroundings—the air a child breathes, the surfaces a child touches, and the food a child eats—affect his or her health and well-being. No one can completely get rid of germs or diseases, but each person who cares for children can learn how to reduce the spread of infectious diseases by reducing the spread of disease-causing germs. Such simple steps as washing hands and diapering properly, cleaning and sanitizing work and play surfaces, airing out rooms, and handling food safely can reduce the risk of infections. This unit will teach you basic skills so you can work to make your child care setting clean and healthful.

What You Will Learn

This unit will teach you—
1. Which are the common infectious childhood diseases.
2. What germs are and how they spread.
3. How to reduce the risk of infections.
4. How the body's immune system works.
5. When and how to wash your hands in a way that prevents the spread of infectious diseases.
6. When and how to clean and sanitize all work and play surfaces in the child care setting in a way that prevents the spread of infectious diseases.
7. How to diaper and to change soiled underwear in a way that prevents the spread of infectious diseases.
8. How to work with parents and health consultants to prevent the spread of infectious diseases.
9. How to handle and store food safely.

Further Information

For further information about preventing infectious diseases, write the American Academy of Pediatrics, P.O. Box 927, Elk Grove Village, IL 60009-0927; the Center for Infectious Diseases, Centers for Disease Control, 1600 Clifton Rd., NE, Atlanta, GA 30333; the National Association for the Education of Young Children, 1834 Connecticut Ave., NW, Washington, DC 20009; or the American Public Health Association, Child Care Project, 1015 15th St., NW, Washington, DC 20005.

Activity 1
Orientation

Objective

After you have finished this activity, you will be able to do the following:
1. Tell the unit requirements

Lessons

- Your instructor will discuss the unit with you and what you must do to pass it. The unit requirements are—
  - Satisfactory performance on the test—80 percent or higher (or 20 correct answers).
  - Attendance of the class for the entire unit.
- You will review the contents of the workbook.

Preventing Infectious Diseases Unit Agenda

Activity	Topic
1	Orientation
2	Introductions
3	About Infectious Diseases
4	*Healthy Child Care—Is It Really Magic?* Video, Part 1: "Germs Away"
5	Germs Away Discussion
Break	
6	*Healthy Child Care—Is It Really Magic?* Video, Part 2: "Clean Scenes"
7	Clean Scenes, Discussion and Skills Test
8	*Healthy Child Care—Is It Really Magic?* Video, Part 3: "The 'We' in Wellness"
9	The "We" in Wellness Discussion
10	Safe Food Rules
11	Test and Unit Evaluation

Activity 2
Introductions

Objectives

After you have finished this activity, you will be able to do the following:
1. Use the All About You sheet to tell the group about yourself
2. Tell why you are taking this unit

Lesson

• Fill out the All About You sheet. The sheet is on the next page.

All About You

Fill in the blanks.

1. What is your name? _____

2. Where do you work? _____

3. What is your job there? _____

4. How old are the children in your group? _____

5. Why are you taking this unit? _____

6. What do you hope to learn? _____

_____

_____

Activity 3
About Infectious Diseases

Learning Objectives

After you have finished this activity, you will be able to do the following:
1. Tell what causes infectious diseases
2. Tell the different ways in which diseases spread
3. List the common infectious childhood diseases
4. List infections that can be prevented by immunizations

Lessons

- Infectious diseases are caused by germs, such as viruses, bacteria, funguses, parasites, and tiny insects that live on the body.
- The most common childhood infections are colds, sore throats, and ear infections. Other common infections include gastrointestinal diseases (diseases of the bowels and stomach) and skin conditions such as impetigo, ringworm, lice, and scabies. You should learn which infectious diseases the children you care for might get. For further information, turn to Appendix A, More About Infectious Diseases.
- Diseases can be spread by germs that live in many different places, and these germs can enter our bodies in many different ways. In all cases, proper hand washing, proper care of children, proper washing of bedding and clothing, proper handling of food, and proper cleaning of the child care setting can reduce the spread of infections.
- Many diseases can be prevented by immunization. (An *immunization* is also known as a *vaccine*.) The instructor will write a list of the common diseases prevented by immunization on the flip chart. Turn to Appendix B, The Immunization Chart. This shows an immunization schedule for children.
- Young children have several common respiratory illnesses and several bouts of diarrhea per year. These tend to occur mainly in the winter. During their first year in the child care setting, children may have a greater number of infectious diseases than children cared for at home, especially if you do not help stop the spread of infections. After the first year, children in the child care setting tend to be sick less often. You can control the introduction of new germs into a group by keeping the same children together with the same caregivers. Young children, whether they are cared for only at home by parents or are cared for in the child care setting by caregivers, can have the same kinds of diseases. In fact, anyone may get any of these diseases at any time in life.

Activity 4
Healthy Child Care—
Is It Really Magic?
Video, Part 1: "Germs Away"

• Watch the video.

Activity 5
Germs Away Discussion

Learning Objective

After you have finished this activity, you will be able to do the following:
1. Tell ways to control the spread of infections

Lessons

• The infection-control triangle reminds you how to control the spread of infections in 3 ways, as you saw in the video. As you discuss this topic, write down the 3 ways in the blanks below. Then label your own triangle to match the triangle the instructor has labeled on the flip chart.

1. People _____

2. Germs _____

3. Places _____

• The immune system of the body fights off infectious diseases. It builds up the body's defenses against each type of germ and it remembers germs it has met before. It can fight familiar germs better and faster when the body meets them again. One of the best ways to prevent infectious diseases is to strengthen people's resistance to infection by immunization. Immunizations are medicines that teach the immune system to recognize certain germs and then to remember how to fight them off. Other ways in which people, especially children, can fight off diseases are rest, exercise, and proper nutrition.

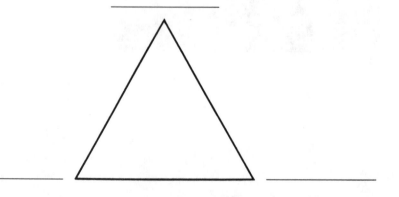

- Germs are everywhere. Germs are spread most commonly and easily by contact with dirty hands. Hands touch places where many germs live, such as in mouths and noses, and on work, play, or other surfaces. Children and adults can easily bring germs into their bodies when eating, handling food, or putting their hands in or around their mouths and noses. You should wash your hands when you arrive at the child care setting, before handling or eating foods, after using the toilet or diapering a child, and after handling other body secretions. Proper hand washing helps stop the spread of germs. You should also wash and sanitize surfaces in the child care setting to stop the spread of germs.
- Sneezing and coughing can spread germs. Direct your sneezes and coughs away from others. Wash your hands after covering a sneeze or a cough, even if you use a tissue, and after wiping your nose or a child's nose.
- Kissing can pass germs. Ill people and people outside of the child's family must never kiss a child directly on the lips. You can show affection by kissing the child on the cheek or forehead instead.
- The instructor will ask you to tell how to alter places in ways that keep people and germs apart in the child care setting. Remember what you learned in the video. You may refer to the following list, adding your own suggestions during the discussion:
  - Clean and sanitize all work and play surfaces.
  - Handle and store cooked foods safely.
  - Cook raw foods that may spoil.
  - Space cribs and cots so air can circulate.
  - Set up separate diaper-changing and toileting areas away from surfaces used for food preparation or food service.
  - Install sinks with running water near diaper-changing and toileting areas.
  - Put all diapering needs in easy reach, but out of the reach of children, so you do not have to use germy hands to open cabinet doors or drawers.
  - Use step trash cans. That way, you do not have to touch the lid.
  - Use toilets instead of potty or training chairs, which need special cleaning by hand.
  - Have lots of washable toys for children who put toys in their mouths. That way, you can wash and sanitize dirty toys after a child has finished playing with them. (To wash mouthed toys properly, use a wash basin to soak off sticky food and mucous. Fill it fresh each day with soap and water and label it "soiled toys." Then wash the toys in the dishwasher, clothes washer, or by hand as you would dishes.)
  - Store toothbrushes separately from one another and with their bristles up, exposed to the air.

● You can help children stay healthy and fight infectious diseases. For further information, turn to Appendix C, Helping Children Stay Healthy. You can also teach children the song about hand washing. You will practice this song in class using the words and hand movements below:

(Sung to the tune of "Row Your Boat")

Words	**Motions**
Wash, wash, wash your hands.	(vertical rubbing of hands)
Play your handy game.	(hands palms out, fingers up)
Rub and scrub and scrub and rub.	(rub hands in washing motion)
Germs go down the drain.	(hands palms out, fingers up, wiggle fingers, lowering arms)
Ha!	(clap)

Song printed with the permission of InSight Productions, Berkeley, California, from the video *Healthy Child Care: Is It Really Magic?*

Activity 6
Healthy Child Care—
Is It Really Magic?
Video, Part 2: "Clean Scenes"

Lesson

• Watch the video.

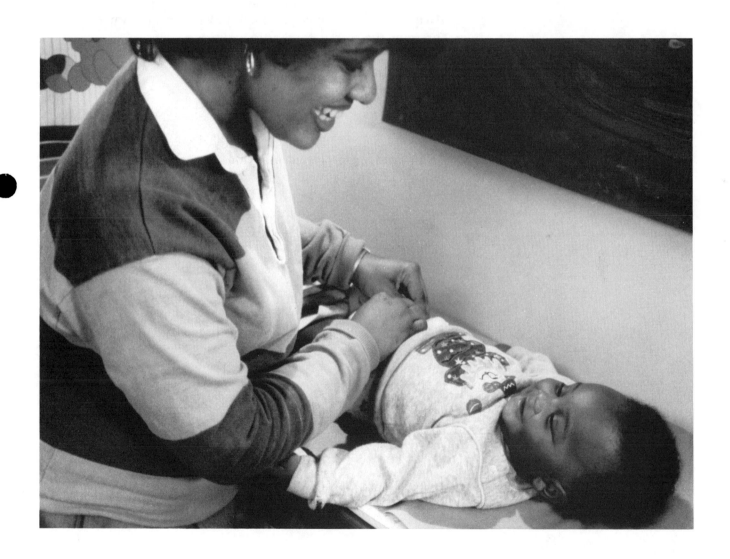

Activity 7
Clean Scenes, Discussion and Skills Check

Learning Objectives

After you have finished this activity, you will be able to do the following:

1. Tell when and how to wash your hands in a way that prevents the spread of infectious diseases
2. Diaper a child, or change soiled underwear, in a way that prevents the spread of infectious diseases
3. Tell when and how to clean and sanitize all work and play surfaces in the child care setting

Lessons

- Clean hands help prevent infectious diseases. You must learn when and how to wash your hands and how to do it in a way that prevents the spread of infectious diseases. You must always wash hands before handling, preparing, or eating food, and after touching body fluids and waste such as blood, saliva, vomit, stool, and urine. You must also teach children about hand washing. Watch the instructor demonstrate the Hand-Washing Instructions on page C-13. Then practice hand washing with a partner using the same instructions. Your instructor will check you.
- Turn to Hand Washing—Do It Right! on page C-14. You can make copies of the page to hang by each sink area in your child care setting.

Hand-Washing Instructions

- Have everything ready, including—
  - Liquid or powdered soap in a dispenser.
  - Paper towels.
  - Hand lotion.
- Use warm, running water and soap.
- Lather the fronts and the backs of hands, under fingernails, and between the fingers for at least 15 seconds.

- Rinse off all the soap under running water. Run water from wrists to fingertips.
- Dry hands with a paper towel.
- Turn the faucet off with the paper towel to avoid picking up the germs on the faucet.
- Drop paper towel into the trash can.
- Apply hand lotion to prevent dry, cracked, or chapped hands.

Hand Washing—Do It Right!

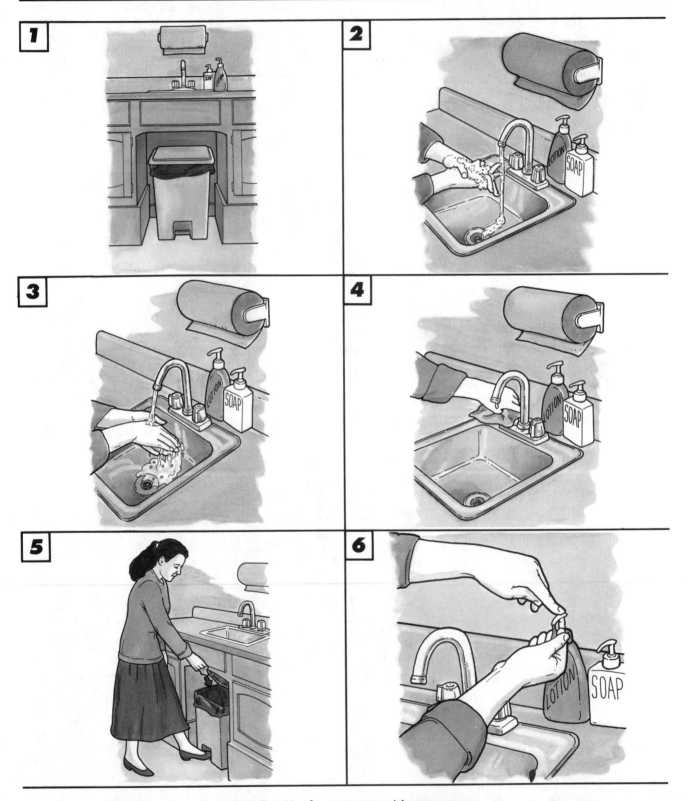

- Proper diapering or changing techniques also help prevent the spread of infections. You may already know how to diaper and how to change soiled underwear. But you may not know how to do these things in a way that prevents the spread of infectious diseases. Read the Diapering Instructions on page C-16. Then watch the diapering demonstration.

  Note: Use the same procedure when you change a child's soiled underwear.
- Turn to the Diapering Self-Test on page C-17. Number the pictures in the correct order. After you have taken the self-test, check your answers with Diapering—Do it Right! on page C-19. (When you return to your child care setting, you may want to make copies of Diapering—Do It Right! and hang a copy in each diapering or changing area.)

Diapering Instructions

- Change diapers in a special place that is away from food, and where nothing else is done.
- Cover the flat, clean diapering surface with nonporous paper.
- Have the following supplies ready before bringing the child to the diapering area:
  - Disposable wipes or fresh, wet paper towels
  - Diapers
  - Disposable plastic gloves and bags, if using them is part of the program's health policy
  - Step trash can
  - Soap and a source of running water
  - Skin preparation such as petroleum jelly or zinc oxide, if the child's doctor has prescribed it
  - Sanitizing solution and paper towels for cleaning up
- Avoid any contact with the child's soiled clothing except with your hands.
- Lay the child down on the paper-covered changing table.
- Put on disposable gloves.
- Take off the child's clothes.
- Open the diaper. Clean off any stool with the inside of the soiled surface or with disposable wipes.

- Wipe the child from front to back. Use a fresh disposable wipe or a fresh, wet paper towel for each wipe.
- Drop the soiled diaper and diaper wipes into the step trash can lined with a plastic bag, or into a plastic bag. (Place cloth diapers or soiled underwear in a plastic bag, seal the bag, and give it to the parent to take home.)
- Put a clean diaper on the child. Make sure the child's clothing is clean and dry.
- Remove the child from the changing table.
- Wash the child's hands under running water with soap, or wipe the child's hands with a disposable wipe.
- Drop the used paper from the changing table into the step trash can or plastic bag.
- Clean any visible soil from the changing table with paper towels or disposable wipes.
- Wipe the surface of the changing table with the sanitizing solution, and let the surface air dry.
- Drop any used disposable gloves into the step trash can or plastic bag.
- Wash and dry your own hands.
- Apply hand lotion to prevent dry, cracked, or chapped skin.

Note: Never leave the child unattended while changing diapers or underwear. Wear disposable gloves if the child has diarrhea.

Diapering Self-Test

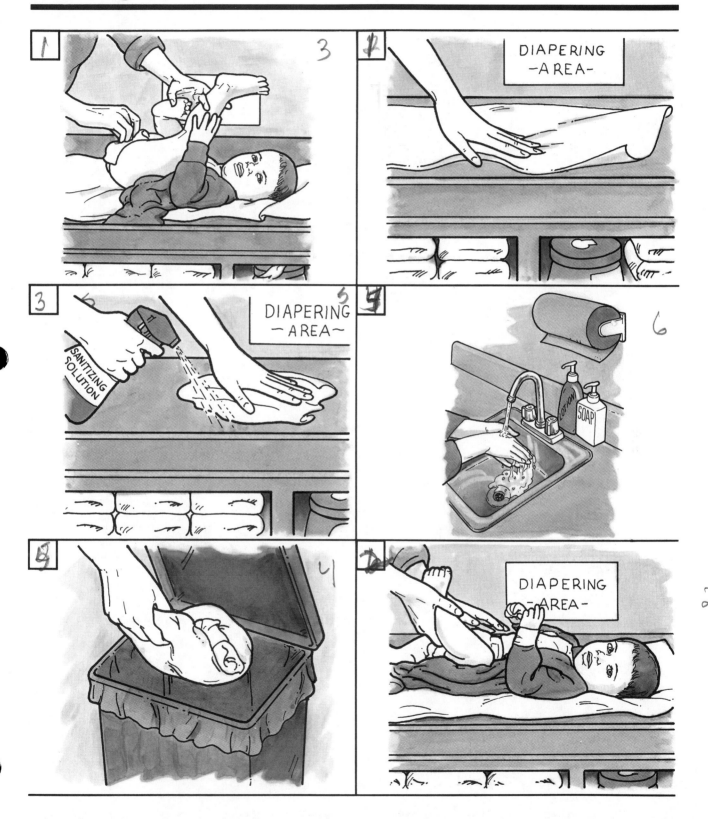

Diapering—Do It Right!

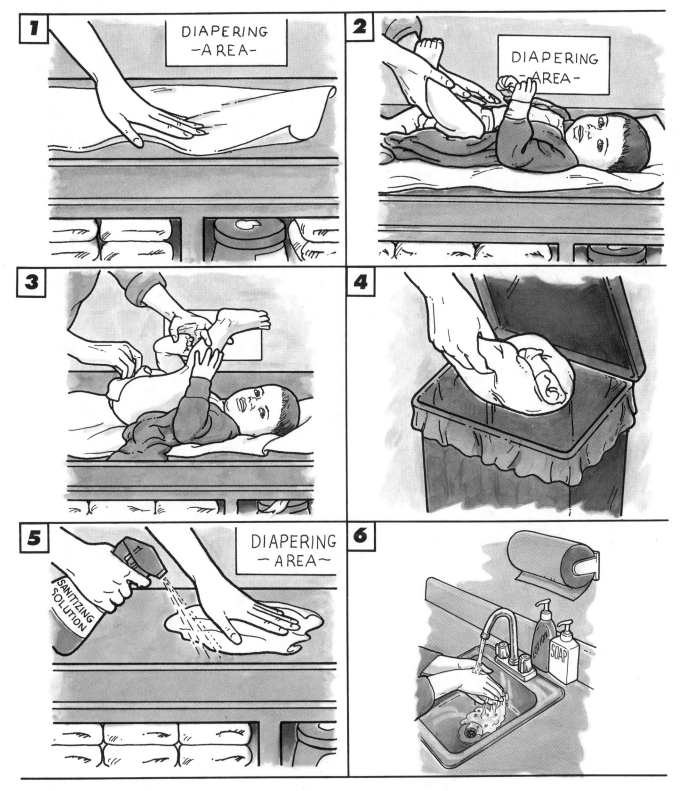

- You must clean and sanitize the surfaces in your child care setting regularly. There are 2 steps. First, wash the surface with a good cleaning solution. Then sanitize it. Use a sanitizing solution of one tablespoonful of liquid household chlorine bleach to one quart of water, or ¼ cup of bleach to one gallon of water.

   Always read the label when you are using a commercial cleaning product. Follow directions and pay attention to any warnings. Some cleaning products contain ammonia, which must never be mixed with the bleach solution.

   You should always make a fresh batch of sanitizing solution each day. The bleach evaporates and makes the solution too weak to kill germs. Keep the bleach solution and all cleaning products out of the reach of children at all times. When using the solution in a spray bottle, be careful to aim the spray away from your face and away from children.

- You must regularly clean and/or sanitize the following places in the child care setting:

   After each use—Counters used for preparing and serving food, tables used for eating, changing tables, toys put in a child's mouth, and other germ-covered surfaces such as dishes and utensils. (Avoid using potty training chairs because these need special cleaning by hand after each use.)

   Daily—Sinks, kitchen floors and counters, toilets and toilet areas, tables, toys, door knobs and other handled surfaces, and rugs.

   Weekly (or more often)—Cubbies, cribs, drinking fountains, uncarpeted floors, refrigerators, and trash cans.

   You should spot-clean walls and carpets monthly, and deep-clean them every 6 months. You must discard rubbish daily. Keep soiled laundry in suitable containers and wash it regularly. All housekeeping equipment and supplies should be kept out of the reach of children.

   To help control the spread of disease-causing germs, children must never share the following: eating utensils, dishes, cups, water-play basins, towels, bedding, and clothing. Remember, fresh air helps to ventilate rooms and to reduce the number of germs in the air. Even in very cold weather, you should ventilate the following areas every day: kitchen, dining room, bathroom, office, and playroom.

- Turn to and review Appendix D, Germs Away Checklist. Follow this checklist to improve the procedures in your child care setting. The words of the closing song from the video, Part 2, will remind you to keep your child care setting clean:

> *Take the time to make it shine;*
> *Disinfect to keep things healthy.*
> *If you clean with care*
> *Germs won't be there.*
> *You'll protect against infection.*
> *Take the time to make it sparkle.*
> *Show the children love, a heart full.*
> *You can rest at ease*
> *When she's fighting off disease*
> *Every day sweep dirt away.*
> *Disinfect to make things healthy.*

Copyright Frank Harris. Used with permission.

Activity 8
Healthy Child Care—
Is It Really Magic?
Video, Part 3:
"The 'We' in Wellness"

Lesson

- Watch the video.

Activity 9
The "We" In Wellness Discussion

Learning Objectives

After you have finished this activity, you will be able to do the following:

1. Name a health consultant to call for advice
2. Do correctly a daily health check
3. List the changes in how a child acts or looks that tell you a child may have an infectious disease
4. Tell how to decide when an ill child should stay home or should go home
5. List what to tell the parent about an infectious disease

Lessons

- Public health nurses, visiting nurses, community nursing associations, local chapters of the National Association of Pediatric Nurse Practitioners (NAPNP), local chapters of the American Academy of Pediatrics, and pediatricians are good sources for professional health advice.

    Turn to and read the Source List of Health Consultants on page C-26. This will tell you whom you may call for health advice.

- Every child care program must have a health policy. Turn to Appendix E, Health Policy Guidelines. Read about the things that a health policy should include in order to prevent infectious diseases. When a parent registers his or her child for the program, you should discuss the program's health policy.

- You must do a health check when the child first arrives each day at the child care setting. When you do the health check every day, you will learn what is normal for each child. That way, you will know when something is different about the child.

    Do the health check before the parent leaves the child care setting. This gives you a chance to find out if the child may be ill. If so, you can ask the parent to take the child home. Remember, you are not supposed to diagnose an illness or care for a very ill child.

    Turn to the Daily Health Check Instructions on page C-27 and read along during the daily health check demonstration. After the demonstration, get a partner and use the instructions to practice the daily health check.

- You may suspect a child has an infectious disease if the child has any of the following symptoms:

  1. Acts or looks ill or seems to be getting worse quickly
  2. Pale or flushed skin, or a rash
  3. Shiny or red eyes, or dark circles under the eyes
  4. Warmer than normal body
  5. Pain or other unpleasant sensation
  6. Changes in body functions; for example, vomiting, diarrhea, lack of appetite, or nasal discharge

- When a child has certain symptoms, he or she should stay home or be cared for in a special care setting, unless the child's doctor says that he or she can be in the child care setting and the child is able to participate fully in the program's activities. These symptoms include the following:

  - An infant under 4 months of age has an axillary (underarm) temperature of 100 degrees Fahrenheit or higher or a rectal temperature of 101 degrees Fahrenheit or higher. (Get medical help immediately.)
  - A child between the ages of 4 months and 24 months has a rectal temperature of 102 degrees Fahrenheit or higher, or an axillary temperature of 101 degrees Fahrenheit or higher.
  - A child over 24 months of age has an oral or axillary temperature of 102 degrees Fahrenheit or higher.
  - You believe the child has an infectious disease that the other children might catch.
  - The child has a special condition that a health consultant has advised puts him or her at increased risk from a contagious illness.
  - The child has a fever and is feeling or acting ill.
  - The child is vomiting and has an upset stomach.
  - The child has looser and more frequent stools than usual (diarrhea) and the stool cannot be contained in the diaper, or the child cannot reach the toilet in time.
  - The child has a constant runny nose not caused by allergies.
  - The child is in pain.
  - You don't have the training or the time to take care of the child's needs.

- For further information, turn to the Exclusion Guidelines and to the Preventing Infectious Diseases guidelines in Appendix E, Health Policy Guidelines.

- Sending an ill child home and notifying all other parents of the presence of an infectious disease are 2 steps that may help stop the spread of the following diseases:
  - Chicken pox (varicella)
  - Hepatitis A
  - Impetigo
  - Infectious conjunctivitis (pink eye)
  - Infectious diarrhea
  - Lice
  - Ringworm
  - Scabies
  - Strep throat, scarlet fever
  - Vaccine-preventable diseases (diseases prevented by immunizations)

  For further information, turn to Appendix A, More About Infectious Diseases.
- You must notify all parents by letter when a child has been exposed to an infectious disease in the child care setting. Turn to Appendix F, Sample Letter. Does your program use a similar letter?
- Parents, health professionals, and caregivers must cooperate to keep children healthy.

Source List of Health Consultants

Many health professionals have skills and knowledge that caregivers can use. Some professionals may have special knowledge for one part of the program; others can serve as overall health consultants. Examples of health professionals who may be able to help include—

- Physicians, preferably pediatricians (specialists in child health).
- Physician assistants.
- Nurses.
- Public health nurses.
- Nurse epidemiologists.
- Nurse practitioners or nurse clinicians—preferably pediatric specialists.
- Infection-control nurses.
- Public health specialists (with a masters degree in Public Health).
- School nurses.
- Sanitarians.

Daily Health Check Instructions

Note: When you perform the health check, be at the child's level—kneel down if the child is sitting or standing, hold the child, or have the parent hold the child at your level.

- Look at how the child acts and looks.
    1. Is the child's behavior normal for this time of day or is there some difference?
    2. Is the child clinging to the parent, acting cranky, or acting normally?

3. Does the child look pale or flushed?
4. Do you see a rash?
5. Do the child's eyes look shiny or red?
6. Are there dark circles under the child's eyes?
7. Is the child's nose running?
8. Is the child coughing or having any difficulty breathing?
9. Does the child seem itchy?

• Listen to the child and to the parent. What do they tell you about how the child feels and acts? Does the child's voice sound normal?

1. If the child can talk, ask "How are you today? Is everything okay?" Listen to the child's voice. Is the child hoarse?

2. Ask the parent how the child has been feeling and acting:
   • Did the child have a good night?
   • Did the child eat normally?
   • Did anything unusual happen?

- Touch the child's skin.
  1. Gently run the back of your hand over the child's cheek, forehead, and the back of the child's neck. See if the child feels unusually warm to the touch, or if the skin feels different (for example, bumpy) and should be looked at more closely.
  2. Use your hand, not your lips, to touch children. Your lips could pick up germs from the child's body, and you might give your germs to the child.
- Sniff for unusual odors.
  1. Children who have not eaten for many hours may have a fruity mouth odor.
  2. Some children may arrive with stool in their diapers and need to be changed right away.
  3. Parents may have used some medication with a distinctive odor that you will want to know about.

Activity 10
Safe Food Rules

Learning Objectives

After you have finished this activity, you will be able to do the following:
1. Describe the ways germs are spread through contaminated foods and when dirty hands touch food
2. List how to keep foods safe until they are used

Lessons

- Germs can contaminate food when carried to food by insects or rodents, or when dirty utensils or dirty hands touch food. For example, flies landing on food may have recently landed on dog feces or garbage. All food must be covered and stored safely to protect it from germs.

  You must always wash your hands properly with soap and water before preparing or handling food, between handling raw and cooked foods, and whenever handling food preparation surfaces, dishes, and utensils. You must never serve or prepare food when you have an infectious disease or skin infection.
- Germs can double in quantity in 15 to 20 minutes. Warmth plus moisture and nutrients cause germs to multiply to a level that can cause disease. For example, suppose potato salad has 100 germs in it. After it has been allowed to sit in an uncovered dish at room temperature for 2 ½ hours, it could contain over 100,000 germs.
- To store or keep food at temperatures that stop or slow germ growth, you must—
  - Keep cold foods in the refrigerator at or below 40 degrees Fahrenheit.
  - Be sure hot foods are heated to and kept at or above 140 degrees Fahrenheit.
- Throw out all perishable foods not kept at safe cold or hot temperatures. Throw out all perishable foods left out at room temperature for 2 hours or more.
- If you prepare food in the child care setting, you should get specific information about food handling and preparation from the United States Department of Agriculture or a public health agency.

- To handle and store foods safely, you must—
  - Rinse thoroughly all raw fruits and vegetables before use.
  - Wash and dry tops of canned goods before opening.
  - Wrap or cover all perishable foods tightly before storing.
  - Store or hold all perishable foods at proper temperatures.
  - Put dry foods such as flour, sugar, and cereal in glass, plastic, or metal containers with tight lids.
  - Be sure all dry or canned goods are on clean shelves that are free from rodents and insects.
  - Separate food from nonfood items.
  - Use an up-to-date inventory system to rotate and to use up all food items.
- For further information, turn to Appendix G, Handling Food Safely.

Activity 11
Test and Unit Evaluation

Objective

After you have finished this activity, you will be able to do the following:
1. Complete the test

Lessons

- The test that the instructor will give you has 25 questions about what you learned in this class. Answer the questions on the answer sheet. You must score 80 percent or higher (or answer 20 or more questions correctly) to pass this unit.
- Your instructor will also give you a unit evaluation sheet. Please tell us what you thought of this unit by filling out this sheet and returning it to the instructor.
- Thank you for your participation in the American Red Cross Child Care Course. By taking all of the units of the Child Care Course, you are showing your commitment to giving the best possible child care. Now that you understand the information and skills presented, you will be able to put your caring and concern for children into action.

 **Appendixes**

More About Infectious Diseases

Bronchitis or Bronchiolitis

Signs and symptoms—Coughing and breathing difficulties.
How disease spreads—By contact with germs from saliva, mucous, or tears of an infected person from one to 2 days before symptoms appear and for several days after they appear.
Child may return—When the caregiver can meet the child's needs.

Chicken Pox

Signs and symptoms—Like those of a cold, with a mild fever and an itchy rash that starts as pink bumps that turn into blisters and finally into scabs.
How disease spreads—By close contact or from airborne droplets from one to 2 days before, until about 5 days after the rash appears. If everyone has already been exposed during this time, keeping a child home will not prevent the disease from spreading. New cases can appear up to 20 days after contact. Chicken pox is very contagious.
Child may return—When the caregiver can meet the child's needs, or when all blisters are crusted over and dry, which is usually not until the sixth day after the rash starts. In mild cases, the child may return sooner if he or she is well.

Colds

Signs and symptoms—Sneezing, runny nose, sore throat, cough, watery or irritated eyes, headache, and crankiness; sometimes a fever.
How disease spreads—By contact with germs from the saliva or nose mucous of an infected person, from one to 2 days before symptoms appear until several days after symptoms appear.
Child may return—When the caregiver can meet the child's needs.

Ear Infections (otitis)

Signs and symptoms—Earache, pulling at the ear, unusual crankiness, difficulty in hearing, or funny sensations in the ear caused by a mucous and/or pus backup in the middle ear and eustachian tube.
How disease spreads—Not contagious.
Child may return—When well enough to participate in the program's activities.

Fifth Disease

Signs and symptoms—A distinctive rash beginning on the face that makes the child appear to have very red slapped cheeks. After one to 4 days, a lacy-looking rash appears on the arms and moves to the trunk, buttocks, and thighs. The body rash may come and go for one to 3 weeks, usually appearing when the child is hot or has been in the sun. Some children have a fever when the illness begins.
How disease spreads—By virus, probably found in respiratory secretions.
Child may return—A few days after the rash appears or when the rash starts to fade.

Hepatitis A

Signs and symptoms—Fever, weakness, loss of appetite, nausea, dark urine, and yellowing of the skin and of the whites of the eyes. Children rarely have any of these symptoms.
How disease spreads—By contact with viral-infected food, stool, water, or environment. The virus is shed for up to 3 weeks, starting 2 weeks before symptoms appear. The illness may occur up to 50 days after contact. The disease is a major problem in the child care setting. The caregiver must contact public health officials about which measures may be needed to control the spread of the disease.

Child may return—One week after illness starts, and when the fever is gone.

Herpes

Signs and symptoms—For herpes simplex of the oral type, fever, irritability, and inflammation of the mouth and gums with cold sores and fever blisters, and blisters around the mouth and sometimes on the fingers. Herpes viruses may be present without symptoms. (Genital herpes is not usually found in children. If present, the possibility of sexual abuse must be considered.)
How disease spreads—By direct contact with infected mucous or saliva; especially contagious the first day after a blister appears.
Child may return—No need to stay home.

Impetigo

Signs and symptoms—Red, oozy rash; blisters; or honey-colored, crusty scabs.
How disease spreads—Through cuts and scrapes in the skin that come in direct contact with bacteria in the soil or from another infected person, or by direct contact with objects that have the bacteria on them.
Child may return—After treatment begins.

Infectious Conjunctivitis (pink eye)

Signs and symptoms—Red, tearing eyes that may hurt or feel itchy; swollen lids; thick, yellow discharge. (Red eyes may also occur with many common respiratory diseases or when a child has eye allergies.)
How disease spreads—By contact, when the infected child rubs his or her eyes and then touches other objects.

Child may return—The day after treatment starts, or when the discharge stops.

Infectious Croup

Signs and symptoms—Difficult breathing, barky cough, and an especially harsh sound when the child inhales, particularly at night. This is caused by swelling in the airway in the neck. (A rare, dangerous form of croup is epiglottitis, or swelling of the tissue cap that keeps food from going into the airway during swallowing. Epiglottitis is caused by the bacteria Haemophilus influenzae type b [Hib], and spreads like the common cold. Hib can be prevented for children over 18 months of age by immunization. Children and staff in contact with a child who has been diagnosed with a disease caused by Hib may need special medicine or a public health official may need to take other measures to control the disease.)
How disease spreads—By contact with germs from the saliva or nose mucous of an infected person.
Child may return—When the child is well enough to attend, and the recommended control measures have been followed.

Infectious Diarrhea: Campylobacter

Signs and symptoms—Abdominal cramps, vomiting, fever, and possibly severe diarrhea.
How disease spreads—Through water or food, or from hands that touch surfaces contaminated by germs from the stools and then go in the mouth. Infections can occur for 7 or more days after exposure to the germ.
Child may return—Forty-eight hours after antibiotic treatment begins and when no fever or severe diarrhea symptoms remain.

Infectious Diarrhea: Common viral

Signs and symptoms—Looser and more frequent stools than normal.

How disease spreads—From hands that touch surfaces contaminated by germs from stools and then go in the mouth. Children may have the virus in their stools for one to 2 days before they have symptoms. The illness usually occurs within one to 3 days after exposure.

Child may return—When the stool can be contained and the child has no other symptoms.

Infectious Diarrhea: Giardia

Signs and symptoms—Symptoms may not always be present, but there may be recurring diarrhea, nausea, bloating, weight loss, and abdominal cramps.

How disease spreads—By cysts contained in infected child's stool. When a case occurs, stool cultures should be taken of all symptomatic people who have had contact with the child.

Child may return—After antibiotic treatment and when all symptoms are gone. Children with no symptoms but with giardia in their stools do not need to stay home if the caregiver and the child follow careful hygiene practices.

Infectious Diarrhea: Salmonellosis

Signs and symptoms—Abdominal cramps, pain, fever, and diarrhea that appear within 24 hours after the germ enters the body.

How disease spreads—By eating contaminated food, or from hands that touch surfaces contaminated by germs from stools and then go in the mouth.

Child may return—When symptoms are gone. The caregiver and child must follow careful hygiene practices. The caregiver should contact public health officials. Stool cultures of caregivers or children in contact with the infected child may be needed. Public health officials may need to take other measures to control the spread of the disease.

Infectious Diarrhea: Shigellosis

Signs and symptoms—Abdominal cramps, diarrhea, or sometimes bloody stool with mucous.

How disease spreads—When hands touch surfaces contaminated by germs from stools and then go in the mouth. When the disease appears, the caregiver must contact public health officials. Stool cultures of caregivers or children in contact with the infected child may be needed. Public health officials may need to take other measures to control the spread of the disease.

Child may return—After antibiotic treatment is completed, and when 3 stool cultures taken 24 hours apart are negative.

Influenza A (winter flu)

Signs and symptoms—Sore throat, fever, chills, headache, muscle aches, loss of appetite, feeling ill.

How disease spreads—By direct contact or by contact with articles recently contaminated by secretions from an infected person's nose or mouth.

Child may return—When the child is well enough to participate.

Lice

Signs and symptoms—Itchy bites on the head.
How disease spreads—By tiny insects that lay eggs (nits) that look like grains of sand on the hair around the neck and ears. Lice crawl from one person or piece of clothing to another. A person can also acquire lice from direct personal contact or contact with infected clothing.
Child may return—The day after treatment begins.

Ringworm

Signs and symptoms—Slightly-raised, itchy, ring-shaped sores anywhere on the body. Ringworm is caused by a fungus.
How disease spreads—By direct contact with infected people, animals, or surfaces that have the ringworm fungus on them.
Child may return—Twenty-four hours after treatment starts.

Roseola

Signs and symptoms—Fever for several days that suddenly disappears at the same time a rash appears. Rash lasts one to 2 days.
How disease spreads—Unknown. The germ is thought to be a virus.
Child may return—When the child is well enough to participate, or if the caregiver can meet the child's needs.

Scabies

Signs and symptoms—Very itchy red rash that appears between the fingers and around the waist, wrists, elbows, underarms, navel, penis, nipples, abdomen, outer borders of the feet, and lower portion of the buttocks. In infants, the rash may look like small blisters on the head, neck, palms, and soles.
How disease spreads—By close personal contact or prolonged casual contact; caused by small insects called mites.
Child may return—Twenty-four hours after treatment starts.

Strep Throat, Scarlet Fever (Streptococcus, Group A Infections)

Signs and symptoms—Sore throat; fever; infections of ears, lymph nodes, skin and other tissue; sometimes a rash.
How disease spreads—By contact with an infected person, or by contaminated food that is improperly refrigerated.
Child may return—The day after antibiotic treatment starts.

Vaccine-Preventable Diseases (diseases prevented by immunizations)

Diseases that can be prevented by immunizations include measles, mumps, polio, rubella, diphtheria, tetanus, whooping cough (pertussis), and Hib (Haemophilus influenzae type b). (Immunizations against chicken pox, winter diarrhea, and other illnesses are being tested, but are not available as of this writing.) Although some of these diseases are rare, they do occur sometimes, and some children are at risk, particularly when they are too young to be immunized fully. (All adults working in the child care setting should either have had the diseases or have been immunized against them.)

Documented cases of measles, mumps, rubella, polio, diphtheria, tetanus, or pertussis should immediately be reported to the local board of health so officials can start identifying and vaccinating any susceptible children or adults. Caregivers should check with their board of health to be sure the doctor who made the diagnosis filed a report.

Diphtheria: A bacterial infection of the nose and throat that causes a sore throat and swollen tonsils and neck glands. The throat or tonsil swelling can actually block breathing. Diphtheria is treated with an antitoxin and antibiotics. Anyone with diphtheria should not return to the child care setting until 2 separate cultures, taken 24 hours apart after treatment is finished, are negative.

Measles: Measles appears first on the face as a brownish-red, itchy rash that then spreads down the body. Measles causes a high fever, cough, and runny nose. The illness lasts up to 2 weeks and may involve complications. Anyone with measles should not return to the child care setting until 4 days after the rash disappears.

Mumps: This viral disease causes fever, headaches, a painful swelling of the salivary glands, and complications such as meningitis, encephalitis, and deafness. Anyone with mumps should not return to the child care setting until 9 days after the swelling starts.

Pertussis (whooping cough): Pertussis starts with mild cold symptoms and develops into severe coughing. Seizures or even death can occur during a coughing spell. The cough continues for a long time, followed by a rapid intake of breath that has a distinctive "whooping" sound. Anyone with pertussis should not return to the child care setting until 5 days after antibiotic therapy starts, or until 3 weeks after the cough starts.

Polio: This viral illness can be mild or so severe that it causes paralysis or death. Anyone with polio should not return to the child care setting until stool tests are negative or public health officials say it is safe for the child to return.

Rubella (German measles): Rubella is a mild viral illness marked by a slight fever and a flat, red rash that starts on the face and spreads quickly to the rest of the body. The illness lasts 3 days. The rash looks the same as many other viral rashes and a sure diagnosis requires 2 blood tests, one at the beginning of the illness and one several weeks later. Anyone with rubella should not return to the child care setting until 5 days after the rash starts.

Tetanus (lockjaw): This bacteria is found in soil and enters the body through an open skin wound. The infection causes muscle spasms and sometimes, paralysis and death. Tetanus is not contagious; anyone with tetanus may return to the child care setting whenever he or she feels well enough to attend.

The Immunization Chart

In January 1995, representatives from the American Academy of Pediatrics, Centers for Disease Control, American Academy of Family Practice, American Medical Association, U.S. Food & Drug Administration, and National Institutes of Health agreed to produce a unified childhood immunization schedule. On the unified immunization schedule printed below, shaded bars represent the acceptable period when each vaccine dose can be given. Accompanying footnotes explain additional recommendations. The changes are mainly that children can receive some vaccines at younger ages. The outer limit of the recommended age range has not changed. Children are not over-due for vaccines until they have passed their outer limit. Updated schedules will be available as soon as the manufacturer ships the chicken pox vaccine. Expect the first vaccine to be in doctors' offices around June, 1995.

So continue to use your second edition of the Immunization Dose Counter to check if children in your care are up-to-date for their shots. Check for updates annually with your health care provider.

Recommended Ages for Administration of Currently Licensed Childhood Vaccines — August 1995

Vaccines are listed under the routinely recommended ages. Solid bars indicate range of acceptable ages for vaccination. Shaded bars indicate new recommendations or vaccines licensed since publication of the Recommended Childhood Immunization Schedule in January 1995. Hepatitis B vaccine is recommended at 11–12 years of age for children not previously vaccinated. Varicella Zoster Virus vaccine is recommended at 11–12 years of age for children not previously vaccinated, and who lack a reliable history of chickenpox.

Age / Vaccine	Birth	2 mos	4 mos	6 mos	12[1] mos	15 mos	18 mos	4–6 yrs	11–12 yrs	14–16 yrs
Hepatitis B[2,3]	Hep B-1	Hep B-2		Hep B-3					Hep B[3]	
Diphtheria, Tetanus, Pertussis[4]		DTP	DTP	DTP	DTP[1,4] DTaP at 15+ m			DTP or DtaP	Td	
H. influenzae type b[5]		Hib	Hib	Hib[5]	HIB[1,5]					
Polio		OPV	OPV	OPV				OPV		
Measles, Mumps, Rubella[6]					MMR[1,6]			MMR or	[6]MMR	
Varicella Zoster[7]					VZV[7]				VZV[7]	

[1] Vaccines recommended in the second year of life (12–15 months of age) may be given at either one or two visits.

[2] **Infants born to HBsAg-negative mothers** should receive 2.5 µg of Merck Sharp & Dohme (MSD) vaccine (Recombivax HB) or 10 µg of SmithKline Beecham (SKB) vaccine (Engerix–B). The second dose should be given between 1 and 4 months of age, if at least 1 month has elapsed since receipt of the first dose. The third dose is recommended between 6 and 18 months of age.
Infants born to HBsAg-positive mothers should receive immunoprophylaxis for hepatitis B with 0.5 ml Hepatitis B Immune Globulin (HBIG) within 12 hours of birth, and either 5 µg of MSD vaccine (Recombivax HB) or 10 µg of SKB vaccine (Engerix-B) at a separate site. In these infants, the second dose of vaccine is recommended at 1 month of age and the third dose at 6 months of age. All pregnant women should be screened for HBsAg in an early prenatal visit.

[3] Hepatitis B vaccine is recommended for adolescents who have not previously received 3 doses of vaccine. The 3-dose series should be initiated or completed at the 11–12 year-old visit for persons not previously fully vaccinated. The 2nd dose should be administered at least 1 month after the first dose, and the 3rd dose should be administered at least 4 months after the first dose.

[4] The fourth dose of DTP may be administered as early as 12 months of age, provided at least 6 months have elapsed since DTP3. Combined DTP-Hib products may be used when these two vaccines are to be administered simultaneously. DTaP (diphtheria and tetanus toxoids and acellular pertussis vaccine) is licensed for use for the 4th and/or 5th dose of DTP vaccine in children 15 months of age or older and may be preferred for these doses in children in this age group. Td (tetanus and diphtheria toxoids, absorbed, for adult use) is recommended at 11–12 years of age if at least 5 years have elapsed since the lst dose of DTP, DTP-Hib, or DT.

[5] Three H. influenzae type b conjugate vaccines are available for use in infants: HbOC [HibTITER] (Lederle Praxis); PRP-T [ActHIB; OmniHIB] (Pasteur Mérieux, distributed by SmithKline Beecham; Connaught); and PRP-OMP [PedvaxHIB] (Merck Sharp & Dohme). Children who have received PRP-OMP at 2 and 4 months of age do not require a dose at 6 months of age. After the primary infant Hib conjugate vaccine series is completed, any licensed Hib conjugate vaccine may be used as a booster dose at 12–15 months.

[6] The second dose of MMR vaccine should be administered EITHER at 4–6 years of age OR at 11–12 years of age, consistent with state school immunization requirements.

[7] Varicella zoster virus vaccine (VZV) is routinely recommended at 12–18 months of age. Children who have not been vaccinated previously and who lack a reliable history of chickenpox should be vaccinated by 13 years of age. VZV can be administered to susceptible children any time after 12 months of age. Children under 13 years of age should receive a single 0.5 mL dose; persons 13 years of age and older should receive two 0.5 mL doses 4–8 weeks apart.

DTP is an immunization shot that combines diphtheria, tetanus, and pertussis vaccines.
Td combines tetanus and diphtheria vaccines (given to children age 6 and older).
MMR combines measles, mumps, and rubella vaccines.

Helping Children Stay Healthy

Caregivers, parents, and children themselves can help fight off infections and diseases. They can strengthen their resistance to germs by keeping their bodies healthy. Share with parents the other ways you are teaching their children to stay healthy.

Songs

Teach children about cleanliness with songs like the one below.

Take the Time to Make It Shine

Take the time to make it shine,
Make it shine, make it shine.
Take the time to make it shine.
Clean up to keep us healthy.

Wash germs away before we eat,
Before we eat, before we eat.
Wash germs away before we eat.
Clean up to keep us healthy.

Circle-Time Talks

You can help children talk and learn about staying healthy as a circle-time activity. As you talk with the children, encourage them to show how they feel with facial expressions and body postures. For example, ask the children to discuss how they feel when they feel well or when they feel sick. Ask them to tell you what they think germs are, then tell them about germs and where germs live. Talk with the children about the importance of hand washing to wash away germs before eating and after using the toilet.

Planning for Illness

Infants, toddlers, and preschoolers are likely to become ill more often than older children because their immature immune systems cannot fight off infections very well.

Parents need to plan ahead for child care for those times when a child is ill. They might want to consider working at home or using their own sick leave to stay home to care for the child. Or parents may want to make arrangements with community home health care workers or other caregivers who can provide care for an ill child at home on short notice. If the child care program has special arrangements for caring for ill children, the caregiver must give parents this information when they register the child for the program.

Parents should know that when their child is ill enough to remain at home, they must tell the caregiver about the illness. Parents must also tell the child's doctor about the illness, and then tell the caregiver about any special information or recommendations the doctor may have given.

Healthful Routines

You can teach children about healthful routines by talking about sleep time and the importance of a regular bedtime routine that includes a quiet period before the child actually goes to bed. This allows the child time to calm down after a busy day of play. You can talk about exercise and show children an exercise chart with developmentally appropriate activities for each age group. Tell children they should exercise daily outdoors. You can talk about proper nutrition and the importance of eating healthful meals and snacks. Snacks should be like small, nutritious meals and can include fruit, milkshakes with milk and fruit, raw vegetables, graham crackers, cheese, unsalted pretzels, or fruit juice bars.

Checkups

Children need regular checkups to be sure they are healthy and to get disease-preventing immunizations. Checkups can also include special tests to find disease problems so that the child's doctor can take steps to treat them. Children with special health problems need to have checkups more often than other children. If the child has no special problem, the child should have regular checkups at specified ages. See the following checkup table.

Checkup Table		
at birth	12 months	5 years
by 1 month of age	15 months	6 years
2 months	18 months	8 years
4 months	2 years	10 years
6 months	3 years	12 years
9 months	4 years	during adolescence as suggested by child's doctor (at least every 2 years)

Germs Away Checklist

The caregiver must follow strict rules for the regular cleaning and sanitizing of the child care setting. Use the following checklist to make a set of rules for each site. Remember the following definitions:

Clean: To remove any visible soil.

Sanitize: To reduce the number of germs on the surface.

Sanitizing solution: A solution for reducing germs that is made from one tablespoon of bleach (liquid household chlorine bleach) to one quart of water, or from ¼ cup bleach to one gallon of water.

Equipment and Supplies

- **Sinks**—Sinks should have hot and cold running water that mix through one faucet. Have at least one sink in every child care and food preparation area. Or use a refillable water dispenser (for example, a drinking water dispenser or large picnic jug) with a catch basin. The dispenser must be emptied, rinsed, and refilled daily. The catch basin also must be emptied at least daily.
- **Soap**—Liquid or powdered soap should be kept in a disposable or wall-mounted dispenser that is cleaned and refilled when empty. Do not use bar soap.
- **Towels**—Provide paper towels, which are kept in a dispenser, or one color-coded or labeled cloth towel per child. Cloth towels should be washed daily.
- **Cleaning supplies**—Necessary supplies include wet and dry mops, broom and dustpan, wash pail, spray bottle for sanitizing solution, dust cloths, sponges, and a vacuum cleaner.
- **Changing surface**—Use a smooth, non-porous, moisture-proof, and easily cleaned surface near a hand-washing area. The surface should be at a convenient height for adults, and it should be at least 3 feet off the floor to keep children from climbing on it easily. The caregiver should use nonporous disposable paper, such as computer paper, that is wide enough to cover the surface.

- **Diapers**—Disposable diapers prevent extra handling of stool and urine. If cloth diapers are used, they should not be rinsed or laundered at the child care setting. The caregiver should place a child's soiled cloth diapers in a plastic bag, seal it, and give the bag to the parent.
- **Disposable wipes**—Disposable wipes come in containers that dispense one wipe at a time. Or the caregiver can use fresh, wet paper towels.
- **Plastic bags**—Food storage bags, or bags left over from bread or other foods, can be used to wrap soiled clothing and disposable waste. Seal with a twist-tie or other closing device, or knot bag closed.
- **Disposable gloves**—Gloves provide a barrier against germs. Disposable gloves, or plastic bags, can be worn when handling stool, urine, or blood-soiled and other contaminated surfaces. The caregiver must wash hands even after using gloves.
- **Waste containers**—Containers should be lined with plastic bags and have tight lids so that they are waterproof and rodent-proof. Trash cans in the kitchen and diaper-changing areas should open with a foot pedal. All trash cans need to be wiped out daily with a paper towel and sanitizing solution.
- **Toilets**—Toilets should have molded plastic seats that are in good condition. Ideally, they should be low enough for easy use by

children. Avoid using potty training chairs because they need handling after each use and special cleaning and sanitizing by hand. If potty chairs are used, the entire frame and bowl must be made of nonporous, easily-cleaned material; after each use, the bowl must be removed and the contents emptied into the toilet; the entire frame and bowl must be washed in a sink used for no other purpose; and the washed chair and bowl must be wiped with a sanitizing solution and allowed to air dry.

- **Toilet paper**—Toilet paper should be soft and should be in a place that children on the toilet can easily reach.

Clean and Sanitize

After Each Use
- Counters used for food or brushing teeth
- Tables used for eating
- Changing tables
- Mouthed toys
- Dishes and utensils

Daily
- Toilets
- Sinks
- Kitchen floors, counters, and tables
- Waste cans
- Toys and surfaces in the child care setting
- Door knobs

Weekly
- Cubbies
- Cribs
- Drinking fountains
- Refrigerators
- Trash cans

Vacuum, Mop, or Sweep

Daily
- All rugs and floors

Wash

At Least Weekly, Preferably Daily
- Laundry
- Uncarpeted floors
- Mop heads

Spot Clean

Monthly
(Deep Clean Every 6 Months)
- Walls
- Carpets

Health Policy Guidelines

Caregivers play an important role in promoting ideas about good health for children. Caregivers can practice good health rules by making them a part of their daily lives and acting as role models for children. Caregivers can follow them in the child care setting with a health policy that clearly expresses the good health rules. Caregivers should use the following outline when working with the program's health consultant to develop a health policy for their setting.

Many programs have a doctor, usually a pediatrician (specialist in child health), as the health consultant. Some programs may use other health professionals such as nurses, physician assistants, public health nurses, nurse epidemiologists, nurse practitioners, or nurse clinicians (preferably pediatric specialists), infection-control nurses, public health specialists (with a Master's degree in Public Health), school nurses, and sanitarians.

This outline lists factors that should be incorporated into a health policy.

Exclusion Guidelines
(Also see page C-24.)

Very few illnesses make it necessary to keep a child at home. If the child has already exposed others to the infection and is being treated, the disease usually cannot be passed. However, children with certain infectious diseases should stay home. These include:

Chicken pox (varicella): The child should stay home for 6 days if the child has not been in contact with the other children in the group in the day or 2 before the rash appeared; if the child is too ill to participate; or if the child needs more care than the caregiver can provide. In general, keeping a child with chicken pox at home will not stop its spread if the other children already were exposed to the child one day before the rash developed.

Hepatitis A: The child should stay home until all those who should be protected have received gamma globulin shots.

Impetigo: The child should stay home until treatment starts.

Infectious conjunctivitis (pink eye): The child should stay home until the day after treatment begins.

Infectious diarrhea: The child should stay home until the diarrhea stays in the diapers or the child can get to the toilet; and/or until a health consultant says the child can return.

Lice: The child should stay home until the day after treatment starts.

Ringworm: The child should stay home until treated for 24 hours, but need not be sent home if the sore can be covered.

Scabies: The child should stay home until treatment starts.

Strep throat, scarlet fever: The child should stay home until the day after treatment with antibiotics.

Vaccine-preventable diseases (diseases prevented by immunizations): The child should stay home until a health consultant says the child may return.

When a child has certain symptoms, he or she should stay home or be cared for in a special care setting. The child may return when a physician has said that the child does not put the other children at risk of getting ill and the child is well enough to participate in the activities. These symptoms include the following:

A fever and the child is feeling or acting ill.

- Fever is a sign that the body is fighting some problem. Fever is not a disease. The importance of a raised temperature depends on what is causing the fever and how the child is behaving. For example, if nothing else is wrong and the child had a diphtheria-tetanus-pertussis (DTP) shot the day before, or had a measles-mumps-rubella (MMR) shot 7 to 10 days before, fever alone does not mean that the child should have to stay home. There are certain times when a fever means a child should stay home. These include those times when—

- An infant under 4 months of age has an axillary (underarm) temperature of 100 degrees Fahrenheit or higher or a rectal temperature of 101 degrees Fahrenheit or higher. (Get medical help immediately.)
- A child between the ages of 4 months and 24 months has a rectal temperature of 102 degrees Fahrenheit or higher or an axillary temperature of 101 degrees Fahrenheit or higher.
- A child over 24 months of age has an oral or axillary temperature of 102 degrees Fahrenheit or higher.
- Body temperature usually goes up during the day. A child may have no fever and may act normal in the morning, but might become ill as the day goes on.

Vomiting or upset stomach

- A child with repeated vomiting can easily spread germs through the vomit. The child will also need a caregiver's attention. Unless the child care program can provide one-to-one attention, a child who vomits repeatedly should be sent home.
- If the child vomits only once and has no other symptoms, the child probably does not have to go home immediately. Some children vomit in the morning when they have swallowed mucous the night before. If the child is vomiting and also has other symptoms such as abdominal pain, diarrhea, and significant behavior changes, the child should stay home.

Looser and more frequent stools than usual (diarrhea)

- When a child has a single loose stool, he or she does not need to be at home. However, if the child has very runny stools that cannot be contained in a diaper, or the child cannot reach the toilet in time, the stool may contaminate the child care setting.
- Sometimes children get diarrhea when they take antibiotics. The children feel and act perfectly well and may not require extra caregiver attention.
- Children may also eat something (for example, prunes, too many strawberries, or melon) that causes loose stools. If they feel well, do not need extra caregiver attention, and are able to participate fully in the child care program activities, they do not have to stay home.
- Children with diarrhea who look or feel sick, or have a fever with their diarrhea, need close attention, need help washing up, or need added fluid intake, should stay home unless the caregiver can pay close attention to them.

Runny nose

- Children with constant runny noses that are not caused by allergies may spread germs everywhere. They may wipe their noses with their hands, then rub them on their own and other people's clothing and on other surfaces.
- Remove secretions from children's noses with facial tissues. You may also use a suction bulb for infants and younger children. This will help prevent the secretions from backing up into the child's ears or sinuses, where they can cause secondary bacterial infection.

Pain

- When a child is in pain, the child needs a parent's attention. The parent must take care of whatever is causing the pain and must comfort the child.

Too sick to fully participate

- Caregivers care for more than one child. When one child cannot participate, the caregiver must care for both the ill child and the other children. Unless the caregiver can provide sick-child care, the child should be cared for elsewhere.

Preventing Infectious Diseases Guidelines

Your program's health policy guidelines for preventing infectious diseases should include the following points:

- Staff health issues, including preemployment and periodic health assessments, immunizations, rest breaks, sick leave, and other benefits
- Requirements for children to keep up with health maintenance routines, including immunizations
- Daily health checks
- Preparing and handling food
- Cleaning and maintenance routines for the child care setting
- Notifying parents of a child's exposure to infectious disease
- Reporting of infectious disease problems to public health authorities

Caring for Ill Children Guidelines

Your program's health policy guidelines for caring for ill children should include the following points:

- The parents' advance plans for sick-care arrangements
- How to arrange for care when the child is too ill for the child care setting, but the parent can't stay home
- Exclusion of children who may be ill before arriving at the program, and those who become ill during the day
- The program's guidelines for caring for ill children and for sending ill children home
- The symptoms of illness to look for
- How to care for ill children in the child care setting
- Coordination of information between the caregiver and the child's health professional
- Giving medicines and taking temperatures
- Appropriate activities for ill children

Sample Letter

_____
(name of child care program)

_____
(address of child care program)

_____
(telephone number of child care program)

_____
(date)

Dear Parents:

A child in our child care program has _____.
                                            (name of infectious disease)

We'd like you to know some of the common symptoms of this illness.

_____

_____

_____

_____

_____

_____

_____

_____

_____

_____

_____

_____

    If your child has any symptoms of this disease, call your doctor to find out what to do. Be sure to tell your doctor about this notice. If you do not have a regular doctor to care for your child, contact your local health department for instructions on how to find a doctor, or ask other parents for names of their children's doctors. If you have any questions, please contact: _____
                                                                                            (caregiver's name)

at (____) _____.
            (telephone number)

Handling Food Safely

Caregivers can help children stay healthy by keeping all utensils, dishes, and food handling surfaces as free from disease-causing germs as possible. Caregivers can also help children stay healthy by making sure the food they serve contains as few disease-causing germs as possible.

The following basic rules should remind caregivers how to prepare and handle food for children in a sanitary way. But if caregivers prepare or handle food in the child care setting, they must get complete and specific information about food preparation and handling from the U. S. Department of Agriculture or a public health agency.

Personal Cleanliness

- Always wash hands with soap and water before, during, and after handling and serving food.
- Cover hair with a hairnet while working with food.
- Wear clean clothes, and put a clean apron over clothes while working with food so clothes don't pick up germs.
- Do not prepare, handle, or serve food when you have any skin infection (sores or cuts), or when you are ill with any infectious disease.
- Always wash hands with soap and water after touching body fluids and waste such as blood, saliva, vomit, stool, and urine. Also wash hands after blowing noses, toileting, or diapering.

Food Storage

- Check that all perishable foods brought into the child care setting have not spoiled. (Perishable foods are foods that can go bad. Examples are fresh meat, poultry, dairy products, and fresh fruits and vegetables.) For example, especially with dairy products, check that the food is not out of date, and smell or taste the food before serving.
- Refrigerate all perishable foods until the last moment before serving. Or hold all perishable foods at a safe temperature to prevent the rapid growth of germs.

- Thaw all frozen meats, poultry, or fish in the refrigerator, not at room temperature.
- Wash the inside of the refrigerator at least once a week with a sanitizing solution.
- Put a refrigerator thermometer inside the refrigerator by the door. Check it daily to be sure that the temperature inside the refrigerator is always between 33 degrees and 40 degrees Fahrenheit.
- Store all foods in containers that are clean, have tight-fitting covers, and are insect- and rodent-resistant.
- Store all leftover foods in the refrigerator. Put them in clean containers with tight lids, and label and date them.
- Never store poisonous chemicals (including cleaning products), cleaning equipment, or any nonfood items near any food.
- Make sure cold cuts aren't discolored. If their surface is slimy, throw them away.

Food Preparation and Service

- Use clean utensils for cutting, stirring, and serving foods. Do not taste or test foods with fingers.
- Wipe food preparation surfaces with a sanitizing solution before and after each use. Wipe with a clean paper towel.
- Wash and sanitize utensils, platters, counter tops, and cutting boards before and after contact with raw meat, poultry, or fish.

- Wash, sanitize, and air dry all eating, drinking, and serving utensils after each use. Use a safe dish-washing procedure: by hand, wash dishes in hot, soapy water, rinse in clear water before dipping in a sanitizing solution, and rinse again in clear water. Better yet, use an automatic dishwasher with a heating element that will bring the water temperature to at least 170 degrees Fahrenheit.
- Wash and sanitize all food preparation and service surfaces before and after serving food.
- Use foods prepared at the child's home only if the food is kept covered and properly stored—that is, refrigerated below 40 degrees Fahrenheit or kept heated above 140 degrees Fahrenheit.
- Accept from the parent only sealed containers of formula or refrigerated breast milk in a bottle with the infant's name on it. Discard leftover formula or breast milk or any milk unrefrigerated for more than 2 hours.
- Serve foods as soon as possible after preparing them.
- Supervise mealtimes to be sure children do not share food, plates, or utensils or eat foods that drop to the floor.
- Throw away all food left on the plates at the end of mealtime.
- Put all discarded food in tightly covered trash cans so it won't attract flies.

American Red Cross Child Care Course: Caring for Ill Children

Contents

About the Caring for Ill Children Unit

Caregivers need to know about childhood illnesses because infants, toddlers, and young children are ill often. The average preschooler has 6 to 8 common respiratory infections and one to 2 bouts of vomiting and/or diarrhea per year. Infants and toddlers may have a few more colds than do preschoolers. Ill children may run a mild fever and feel tired, upset, or uncomfortable. They may need to rest in a quiet area under caregiver supervision. Ill children may require medical attention and may need care at home.

But some ill children can play normally while they recover and can participate in the regular child care program. Some ill children can stay in the child care setting by special arrangement and when caregivers follow their program's policies and procedures to care for mildly ill children. You need to know enough about childhood illnesses to decide the best kind of care to give to ill children. Your skill in coping with ill children makes a difference in the quality of care all children receive.

Some caregivers are able to provide sick-child care, and all caregivers must care for children who become ill until a parent can arrive. The information in this unit can be used in either of these situations.

According to the American Academy of Pediatrics (*Health in Day Care, A Manual for Health Professionals*, 1987), "The center should have a written policy concerning the management of sick children. It should be conveyed in writing at the time a child is registered. This policy, arrived at after consultation with health care providers, should take into consideration the physical facilities and the number and qualifications of the center's personnel." This recommendation, which enables child care center staff to care for mildy ill children on an ongoing basis, is a good one for caregivers in homes to follow, too.

What You Will Learn

This unit will teach you—
1. Which are the most common childhood illnesses.
2. Which symptoms to look for.
3. How the caregiver and the parent can plan for a child's care in the event of illness.
4. How to use thermometers and medicine measuring devices.
5. How to give medicines safely.
6. How to fill out the Symptom Checklist.
7. How to care for an ill child in the child care setting.

   By taking this unit, and all units in the American Red Cross Child Care Course, you are showing your commitment to giving the best possible child care. When you understand the information and skills presented, you will be able to put your caring and concern for children into action.

Further Information

For further information about caring for ill children, write the American Academy of Pediatrics, P.O. Box 927, Elk Grove Village, IL 60009-0927; the National Association for the Education of Young Children, 1834 Connecticut Ave., NW, Washington, DC 20009; or the American Public Health Association, Child Care Project, 1015 15th St., NW, Washington, DC 20005.

Activity 1
Orientation

Objective

After you have finished this activity, you will be able to do the following:
1. Tell the unit requirements

Lessons

- Your instructor will discuss the unit with you and what you must do to pass it. The unit requirements are—
  - Satisfactory performance on the test—80 percent or higher (or 20 correct answers).
  - Attendance of the class for the entire unit.
- You will review the contents of the workbook.

Caring for Ill Children Unit Agenda

Activity	Topic
1	Orientation
2	Introductions
3	About Common Childhood Illnesses
4	Planning for Illness
5	How to Use Thermometers, Measuring Spoons, and Medicines
Break	
6	Using the Symptom Checklist
7	Care Plans for Common Symptoms
8	*Caring for Ill Children* Video
9	Test and Unit Evaluation

Activity 2
Introductions

Objectives

After you have finished this activity, you will be able to do the following:
1. Use the All About You sheet to tell the group about yourself
2. Tell why you are taking this unit

Lesson
- Fill out the All About You sheet. The sheet is on the next page.

All About You

Fill in the blanks.

1. What is your name? _____

2. Where do you work? _____

3. What is your job there? _____

4. How old are the children in your group? _____

5. Why are you taking this unit? _____

6. What do you hope to learn? _____

_____

_____

Activity 3
About Common Childhood Illnesses

Learning Objectives

After you have finished this activity, you will be able to do the following:
1. Name some of the symptoms of common childhood illnesses
2. Name several common childhood illnesses
3. Name some common childhood illnesses that can be prevented by immunizations

Lessons

• As an adult, you may be familiar with many of the symptoms of common childhood illnesses. These symptoms tell you that something may be wrong with the body. The instructor will ask you to name some of these symptoms. After you have named as many as you can, look at the symptom list. As you talk about the symptoms, you may want to make notes.

Symptom List

Symptoms of common childhood illnesses include—

- Diarrhea
- Earache
- Fever
- Headache
- Rash or itching
- Stomachache (Abdominal pain)
- Upper respiratory or cold symptoms
- Urinating problems
- Vomiting or nausea
- Wheezing

Some examples of the less common symptoms of illness are—

- Yellowish tint to the eyes or skin (jaundice)
- Stiff neck

- Young children are more likely to catch infectious diseases than older children and adults for several reasons. They have immature immune systems that do not fight infections as well as more mature immune systems. Young children also are meeting many infections for the first time. Unlike older children and adults whose bodies remember having fought off many similar infections, young children's bodies do not have the same experience.

- Children have the same kinds of infectious childhood illnesses whether they are cared for only at home by parents or in the child care setting by a caregiver. You may be familiar with the names of many of the illnesses listed below.

Common Childhood Illnesses

- Asthma
- Bronchitis or bronchiolitis
- Chicken pox (Varicella)
- Colds
- Fifth disease
- Hepatitis A
- Impetigo
- Infectious conjunctivitis (pink eye)
- Infectious diarrhea
- Influenza and other flu-like infections
- Lice
- Measles
- Mumps
- Pertussis (whooping cough)
- Ringworm
- Rubella (German measles)
- Scabies
- Strep throat or scarlet fever (Streptococcus)

- Immunizations (also known as vaccines) can help prevent infectious diseases for children in the child care setting. Some immunization shots combine more than one vaccine. For example, measles, mumps, and rubella vaccines are often given together in one shot called MMR. Read the table below. The table lists the types of immunizations that most children should receive to prevent infections, what the vaccine is called, and how the vaccine is administered.

Name of Infection	Name of Vaccine	How Administered
Diphtheria	DTP, Td, DT	Injection (shot)
Haemophilus influenzae type b	Hib	Injection (shot)
Hepatitis B	Hepatitis B	Injection (shot)
Influenza	Flu	Injection (shot)
Measles	Measles, MMR	Injection (shot)
Mumps	Mumps, MMR	Injection (shot)
Pertussis (whooping cough)	DTP	Injection (shot)
Polio	Oral Polio (OPV) Inactivated Polio (IPV)	Mouth (oral) Injection (shot)
Rubella (German measles)	Rubella, MMR	Injection (shot)
Tetanus	DTP, Td, DT	Injection (shot)

DTP is an immunization shot that combines diptheria, tetanus, and pertussis vaccines.

Td combines tetanus and diptheria vaccines (given to children age 6 and older).

MMR combines measles, mumps, and rubella vaccines.

The schedule below is the recommended immunization schedule at the time of publication.

Age	DTP	Polio	MMR	Hepatitis B ★	Haemophilus	Tetanus-Diptheria
Birth				✓		
1-2 months				✓		
2 months	✓	✓			✓	
4 months	✓	✓			✓	
6 months	✓				◆	
6-18 months				✓		
12-15 months					◆	
15 months			✓		◆	
15-18 months	✓	✓				
4-6 years	✓	✓				
11-12 years			(✓)			
14-16 years						✓

(✓) Except where public health authorities require otherwise.

◆ As of March 1991, two vaccines for *Haemophilus influenzae* infections have been approved for use in children younger than 15 months of age. The schedule varies for doses after 4 months of age depending on which vaccine for *Haemophilus influenzae* infections was previously given.

★ Infants of mothers who tested seropositive for hepatitis B (HBsAg+) must also receive hepatitis B immune globulin (HBIG) at or shortly after the first dose, a second hepatitis B vaccine dose at 1 month, and a third hepatitis B vaccine injection at 6 months of age. Pediatricians may decide that infants of mothers who tested seronegative begin the three-dose schedule after the baby has left the hospital.

• Healthy children need checkups to get disease-preventing immunizations. Checkups can also include special tests to find problems when they start and are easy to treat. Children with special health problems need to have checkups more often than other children. Read the table below. It shows the ages at which children should have regular checkups.

Checkup Table		
at birth	12 months	5 years
by 1 month of age	15 months	6 years
2 months	18 months	8 years
4 months	2 years	10 years
6 months	3 years	12 years
9 months	4 years	
during adolescence as suggested by the child's doctor (at least every 2 years)		

• When a child is ill in the child care setting, follow the health policy of your program. Comfort the child, check the child's condition and need for further care, and call the parent.

Activity 4
Planning for Illness

Learning Objectives

After you have finished this activity, you will be able to do the following:

1. Tell when an ill child may remain in the child care setting and when an ill child should be at home
2. Tell why parents may have problems caring for an ill child
3. Tell how you can help parents care for an ill child

Lessons

- Every child care program should have a health policy or a way of caring for ill children. If you are going to provide sick-child care, you must have—
  - Written procedures for handling medicines and illnesses.
  - Proper training for caring for ill children.
  - A quiet area where the ill child can rest, along with ample supplies and easy access to hand-washing areas.
  - Access to professional medical advice at all times.
  For further information, turn to Appendix A, Health Policy Guidelines.
- In general, a child with a mild illness, such as a cold, bronchitis, or a treated ear infection, can remain in the child care setting if the child is well enough to participate, if the child does not need too much extra attention and cuddling, and if the child does not represent a new source of infection. This means that the child is not bringing into the setting a new infection to which the other children have not been exposed. Of course, because each child is different, the caregiver, the parent, and the health consultant should decide each case on its own. The decision must also agree with the health policy.
- There are certain times when an ill child should stay home. These include those times when—
  - An infant under 4 months of age has an axillary (underarm) temperature of 100 degrees Fahrenheit or higher or a rectal temperature of 101 degrees Fahrenheit or higher. (Get medical help immediately.)
  - A child between the ages of 4 months and 24 months has a rectal temperature of 102 degrees Fahrenheit or higher or an axillary temperature of 101 degrees or higher.
  - A child over 24 months of age has an oral or axillary temperature of 102 degrees Fahrenheit or higher.

- A child has a serious and/or contagious illness.
- A child has a special condition that a health consultant has advised may put him or her at increased risk from a contagious illness.
- You cannot provide the care the ill child needs while also taking care of the other children.
- The child needs more care than you have been trained to provide.

The caregiver generally should not care for children with the following infectious illnesses except as noted:

- Chicken pox (according to the program's health policy)
- Hepatitis A (until all those exposed have received gamma globulin)
- Impetigo (until treatment starts)
- Infectious conjunctivitis (pink eye) (until the day after treatment starts)
- Infectious diarrhea (according to the program's health policy)
- Lice (until the day after treatment starts)
- Measles (can return the 5th day after the rash appears)
- Mumps (until 9 days after swelling begins)
- Ringworm (until treatment starts)
- Scabies (until treated)
- Strep throat or scarlet fever (until the day after treatment with antibiotics)
- Whooping cough (until the health consultant approves)

- You may need to get medical help in a medical emergency. You must have available the name and phone number of each child's doctor, of the health consultant, and of the local emergency medical services (EMS) system. You must also have a current, signed Consent and Contact Form or similar form signed by the parent or legal guardian that gives you permission to get medical help and to transport the ill child. For a sample of the form, turn to Appendix B, Consent and Contact Form.
- You will join with a group to discuss one of the following 4 topics, which will be assigned by the instructor. Be prepared to report what your group discussed. You also may want to take notes during the discussion. The topics are as follows:
  1. How do parents and caregivers know when a child is ill?
  2. Why do parents send an ill child to the child care setting?
  3. How do parents and caregivers care for an ill child?
  4. What can caregivers do to help parents handle an ill child?

Activity 5
How to Use Thermometers, Measuring Spoons, and Medicines

Learning Objectives

After you have finished this activity, you will be able to do the following:

1. Read correctly the temperature on standard oral mercury and digital thermometers
2. Choose an accurate measuring device for giving medicine
3. Tell when to give medicines and how to store them safely
4. Fill out all the necessary forms when you give medicines to an ill child

Lessons

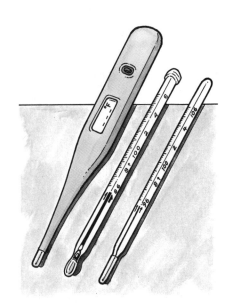

• You may use several types of thermometers to take a child's temperature—a glass oral or rectal (bulb type) thermometer, or a digital thermometer. An oral thermometer has a long, thin bulb. It can be used in the mouth, where it is placed under the tongue, to take an oral temperature. And it can be used under a child's arm to take what is called an axillary temperature. An oral thermometer must *never* be used to take a rectal temperature. The long, thin bulb might hurt the child or even break.

A rectal thermometer has a short, thick bulb that is the right shape to use when taking a rectal temperature. This shape means that a rectal thermometer may also be more comfortable to use when taking a young child's oral temperature. But you do not want to use the same thermometer to take an oral temperature that you have used to take a rectal temperature. If you want to use a rectal thermometer to take temperatures by mouth, label it and save it to be used only for oral temperatures.

Digital thermometers look like standard glass thermometers, but they are put into a disposable plastic sheath before use. Digital thermometers are plastic so they are harder to break. They give a fast, accurate readout that looks like the face of an electronic clock.

All thermometers should be cleaned with soapy water after use, wiped with alcohol, and allowed to air dry before the next use. Remember to follow your program's health policy guidelines on taking temperatures. For further information, turn to Appendix C, How to Use a Thermometer to Take a Temperature and Appendix D, How to Read a Thermometer.

- You will join a group to learn how to read a thermometer. Your instructor will give your group a preset thermometer and an answer card. Read the thermometer and write your reading below. Compare your reading to the answer card.

> **The temperature on my group's thermometer is _____ degrees Fahrenheit.**

- You must get medical help immediately and must tell the parent to come right away when—
  - An infant under 4 months of age has an axillary temperature of 100 degrees Fahrenheit or higher or a rectal temperature of 101 degrees Fahrenheit or higher.
  - A child over 4 months of age has a temperature of 105 degrees Fahrenheit or higher.
- You must ask the parent to come soon and must tell the parent to get medical advice within the next few hours when—
  - A child between the ages of 4 months and 24 months has a rectal temperature of 102 degrees Fahrenheit or higher or an axillary temperature of 101 degrees Fahrenheit or higher.
  - A child over 24 months of age has an oral or axillary temperature of 102 degrees Fahrenheit or higher.
- Medicines come in many forms—for example, eye, nose, and ear drops; tablets, capsules, and liquids; suppositories; topical applications such as creams and ointments; and injections. If you agree to give medicine to an ill child, you must learn how to measure medicine accurately and to give and to store medicine safely. All medicines must be labeled with the child's name, the medicine's name, and directions for use.

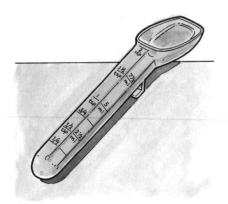

- Before you can give any medicine to a child, you must have the written approval of a doctor and of the parent. You must also have a doctor's written instructions, a filled-out Parent's Medicine Consent Form, and a filled-out Caregiver Medicine Check form. After you have given the medicine to the child, you must fill out a Medicine Record. See pages D-15 through D-17 to read these forms.
- You must use the correct measuring device for giving medicine. A household spoon, for example, may not hold the same amount of liquid that an accurate medicine measuring device does. Other important safety measures for handling medicines include the following:
  - Discard out-of-date medicines and any medicines more than one year old unless the druggist says the medicine is still safe and effective. (Flush the medicines down the toilet. Rinse out containers that held liquids before throwing them away.)
  - Keep all adult medicines out of the child care setting.
  - Store all medicines in child-proof containers refrigerated or locked up in a cool, dark, dry place out of reach of children.

For further information, turn to Appendix E, Safe Handling of Medicines.

Parent's Medicine Consent Form

I, _____ ,
(Name of parent)

give permission to _____
(Name of caregiver)

to give my child _____
(Name of child)

the following medicine _____
(Name of medicine)

for _____
(Problem or illness)

on _____
(Date or dates)

at _____
(Time or times)

in the amount of _____
(Amount or amounts)

by _____
(Body location and method of use)

Side effects of the medicine to watch for _____

_____
(Possible side effects)

This medicine has been prescribed by _____
(Name of doctor)

The telephone number of the doctor is _____

By _____   _____
(Signature of parent or legal guardian)   (Date)

Caregiver Medicine Check

Child's name _____

Type of medicine _____

Accept medicine only if you can answer Yes to all the questions below. (Circle an answer for each one.)

Medicine consent form complete	Yes	No
Medicine in child-proof container	Yes	No
Medicine has original label	Yes	No
Child's name is on medicine	Yes	No
Label and parent's instructions match	Yes	No
Written instructions from the doctor	Yes	No

Caregiver signature _____

Medicine Record

Child's name _____

Name of Medicine	Dose	Date	Time	Given By	Comments

This page may be duplicated by individuals and entities for noncommercial purposes.

Activity 6
Using the Symptom Checklist

Learning Objectives

After you have finished this lesson, you will be able to do the following:
1. Note the symptoms of an ill child
2. Fill out the Symptom Checklist to record your observations about an ill child

Lesson

- You must write down the symptoms of an ill child. This helps you decide how to care for the child in the child care setting. It also helps the parents know how to care for the child at home and helps the doctor give useful advice to the parent. Remember, you are not expected to make a diagnosis. You must always use the Symptom Checklist or a similar form. You must give a copy of the form to the parent and file a copy for the records. Please look at the Symptom Checklist on the next page. Notice that on the back of the Symptom Checklist, you will find a listing of symptoms and conditions that tell you when to get medical help immediately.

Symptom Checklist

Child's Name _____

Symptom(s)*	Time	Description (how long, how severe, how often)	Action (care, call)
Temperature		(Degrees)　　　　(Oral, rectal, axillary)	

*See reverse for when to get medical help immediately.

Food or Drink	Amount	Time	Describe Urine, Stool, Vomiting	Amount	Time

Other Information

Exposure to new items (foods, soaps, insects, animals, medicine, etc.)	Recent injuries
Exposure to other children's illnesses	Child's complicating condition (asthma, sickle cell disease, diabetes, allergies, emotional trauma)

Caregiver's Signature: _____　Date: _____

This page may be duplicated by individuals and entities for noncommercial purposes.

Get Medical Help Immediately

For some conditions, you need to get medical help immediately. When this is necessary, and you can reach the parent without delay, tell the parent to come right away. You may also have to have the parent tell the doctor that you will be calling because you are with the child. If the parent or the child's doctor is not immediately available, contact the program's health consultant or EMS for immediate medical help.

Tell the parent to come right away and get medical help immediately when any of the following things happens:

- An infant under 4 months of age has an axillary temperature of 100 degrees Fahrenheit or higher or a rectal temperature of 101 degrees Fahrenheit or higher.
- A child over 4 months of age has a temperature of 105 degrees Fahrenheit or higher.
- An infant under 4 months of age has forceful vomiting (more than once) after eating.
- Any child looks or acts very ill or seems to be getting worse quickly.
- Any child has neck pain when the head is moved or touched.
- Any child has a stiff neck or severe headache.
- Any child has a seizure for the first time.
- Any child has a seizure that lasts more than 15 minutes.
- Any child acts unusually confused.
- Any child has uneven pupils (black centers of the eyes).
- Any child has a blood-red or purple rash made up of pinhead-sized spots or bruises that are not associated with injury.
- Any child has a rash of hives or welts that appears quickly.
- Any child breathes so fast or hard that he or she cannot play, talk, cry, or drink.
- Any child has a severe stomachache that causes the child to double up and scream.
- Any child has a stomachache without vomiting or diarrhea after a recent injury, blow to the abdomen, or hard fall.
- Any child has stools that are black or have blood mixed through them.
- Any child has not urinated in more than 8 hours; the mouth and tongue look dry.
- Any child has continuous clear drainage from the nose after a hard blow to the head.

Note for programs that provide care for sick children: If any of the conditions listed above appear after the child's care has been planned, medical advice must be obtained before continuing child care can be provided.

Activity 7
Care Plans for Common Symptoms

Learning Objectives

After finishing this activity, you will be able to do the following:
1. List some symptoms that tell you a child may be ill
2. Tell how to care for an ill child by comforting the child, completing the symptom checklist, and calling the parent

Lesson

- Many childhood illnesses start with a fever. You must know that you should give the ill child clear fluids to drink. A clear fluid is one that you can see through when the fluid is held up to the light. Clear fluids include water, weak tea, chicken broth, gelatine, or apple or grape juice diluted with water.

- The instructor will pair up members of the class and assign each pair one or 2 symptoms with case studies. You and your partner will develop care plans for your assigned symptom. Use your personal experience, common sense, and your program's health policy when deciding how to care for an ill child. You and your partner will write your care plan for one or 2 symptoms. Please do not turn to the Care Plans that are printed in this book until later in this activity. Then you can make notes on the Care Plan pages if you wish.

Care Plans

Symptoms may be known by many different names. The following words or terms are commonly used. Use this list to guide you to one of the Care Plans on the pages that follow. The Care Plans are in alphabetical order.

Abdominal distress. *See* Stomachache

Allergies. *See* Headache; Upper Respiratory Symptoms; Rashes

Asthma. *See* Wheezing

Breathing problems. *See* Wheezing; Upper Respiratory Symptoms

Bronchiolitis. *See* Wheezing

Bumps. *See* Rashes

Chest cold. *See* Upper Respiratory Symptoms

Colds. *See* Upper Respiratory Symptoms

Colic. *See* Stomachache

Congestion. *See* Upper Respiratory Symptoms

Coughing. *See* Upper Respiratory Symptoms; Wheezing

Cramps. *See* Stomachache

Croup. *See* Upper Respiratory Symptoms

Draining, from ear. *See* Earache

Flu. *See* Upper Respiratory Symptoms

Gas. *See* Stomachache

Gasping. *See* Upper Respiratory Symptoms

Grippe. *See* Upper Respiratory Symptoms

Head cold. *See* Upper Respiratory Symptoms

Headache. *See also* Upper Respiratory Symptoms; Vomiting or Nausea

Hearing loss. *See* Earache

Heartburn. *See* Stomachache

Hives. *See* Rashes

Hot. *See* Fever

Huskiness. *See* Wheezing

Indigestion. *See* Stomachache

Itchiness. *See* Rashes

Loose bowels. *See* Diarrhea

Peeing problems. *See* Urinating Problems

Puking. *See* Vomiting or Nausea

Pupils, uneven. *See* Fever; Headache; Rashes; Stomachache; Upper Respiratory Symptoms; Vomiting or Nausea

Queasiness. *See* Vomiting or Nausea

Redness. *See* Rashes

Retching. *See* Vomiting or Nausea

Runny nose. *See* Upper Respiratory Symptoms

Runs. *See* Diarrhea

Seizure. *See* Fever

Shakes. *See* Fever

Shivering. *See* Fever

Sneezing. *See* Upper Respiratory Symptoms

Sniffles. *See* Upper Respiratory Symptoms

Sore ear. *See* Earache

Sore throat. *See* Upper Respiratory Symptoms

Spitting up. *See* Vomiting or Nausea

Spots. *See* Rashes

Stuffed up. *See* Upper Respiratory Symptoms

Stuffiness. *See* Upper Respiratory Symptoms

Temperature. *See* Fever

Throat, sore. *See* Upper Respiratory Symptoms

Throwing up. *See* Vomiting or nausea

Tight chest. *See* Wheezing

Tummy ache. *See* Stomachache

Upset stomach. *See* Stomachache

Welts. *See* Rashes

Care Plan
Symptom—DIARRHEA

- *Comfort* the child.
- *Complete* Symptom Checklist.
- *Call* the parent.
- *Care* for the child.

What You Need to Know

- A child with diarrhea has frequent, unformed bowel movements.
- Diarrhea may result from an infection of the bowel, but certain antibiotics, foods, and other health problems may also cause diarrhea.
- Infectious diarrhea can spread easily from child to child by contact with vomit or stool or by hands that have touched a surface covered with germs from stool. This can happen a few days before the child is ill and for a long time after the child no longer seems ill.
- To stop the spread of diarrhea, the caregiver must pay special attention to hand washing and to cleaning surfaces (especially diaper-changing tables, play tables, beds, and floors) that may have come in contact with the stool or have been touched by someone who has been in contact with the stool. Caregivers must always wash their hands and the child's hands with soap and water before handling food or eating, after changing a diaper or taking a child to the toilet, or after going to the toilet themselves.
- The caregiver should call the program's health consultant if more than one child in the same group has diarrhea.

What You Need to Do

- *Comfort* the child.
- *Complete* the Symptom Checklist.
- *Call.*
  Tell the parent to come right away and get medical help immediately when any of the following things happens:
  - An infant under 4 months of age has an axillary temperature of 100 degrees Fahrenheit or higher or a rectal temperature of 101 degrees Fahrenheit or higher.
  - A child over 4 months of age has a temperature of 105 degrees Fahrenheit or higher.
  - An infant under 4 months of age has forceful vomiting (more than once) after eating.
  - Any child looks or acts very ill, or seems to be getting worse quickly.
  - Any child breathes so fast or hard that he or she cannot play, talk, cry, or drink.
  - Any child has a severe stomachache that causes the child to double up and scream.
  - Any child has stools that are black or have blood mixed through them.
  - Any child has not urinated in more than 8 hours; the mouth and tongue look dry.

Ask the parent to come soon and to get medical advice within the next few hours when any of the following things happens:

- A child between the ages of 4 months and 24 months has a rectal temperature of 102 degrees Fahrenheit or higher or an axillary temperature of 101 degrees Fahrenheit or higher.
- A child over 24 months of age has an oral or axillary temperature of 102 degrees Fahrenheit or higher.
- Any child has stool not contained in the diaper.

- Any child has intense thirst.
- Any child refuses to eat or drink at all. **Inform the parent about all of the child's symptoms and any care you give.**

- *Care* for the ill child.
  - Offer clear fluids.
  - Avoid any milk except breast milk.
  - Offer bananas, rice, noodles, dry crackers, bread, or applesauce if the child wants to eat.
  - Make the child comfortable in a quiet area.

Care Plan
Symptom—EARACHE

- **Comfort** the child.
- **Complete** Symptom Checklist.
- **Call** the parent.
- **Care** for the child.

What You Need to Know

- Colds often cause middle-ear infections because mucous may collect in the middle ear (the space behind the eardrum that is connected to the back of the nose and throat). Infection-causing nose and throat germs can grow in mucous in the middle ear.
- A stretched eardrum causes the pain of an earache. Stretching may happen when air from the back of the nose cannot move freely in and out of the middle ear or when mucous or pus is trapped in the middle ear space, behind the eardrum.
- Sometimes children have ear infections without ear pain. They sometimes rub or tug at their ears or they seem to have trouble hearing.
- Sometimes a stretched, painful eardrum breaks and drains; then the pain goes away. Even though the pain goes away, the child still needs to see a doctor for treatment to prevent a more serious illness and possible hearing loss.

What You Need to Do

- **Comfort** the child.

- **Complete** the Symptom Checklist.

- **Call.**
  Tell the parent to come right away and get medical help immediately when any

of the following things happens:
- An infant under 4 months of age has an axillary temperature of 100 degrees Fahrenheit or higher or a rectal temperature of 101 degrees Fahrenheit or higher.
- A child over 4 months of age has a temperature of 105 degrees Fahrenheit or higher.
- An infant under 4 months of age has forceful vomiting (more than once) after eating.
- Any child looks or acts very ill, or seems to be getting worse quickly.
- Any child has neck pain when the head is moved or touched.
- Any child has a stiff neck or severe headache.

Ask the parent to come soon and to get medical advice within the next few hours when any of the following things happens:
- A child between the ages of 4 months and 24 months has a rectal temperature of 102 degrees Fahrenheit or higher or an axillary temperature of 101 degrees Fahrenheit or higher.
- A child over 24 months of age has an oral or axillary temperature of 102 degrees Fahrenheit or higher.
- Any child has any kind of earache or ear pain.

Inform the parent about all of the child's symptoms and any care you give.

- *Care* for the ill child.
  - Use a cool-mist humidifier to moisten the air. Do this especially at nap time so you can place the child closer to the humidifier for better results. The cool-mist humidifier helps loosen the mucous blockage that may be causing the earache.
  - Sit the child up so mucous can drain easily.
  - Give the child acetaminophen if you have the parent's consent and a doctor's written instructions for use.
  - Offer clear fluids.
  - Remind parents to talk to a doctor when the child has an earache, even if the earache seems to go away.

Note: Humidifiers must be cleaned often to prevent mold growth. Cool-mist, water-spinning humidifiers may be cleaned with a solution of one-quarter cup of liquid household chlorine bleach to one gallon of water. Ultrasonic humidifiers must be cleaned by wiping out to avoid damaging the disk. Follow manufacturer's recommendations for cleaning humidifiers.

Care Plan
Symptom—FEVER

- *Comfort* the child.
- *Complete* Symptom Checklist.
- *Call* the parent.
- *Care* for the child.

What You Need to Know

- Fever is a symptom, not an illness.
- Fever means the child's body temperature has risen above that child's normal temperature for that time of day.
- Fever happens when the body heats up too much from any cause, such as infection, strenuous exercise, overdressing, vigorous activity in hot weather, etc.
- Young children get fevers more easily than do older children.
- Temperatures between 100 degrees Fahrenheit and 102 degrees Fahrenheit may help children fight off infections.
- High fevers do not always mean a serious illness.
- Fevers increase the loss of water from the body; children need to drink more as their temperatures rise.
- Fevers may make children feel cold and shiver because normal room-temperature air feels cool to their hot skin. But don't wrap them in blankets or their fevers may go even higher. Keep them lightly dressed.
- Children with a high fever may be cranky.
- Giving acetaminophen to lower a high fever may help the child feel much better, but the illness still needs proper care.
- Sometimes acetaminophen may not lower a high fever, but that does not mean the illness is serious.
- Aspirin is being used less and less for fever control because of concerns about its connection to developing a rare disease called Reye's Syndrome.

- A small number of children under 4 years old may have fevers with seizures (convulsions) when their temperatures are rising. The first sign they are ill may be the seizure. These seizures are brief (less than 15 minutes) and do not cause any permanent damage as long as the child does not choke on saliva or injure himself or herself during the seizure.

What You Need to Do

- *Comfort* the child.
- *Complete* the Symptom Checklist.
- *Call.*
  Tell the parent to come right away and get medical help immediately when any of the following things happens:
  - An infant under 4 months of age has an axillary temperature of 100 degrees Fahrenheit or higher or a rectal temperature of 101 degrees Fahrenheit or higher.
  - A child over 4 months of age has a temperature of 105 degrees Fahrenheit or higher.
  - An infant under 4 months of age has forceful vomiting (more than once) after eating.
  - Any child looks or acts very ill, or seems to be getting worse quickly.
  - Any child has neck pain when the head is moved or touched.

- Any child has a stiff neck or severe headache.
- Any child has a seizure for the first time.
- Any child has a seizure that lasts more than 15 minutes.
- Any child acts unusually confused.
- Any child has uneven pupils (black centers of the eye).
- Any child has a blood-red or purple rash made up of pinhead-sized spots or bruises that are not associated with injury.
- Any child has rash of hives or welts that appears quickly.
- Any child breathes so fast or hard that he or she cannot play, talk, cry, or drink.
- Any child has a severe stomachache that causes the child to double up and scream.
- Any child has a stomachache without vomiting or diarrhea after a recent injury, blow to the abdomen, or hard fall.
- Any child has stools that are black or have blood mixed through them.
- Any child has not urinated in more than 8 hours; the mouth and tongue look dry.

Ask the parent to come soon and to get medical advice within the next few hours when any of the following things happen:

- A child between the ages of 4 months and 24 months has a rectal temperature of 102 degrees Fahrenheit or higher or an axillary temperature of 101 degrees Fahrenheit or higher.
- A child over 24 months of age has an oral or axillary temperature of 102 degrees Fahrenheit or higher.

- Any child has joint pain.
- Any child refuses to eat or drink at all.

Inform the parent about all of the child's symptoms and any care you give.

- *Care* for the ill child.
    - Make the child comfortable in a quiet area.
    - Give acetaminophen if the child's temperature is over 102 degrees Fahrenheit and if you have the parent's consent and a doctor's written instructions for use.
    - Remove extra clothing.
    - Putting the child in a comfortably warm bath (90 degrees Fahrenheit) for up to 30 or 40 minutes may help reduce the fever if the child's temperature is over 102 degrees Fahrenheit.
    - Offer clear fluids.

Note: When a child has a fever with a seizure for the first time, the child should be taken to a doctor as soon as possible for evaluation. When a child has had seizures before, notify the parent about each seizure. Then follow the instructions for care of children with fevers. To manage a seizure, remain calm, place the child on his or her side on the floor to prevent choking on saliva, remove any nearby objects or furniture to avoid injury, and wait for the seizure to stop while you notify the parent and seek emergency medical help. Do not put anything in the child's mouth.

Care Plan
Symptom—HEADACHE

- *Comfort* the child.
- *Complete* Symptom Checklist.
- *Call* the parent.
- *Care* for the child.

What You Need to Know

- Children have headaches for many reasons, including allergies, fatigue, infections, and stress.
- Headaches that do not interfere with normal activity usually do not mean a serious illness.

What You Need to Do

- *Comfort* the child.

- *Complete* the Symptom Checklist.

- *Call.*
  Tell the parent to come right away and get medical help immediately when any of the following things happens:
  - Any child has a temperature of 105 degrees Fahrenheit or higher.
  - Any child looks or acts very ill, or seems to be getting worse quickly.
  - Any child has neck pain when the head is moved or touched.
  - Any child has a stiff neck or severe headache.
  - Any child has a seizure for the first time.
  - Any child has a seizure that lasts more than 15 minutes.
  - Any child acts unusually confused.
  - Any child has uneven pupils (black centers of the eye).
  - Any child has a blood-red or purple rash made up of pinhead-sized spots or bruises that are not associated with injury.
  - Any child has a rash of hives or welts that appears quickly.
  - Any child breathes so fast or hard that he or she cannot play, talk, cry, or drink.
  - Any child has a severe stomachache that causes the child to double up and scream.
  - Any child has a stomachache without vomiting or diarrhea after a recent injury, blow to the abdomen, or hard fall.
  - Any child has a severe headache after a recent injury, blow to the head, or hard fall.
  - Any child has stools that are black or have blood mixed through them.
  - Any child has not urinated in more than 8 hours; the mouth and tongue look dry.

  Ask the parent to come soon and to get medical advice within the next few hours when any of the following things happens:
  - A child between the ages of 4 months and 24 months has a rectal temperature of 102 degrees Fahrenheit or higher or an axillary temperature of 101 degrees Fahrenheit or higher.
  - A child over 24 months of age has an oral or axillary temperature of 102 degrees Fahrenheit or higher.
  - Any child has repeated vomiting.
  - Any child has eyes starting to cross.

Inform the parent about all of the child's symptoms and any care you give.

- *Care* for the ill child.
  - Give the child acetaminophen if you have the parent's consent and a doctor's written instructions for use.

Care Plan
Symptom—RASH

- *Comfort* the child.
- *Complete* Symptom Checklist.
- *Call* the parent.
- *Care* for the child.

What You Need to Know

- Rashes make the skin look or feel abnormal.
- Rashes from different illnesses may look the same.
- Doctors need clear details about other symptoms of a child's illness to diagnose a rash properly.
- Rashes that look like blood under the skin, or that look like lumps (hives or welts) or swelling of the skin, or that come quickly from an allergic reaction need immediate care from a doctor.

What You Need to Do

- *Comfort* the child.
- *Complete* the Symptom Checklist.
- *Call.*
  Tell the parent to come right away and get medical help immediately when any of the following things happens:
  - An infant under 4 months of age has an axillary temperature of 100 degrees Fahrenheit or higher or a rectal temperature of 101 degrees Fahrenheit or higher.
  - A child over 4 months of age has a temperature of 105 degrees Fahrenheit or higher.
  - An infant under 4 months of age has forceful vomiting (more than once) after eating.

- Any child looks or acts very ill, or seems to be getting worse quickly.
- Any child has neck pain when the head is moved or touched.
- Any child has a stiff neck or severe headache.
- Any child has a seizure for the first time.
- Any child has a seizure that lasts more than 15 minutes.
- Any child acts unusually confused.
- Any child has uneven pupils (black centers of the eyes).
- Any child has a blood-red or purple rash made up of pinhead-sized spots or bruises that are not associated with injury.
- Any child has a rash of hives or welts that appears quickly.
- Any child has stools that are black or have blood mixed through them.
- Any child has not urinated in more than 8 hours; the mouth and tongue look dry.

Ask the parent to come soon and to get medical advice within the next few hours when any of the following things happens:
- A child between the ages of 4 months and 24 months has a rectal temperature of 102 degrees Fahrenheit or higher or an axillary temperature of 101 degrees Fahrenheit or higher.
- A child over 24 months of age has an oral or axillary temperature of 102 degrees Fahrenheit or higher.
- Any child has any rash for which the cause is unknown.

- Any child has a rash with blisters that break, developing honey-colored crusts. (This may be impetigo.)

Inform the parent about all of the child's symptoms and any care you give.

- *Care* for the ill child.
  - Use cool water soaks to relieve itchy rashes. Do not apply ointments, creams, powders, or lotions to the child's skin or give medicines unless you have both the doctor's instructions and a parent's consent.

Care Plan
Symptom—STOMACHACHE (ABDOMINAL PAIN)

- *Comfort* the child.
- *Complete* Symptom Checklist.
- *Call* the parent.
- *Care* for the child.

What You Need to Know

- A stomachache may have many causes.
- Severe and constant pain means that the stomachache may be serious.
- Stomach cramps may be caused by an infection, constipation, or a serious bowel problem.
- Some children have stomachaches when they are upset.

What You Need to Do

- *Comfort* the child.

- *Complete* the Symptom Checklist.

- *Call.*
  Tell the parent to come right away and get medical help immediately when any of the following things happens:
  - An infant under 4 months of age has an axillary temperature of 100 degrees Fahrenheit or higher or a rectal temperature of 101 degrees Fahrenheit or higher.
  - A child over 4 months of age has a temperature of 105 degrees Fahrenheit or higher.
  - An infant under 4 months of age has forceful vomiting (more than once) after eating.
  - Any child looks or acts very ill, or seems to be getting worse quickly.
  - Any child has neck pain when the head is moved or touched.
  - Any child has a stiff neck or severe headache.

- Any child has a seizure for the first time.
- Any child has a seizure that lasts more than 15 minutes.
- Any child acts unusually confused.
- Any child has uneven pupils (black centers of the eyes).
- Any child has a blood-red or purple rash made up of pinhead-sized spots or bruises that are not associated with injury.
- Any child has a rash of hives or welts that appears quickly.
- Any child breathes so fast or hard that he or she cannot play, talk, cry, or drink.
- Any child has a severe stomachache that causes the child to double up and scream.
- Any child has a stomachache after vomiting.
- Any child has a stomachache without vomiting or diarrhea after a recent injury, blow to the abdomen, or hard fall.
- Any child has stools that are black or have blood mixed through them.
- Any child has not urinated in more than 8 hours; the mouth and tongue look dry.

Ask the parent to come soon and to get medical advice within the next few hours when any of the following things happens:
- A child between the ages of 4 months and 24 months has a rectal temperature of 102 degrees Fahrenheit or higher or an axillary temperature of 101 degrees Fahrenheit or higher.
- A child over 24 months of age has an oral or axillary temperature of 102 degrees Fahrenheit or higher.

- Any child refuses to eat or drink at all.
- Any child has urinating problems.

Inform the parent about all of the child's symptoms and any care you give.

- *Care* for the ill child.
  - Offer clear fluids.
  - Make the child comfortable in a quiet area.

Care Plan
Symptom—UPPER RESPIRATORY SYMPTOMS (INCLUDING COLDS)

- *Comfort* the child.
- *Complete* Symptom Checklist.
- *Call* the parent.
- *Care* for the child.

What You Need to Know

- Many different kinds of viruses and bacteria can cause upper respiratory infections.
- Viruses cause colds.
- Runny noses, coughs, sore throats, and noisy breathing often mean an upper airway infection.
- Colds may involve the lower airway, too, making the child breathe faster than normal and wheeze and cough often. (See Care Plan for Wheezing.)
- Voice loss (laryngitis) happens when the voice box swells from infection or inflammation.
- A swollen voice box makes an infant's breathing noisy and gives the infant a barking sound while breathing (croup).
- Colds can cause the throat or nose to swell.
- Children with colds may be cranky or sleepy.
- Children usually feel better after the first 4 or 5 days, even if their colds last for weeks.
- Upper respiratory symptoms may be caused by allergies.
- Having something stuck in the throat may make a child's breathing noisy.

What You Need to Do

- *Comfort* the child.
- *Complete* the Symptom Checklist.
- *Call.*
  Tell the parent to come right away and get medical help immediately when any

of the following things happens:
- An infant under 4 months of age has an axillary temperature of 100 degrees Fahrenheit or higher or a rectal temperature of 101 degrees Fahrenheit or higher.
- A child over 4 months of age has a temperature of 105 degrees Fahrenheit or higher.
- An infant under 4 months of age has forceful vomiting (more than once) after eating.
- Any child looks or acts very ill, or seems to be getting worse quickly.
- Any child has neck pain when the head is moved or touched.
- Any child has a stiff neck or severe headache.
- Any child has a seizure for the first time.
- Any child has a seizure that lasts more than 15 minutes.
- Any child acts unusually confused.
- Any child has uneven pupils (black centers of the eye).
- Any child has continuous clear drainage from the nose after a hard blow to the head.
- Any child has a blood-red or purple rash made up of pinhead-sized spots or bruises that are not associated with injury.
- Any child has a rash of hives or welts that appears quickly.
- Any child breathes so fast or hard that he or she cannot play, talk, cry, or drink.
- Any child has a severe stomachache that causes the child to double up and scream.
- Any child has stools that are black or have blood mixed through them.

- Any child has not urinated in more than 8 hours; the mouth and tongue look dry.

Ask the parent to come soon and to get medical advice within the next few hours when any of the following things happens:

- A child between the ages of 4 months and 24 months has a rectal temperature of 102 degrees Fahrenheit or higher or an axillary temperature of 101 degrees Fahrenheit or higher.
- A child over 24 months of age has an oral or axillary temperature of 102 degrees Fahrenheit or higher.
- Any child coughs so much that he or she can't rest or play.

Inform the parent about all of the child's symptoms and any care you give.

- *Care* for the ill child.
  - Use a cool-mist humidifier. Do this especially at nap time so you can place the child closer to the humidifier for better results.
  - Sit the child up so mucous will drain away from the child's ears.
  - Offer clear fluids.
  - Prop the child's head up when he or she sleeps by putting a pillow, books, or a rolled towel or blanket under the head end of the child's mattress or cot. Do not use pillows directly under the child's head since this may push the child's chin onto his or her chest and make it harder to breathe.
  - Make the child comfortable in a quiet area.
  - For infants and young children who cannot blow their noses, use a suction bulb to remove the mucous. A small amount of saline solution put in each nostril before suctioning may help remove thick mucous.

Notes: Give cold or allergy medicines only with a parent's consent and a doctor's written instructions. Giving cold medicines is not a routine thing to do. Most "cold" medicines only thicken mucous so the child cannot expel it easily. Cold medicines may make a child feel drowsy or irritable so you do not know if the cold is getting worse or the medicine is having a side effect.

Humidifiers must be cleaned often to prevent mold growth. Cool-mist and water-spinning humidifiers may be cleaned with a solution of one-quarter cup liquid household chlorine bleach to one gallon of water. Ultrasonic humidifiers must be cleaned by wiping out to avoid damaging the disk. Follow manufacturer's recommendations for cleaning the humidifier.

The same bleach solution is appropriate for sanitizing suction bulbs used with infants and young children.

Care Plan
Symptom—URINATING PROBLEMS

- *Comfort* the child.
- *Complete* Symptom Checklist.
- *Call* the parent.
- *Care* for the child.

What You Need to Know

- Girls have urinary infections more than boys do.
- You may suspect a child has urinating problems when the child urinates often, urinates too little or too much, or urinates with pain, or when a child who can use the toilet wets himself or herself.
- Dark yellow urine usually means the child is not drinking enough.
- Red or cola-colored urine means the child may have an illness that requires urgent medical care.
- Drinking plenty of fluids helps clear up a urinary infection.
- Some serious illnesses such as diabetes make children urinate often.
- Some serious kidney diseases and dehydration may make children urinate less often than they usually do.

What You Need to Do

- *Comfort* the child.

- *Complete* the Symptom Checklist.

- *Call.*
  Tell the parent to come right away and get medical help immediately when any of the following things happens:
  - An infant under 4 months of age has an axillary temperature of 100 degrees Fahrenheit or higher or a rectal temperature of 101 degrees Fahrenheit or higher.
  - A child over 4 months of age has a temperature of 105 degrees Fahrenheit or higher.
  - An infant under 4 months of age has forceful vomiting (more than once) after eating.
  - Any child looks or acts very ill, or seems to be getting worse quickly.
  - Any child breathes so fast or hard that the child cannot play, talk, cry, or drink.
  - Any child has a severe stomachache that causes the child to double up and scream.
  - Any child has a stomachache without vomiting or diarrhea after a recent injury, blow to the abdomen, or hard fall.
  - Any child has stools that are black or have blood mixed through them.
  - Any child has not urinated in more than 8 hours; the mouth and tongue look dry.

  Ask the parent to come soon and to get medical advice within the next few hours when any of the following things happens:
  - A child between the ages of 4 months and 24 months has a rectal temperature of 102 degrees Fahrenheit or higher or an axillary temperature of 101 degrees Fahrenheit or higher.
  - A child over 24 months of age has an oral or axillary temperature of 102 degrees Fahrenheit or higher.
  - Any child has a bad stomachache.

- Any child has red or cola-colored urine.
- Any child refuses to eat or drink at all.

Inform the parent about all of the child's symptoms and any care you give.

- *Care* for the ill child.
  - Offer clear fluids.

Care Plan
Symptom—VOMITING OR NAUSEA

- *Comfort* the child.
- *Complete* Symptom Checklist.
- *Call* the parent.
- *Care* for the child.

What You Need to Know

- Many infectious illnesses such as earaches, pneumonia, and stomach-virus infections can cause vomiting and/or nausea.
- Some serious conditions, like twisting of the bowel, can also cause vomiting.

What You Need to Do

- *Comfort* the child.

- *Complete* the Symptom Checklist.

- *Call.*
  Tell the parent to come right away and get medical help immediately when any of the following things happens:
  - An infant under 4 months of age has an axillary temperature of 100 degrees Fahrenheit or higher or a rectal temperature of 101 degrees Fahrenheit or higher.
  - A child over 4 months of age has a temperature of 105 degrees Fahrenheit or higher.
  - An infant under 4 months of age has forceful vomiting (more than once) after eating.
  - Any child looks or acts very ill, or seems to be getting worse quickly.
  - Any child has neck pain when the head is moved or touched.
  - Any child has a stiff neck or severe headache.
  - Any child acts unusually confused.
  - Any child has uneven pupils (black centers of the eye).
  - Any child has a blood-red or purple rash made up of pinhead-sized spots or bruises that are not associated with injury.
  - Any child has a rash of hives or welts that appears fast.
  - Any child breathes so fast or hard that he or she cannot play, talk, cry, or drink.
  - Any child has a severe stomachache that causes the child to double up and scream.
  - Any child has a stomachache without vomiting or diarrhea after a recent injury, blow to the abdomen, or hard fall.
  - Any child has stools that are black or have blood mixed through them.
  - Any child has not urinated in more than 8 hours; the mouth and tongue look dry.

  Ask the parent to come soon and to get medical advice within the next few hours when any of the following things happens:
  - A child between the ages of 4 months and 24 months has a rectal temperature of 102 degrees Fahrenheit or higher or an axillary temperature of 101 degrees Fahrenheit or higher.
  - A child over 24 months of age has an oral or axillary temperature of 102 degrees Fahrenheit or higher.
  - Any child has repeated vomiting.

Inform the parent about all of the child's symptoms and any care you give.

- *Care* for the ill child.
  - Do not let the child eat or drink for 30 minutes after he or she has vomited. Then offer one teaspoonful of a sweet fluid (not artificially sweetened) such as soda or tea with sugar every 5 minutes for 30 to 60 minutes. If the child does not vomit again, give one tablespoonful of a sweet fluid every 5 minutes for 30 to 60 minutes, increasing the amounts until the child feels better.
  - If the child vomits again, wait 30 minutes and start with one teaspoonful of a sweet fluid again.
  - To clean a child who has vomited on his or her clothing, remove the clothing and sponge off the child with soap and water if necessary. Dress the child in extra clothes or wrap in a blanket or towel. Place the soiled clothes in a plastic bag to give to the parent to wash.
  - Make the child comfortable in a quiet area.

Care Plan
Symptom—WHEEZING

- *Comfort* the child.
- *Complete* Symptom Checklist.
- *Call* the parent.
- *Care* for the child.

What You Need to Know

- Muscle spasms, swelling, or mucous can cause the air tubes in the chest to narrow. The narrowing causes wheezing. As the air moves through the narrowed space, it sounds like whistling or whooshing.
- Children or infants who are wheezing are usually having a harder time breathing out than breathing in.
- Children who have asthma or infants who have bronchiolitis may wheeze.

What You Need to Do

- *Comfort* the child.

- *Complete* the Symptom Checklist.

- *Call.*
  Tell the parent to come right away and get medical help immediately when any of the following things happens:
  - An infant under 4 months of age has an axillary temperature of 100 degrees Fahrenheit or higher or a rectal temperature of 101 degrees Fahrenheit or higher.
  - A child over 4 months of age has a temperature of 105 degrees Fahrenheit or higher.
  - An infant under 4 months of age has forceful vomiting (more than once) after eating.
  - Any child looks or acts very ill, or seems to be getting worse quickly.

- Any child breathes so fast or hard that he or she cannot play, talk, cry, or drink.
- Any child has a severe stomachache that causes the child to double up and scream.
- Any child has not urinated in more than 8 hours; the mouth and tongue look dry.

Ask the parent to come soon and to get medical advice within the next few hours when any of the following things happens:
- A child between the ages of 4 months and 24 months has a rectal temperature of 102 degrees Fahrenheit or higher or an axillary temperature of 101 degrees Fahrenheit or higher.
- A child over 24 months of age has an oral or axillary temperature of 102 degrees Fahrenheit or higher.
- Any child wheezes who has never wheezed before.
- Any child vomits or refuses to take his or her prescribed wheezing medicine and is wheezing hard.

Inform the parent about all of the child's symptoms and any care you give.

- *Care* for the ill child.
  - Give the child's prescribed asthma medicine if you have the parent's consent and a doctor's written instructions.
  - Offer clear fluids.
  - Let the child sit up to make breathing more comfortable.
  - Make the child comfortable in a quiet area.

Activity 8
Caring for Ill Children Video

Lesson

- Watch the video.

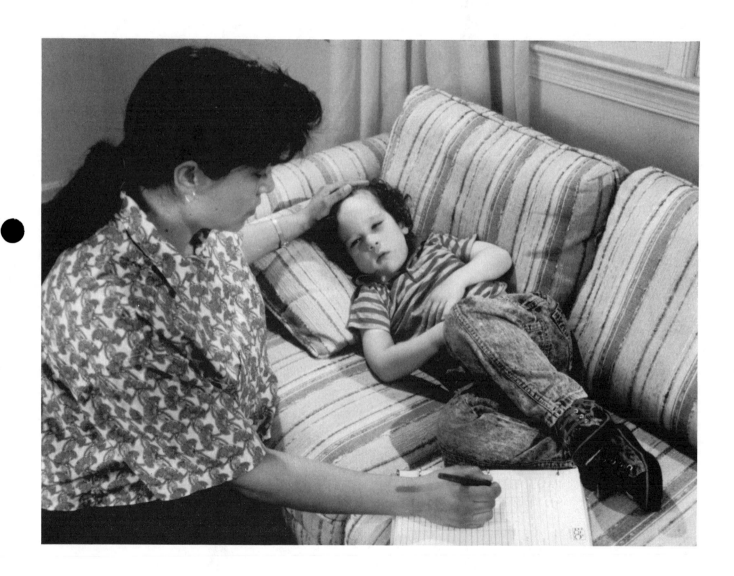

Activity 9
Test and Unit Evaluations

Objective

After you have finished this activity, you will be able to do the following:
1. Complete the test

Lessons

- The test that the instructor will give you has 25 questions about what you learned in this class. Answer the questions on the answer sheet. You must score 80 percent or higher (or answer 20 or more questions correctly) to pass this unit.
- Your instructor will also give you a unit evaluation sheet. Please tell us what you thought of this unit by filling out this sheet and returning it to the instructor.
- Thank you for your participation in the American Red Cross Child Care Course. By taking all of the units of the Child Care Course, you are showing your commitment to giving the best possible child care. Now that you understand the information and skills presented, you will be able to put your caring and concern for children into action.

Appendixes

Health Policy Guidelines

Caregivers play an important role in promoting ideas about good health for children. Caregivers can practice good health rules by making them a part of their daily lives and acting as role models for children. Caregivers can follow them in the child care setting with a health policy that clearly expresses the good health rules. Caregivers should use the following outline when working with the program's health consultant to develop a health policy for their setting.

Many programs have a doctor, usually a pediatrician (specialist in child health), as the health consultant. Some programs may use other health professionals such as nurses, physician's assistants, public health nurses, nurse epidemiologists, nurse practitioners, or nurse clinicians (preferably pediatric specialists), infection-control nurses, public health specialists (with a Masters degree in Public Health), school nurses, and sanitarians.

This outline lists factors that should be incorporated into a health policy.

Exclusion Guidelines
(Also see page D-11)

Very few illnesses make it necessary to keep a child at home. If the child has already exposed others to the infection and is being treated, the disease usually cannot be passed. However, children with certain infectious diseases should stay home. These include:

Chicken pox (varicella): The child should stay home for 6 days if the child has not been in contact with the other children in the group in the day or 2 before the rash appeared; if the child is too ill to participate; or if the child needs more care than the caregiver can provide. In general, keeping a child with chicken pox at home will not stop its spread if the other children already were exposed to the child one day before the rash developed.

Hepatitis A: The child should stay home until all those who should be protected have received gamma globulin shots.

Impetigo: The child should stay home until treatment starts.

Infectious conjunctivitis (pink eye): The child should stay home until the day after treatment begins.

Infectious diarrhea: The child should stay home until the diarrhea stays in the diapers or the child can get to the toilet; and/or until a health consultant says the child can return.

Lice: The child should stay home until the day after treatment starts.

Ringworm: The child should stay home until treated for 24 hours, but need not be sent home if the sore can be covered.

Scabies: The child should stay home until treatment starts.

Strep throat, scarlet fever: The child should stay home until the day after treatment with antibiotics.

Vaccine-preventable diseases (diseases prevented by immunizations): The child should stay home until a health consultant says the child may return.

When a child has certain symptoms, he or she should stay home or be cared for in a special care setting. The child may return when a physician has said that the child does not put the other children at risk of getting ill and the child is well enough to participate in the activities. These symptoms include the following:

A fever and the child is feeling or acting ill
- Fever is a sign that the body is fighting some problem. Fever is not a disease. The importance of a raised temperature depends on what is causing the fever and how the child is behaving. For example, if nothing else is

wrong and the child had a diphtheria-tetanus-pertussis (DTP) shot the day before, or had a measles-mumps-rubella (MMR) shot 7 to 10 days before, fever alone does not mean that the child should have to stay home. There are certain times when a fever means a child should stay home. These include those times when—

- An infant under 4 months of age has an axillary (underarm) temperature of 100 degrees Fahrenheit or higher or a rectal temperature of 101 degrees Fahrenheit or higher. (Get medical help immediately.)
- A child between the ages of 4 months and 24 months has a rectal temperature of 102 degrees Fahrenheit or higher or an axillary temperature of 101 degrees Fahrenheit or higher.
- A child over 24 months of age has an oral or axillary temperature of 102 degrees Fahrenheit or higher.

- Body temperature usually goes up during the day. A child may have no fever and may act normal in the morning, but might become ill as the day goes on.

Vomiting or upset stomach

- A child with repeated vomiting can easily spread germs through the vomit. The child will also need a caregiver's attention. Unless the child care program can provide one-to-one attention, a child who vomits repeatedly should be sent home.
- If the child vomits only once and has no other symptoms, the child probably does not have to go home immediately. Some children vomit in the morning when they have swallowed mucous the night before. If the child is vomiting and also has other symptoms such as abdominal pain, diarrhea, and significant behavior changes, the child should stay home.

Looser and more frequent stools than usual (diarrhea)

- When a child has a single loose stool, he or she does not need to be at home. However, if the child has very runny stools that cannot be contained in a diaper, or the child cannot reach the toilet in time, the stool may contaminate the child care setting.
- Sometimes children get diarrhea when they take antibiotics. The children feel and act perfectly well and may not require extra caregiver attention.
- Children may also eat something (for example, prunes, too many strawberries, or melon) that causes loose stools. If they feel well, do not need extra caregiver attention, and are able to participate fully in the child care program activities, they do not have to stay home.
- Children with diarrhea who look or feel sick, or have a fever with their diarrhea, need close attention, need help washing up, or need added fluid intake, should stay home unless the caregiver can pay close attention to them.

Runny nose

- Children with constant runny noses that are not caused by allergies may spread germs everywhere. They may wipe their noses with their hands, then rub them on their own and other people's clothing and on other surfaces.
- Remove secretions from children's noses with facial tissues. You may also use a suction bulb for infants and younger children. This will help prevent the secretions from backing up into the child's ears or sinuses, where they can cause secondary bacterial infection.

Pain

- When a child is in pain, the child needs a parent's attention. The parent must take care of whatever is causing the pain and must comfort the child.

Too sick to fully participate

- Caregivers care for more than one child. When one child cannot participate, the caregiver must care for both the ill child and the other children. Unless the caregiver can provide sick-child care, the child should be cared for elsewhere.

Caring for Ill Children Guidelines

Your program's health policy guidelines for caring for ill children should include the following points:

- Each parent's plans for care when the child is too sick for the child care setting, but the parent can't stay home
- The program's procedure for recognition and exclusion of children who may be ill before arriving at the program, and those who become ill during the day
- The program's procedures for caring for ill children

- Coordination of information between the caregiver and the child's health care professional
- Giving medicines and taking temperatures
- Appropriate activities for ill children

Preventing Infectious Diseases Guidelines

Your program's health policy guidelines for preventing infectious diseases should include the following points:

- Staff health issues, including preemployment and periodic health assessments, immunizations, rest breaks, sick leave, and other benefits
- Requirements for children to keep up with health maintenance routines, including immunizations
- Daily health checks
- Preparing and handling food
- Cleaning and maintenance routines for the child care setting
- Notifying parents of a child's exposure to infectious disease
- Reporting of infectious disease problems to public health authorities

Consent and Contact Form

This form is to be completed and signed by the child's parent or legal guardian.

Name of child _____

In the event the child named above is injured or ill, I understand that the caregiver will attempt to contact me, the other parent, or the legal guardian at the telephone number provided below.

Parent's (legal guardian's) name _____

    Telephone numbers _____ on _____ (hours/days)

    _____ on _____ (hours/days)

Parent's (legal guardian's) name _____

    Telephone numbers _____ on _____ (hours/days)

    _____ on _____ (hours/days)

In the event that I or the others listed are not available, I give my permission to the caregiver to provide first aid for the child named above and to take the appropriate measures including contacting the emergency medical services (EMS) system and arranging for transportation to _____

_____

or the nearest emergency medical facility. At no time will the caregiver drive an ill or injured child to an emergency medical facility unless accompanied by another adult.

Signature _____ Date _____

How to Use a Thermometer to Take a Temperature

Three Types of Thermometers

Drawings of the three types of thermometers—digital, rectal, and oral—are below.

For standard glass thermometers, the shape of the bulb tells you whether it is for rectal or oral use. Rectal thermometers have a short, thick bulb; oral thermometers have a long, thin bulb. The long, thin bulb of an oral thermometer makes good contact between the mouth and the thermometer. The short, thick bulb of the rectal thermometer, however, fits more comfortably into a small child's mouth than the long, thin bulb of an oral thermometer does.

If you decide to use a rectal thermometer for taking oral temperatures, label the thermometer so you do not use it for taking rectal temperatures. Do not use oral thermometers in the rectum.

Whatever type of thermometer you use, clean it before and after use with soap and water. Then wipe it with rubbing alcohol and allow it to air dry before it is used again. Store the thermometer in its case.

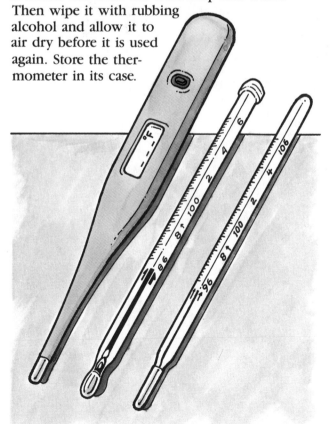

How to Take a Temperature

Shake a glass thermometer down by holding the thermometer by the non-bulb end and snapping your hand. The mercury must go down below the 95-degree mark.

By Mouth (oral)
1. Wait at least 15 minutes after the child eats or drinks to use a thermometer in the mouth. Eating or drinking before taking the temperature can affect mouth temperature and change the reading on the thermometer.
2. Place the bulb of the thermometer under the child's tongue. Have the child close his or her mouth without biting on the thermometer.
3. Leave the thermometer under the child's tongue for 3 minutes. If the child cannot keep the bulb of the thermometer between the bottom of the tongue and the floor of the mouth, the reading will not be accurate.

By Rectum (rectal)
(Be sure you know the program's health policy before taking a rectal temperature.)
1. Use a rectal thermometer for an accurate reading. Use it for children who cannot hold a thermometer in their mouth, generally children 3 years old and younger.
2. Cover the bulb end of the thermometer with a lubricating jelly. This makes putting the thermometer in easy and prevents hurting the child. If possible, ask another adult to observe this procedure to avoid any suspicion that inappropriate genital handling is involved.
3. Use gentle pressure to put the thermometer in about 3/4 of an inch to an inch and hold it there. Never use force.
4. Hold the thermometer in place for 2 to 3 minutes. Never leave the child alone when the thermometer is in place.

Under Arm (axillary)

1. Use an oral thermometer if possible. Its longer bulb means that more skin surface will be in contact with the bulb.
2. Place the bulb end of the thermometer in the child's armpit.
3. Hold the thermometer in place by pressing the child's arm to his or her body for 5 minutes.
4. Use the method only for newborns and very young infants. It does not give an accurate reading for older children.

With a Digital Thermometer

Follow the instructions that come with the thermometer for starting the thermometer and knowing when it is ready to read. Otherwise, use and clean it as described for a glass thermometer. The same digital thermometer can be used to measure oral, rectal, or axillary temperature if you wash it with soap and water, wipe it off with alcohol, allow it to air dry between use, and use a clean sheath each time. Because digital thermometers work quickly, children who can't hold a glass thermometer in their mouths long enough can have an oral temperature taken with a digital thermometer.

How to Read a Thermometer

1. Look at the drawing below. You will see the lines marked on the thermometer. Each short line marks 2/10 of a degree. Each long line marks a full degree. (For example, the first short line to the right of the long line for 99 is 99 and 2/10, or 99.2, degrees. The second short line would be 99 and 4/10, or 99.4; the third, 99 and 6/10 or 99.6; and soon on.)

2. Hold the thermometer in a good light to read it clearly. Have the light behind you.

3. Turn the thermometer until you can see clearly the line of mercury and where it has stopped.

4. Read the long line to the left of where the mercury has stopped. This will give you the whole degree.

5. Count the short lines between the long line you have just read and the point where the mercury has stopped. Remember, each short line means 2/10 of a degree.

6. Add the short lines to the long line for the exact reading.

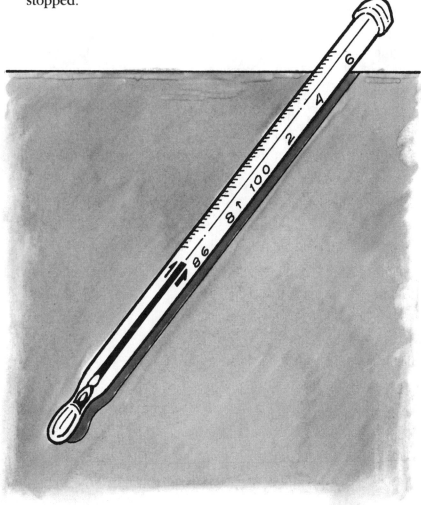

Safe Handling of Medicines

Some children may need medicines during the day for a mild illness or for a chronic problem. If your child care program has agreed with parents that you or another caregiver may give the child his or her medicine, you must know how to handle medicine safely.

1. Only trained caregivers may give a child medicine.
2. Always have a doctor's written instructions stating just how and when to give both prescription and nonprescription medicine. You should also know about any side effects you should look for.
3. Always have the parent's written consent for giving medicines.
4. All medicines must have proper labeling. For prescription medicines, the medicine container must have the original label and carry the following basic information:
   - The name of the child who will be getting the medicine
   - The name of the child's doctor
   - The name of the medicine
   - The issue date of the medicine
   - The dosage
   - How often to give the dosage
   - The route of administration (for example, oral)
   - Storage requirements (for example, refrigeration)

   For nonprescription medicines, the medicine container must have the following:
   - The name of the child who will be getting the medicine
   - Directions for safe use
   - The date the medicine expires
   - A list of active ingredients
   - The name and address of the manufacturer

   Remember, only use medicines that come in their original containers.

5. Caregivers who give medicines must know who each child is. If not, they may give the medicine to the wrong child.
6. Store all medicines safely in child-proof containers. Store them either in a refrigerator (if the label says so) or locked in a cool, dark, dry place out of the reach of children.
7. Discard, or return to the parent, any unused medicine.
8. Prepare, take, and give medicines out of the sight of other children.
9. Always read the label before giving the medicine.
10. Never call medicine "candy."
11. Never leave a container of medicine out or in a purse or a pocket where a child can reach it.
12. Make a note of which child took the medicine, how much the child took, and when the child took it. You may want to use a form such as the Medicine Record.

Medicine Record

Child's Name					
Name of Medicine	**Dose**	**Date**	**Time**	**Given By**	**Comments**

Tips for Giving Medicine Safely

1. Wash your hands before giving any medicine.
2. Be gentle, yet firm, when giving a child medicine. He or she may not want to take it.
3. Medicines come in many forms. They can be given by mouth, sprayed in the nose, dropped into the ear, put into the rectum, or rubbed on the skin. Be sure to follow written instructions.

To give medicine by mouth—
- Measure the exact amount of liquid the child must swallow. Shake the liquid medicine before pouring it if the label says to shake. Use a dropper or other special measuring device for liquids. Give liquids slowly and wait for the child to swallow each portion.
- Break large pills into smaller pieces if there is a line on the pill.

To give ear drops—
Ear drops go in more easily if you gently pull the ear toward the back of the head.

To give eye drops—
Eye drops go in more easily if you gently pull out the lower eyelid and put the drops in the "cup" the lower lid makes when pulled out.

To give nose drops—
Nose drops go in more easily if you lay the child on his or her back. For nose sprays, the child can stand or sit up.

To give a rectal suppository—
Before giving a rectal suppository, ask a doctor about the best way to insert it. (Be sure you know your program's health policy before giving a rectal suppository.)

American Red Cross Child Care Course

Infant and Child First Aid Guides

Emergency Action Principles

Survey the Scene

- Is the scene safe?

- Are the other children safe?

- What happened?

- How many people are injured?

- Are there bystanders who can help?

(Continued)

Do a Primary Survey for Life-threatening Conditions

Find out if the child is unconscious.

- Gently tap or shake the child's shoulder.

- Shout for help if the child does not respond.

Check the ABCs.

- **A**irway—Open the airway.

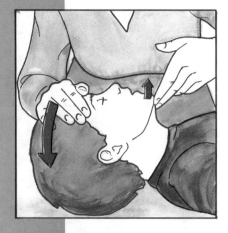

- **B**reathing—Look, listen, and feel for breathing.

- **C**irculation—Check for a pulse. Check for severe bleeding.

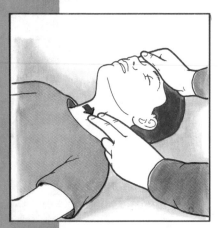

(Continued)

Phone EMS for Help

- Dial 9-1-1 or local emergency medical services (EMS) system
  number: _____

Do a Secondary Survey for Specific Injuries

- If possible, talk with the child and/or bystanders. Ask the
  child simple questions, such as "Do you hurt anywhere?"
- Check breathing, skin appearance, and skin temperature.
- Check all parts of the child's body. Start with the hands
  and arms.
  - Check the hands, arms, and shoulders.
  - Check the feet, legs , and hips.
  - Check the chest and abdomen.
  - Check the neck.
  - Check the scalp, face, ears, nose, and mouth.

While you are checking the child's body for injuries, ask simple

questions, such as "Can you wiggle your toes?" "Can you

wiggle your fingers?" "Can you take a deep breath for me?"

Important

If you suspect the child has a serious head injury, or a neck
or back injury, ask the child to stay still; do not move the
child. Call EMS immediately.

Bites, Animal or Human

What to Do

1. Follow the emergency action principles. Phone EMS or get medical help immediately if the wound is large or deep, if there is severe bleeding, or if the bite comes from an unknown or wild animal.

(Continued)

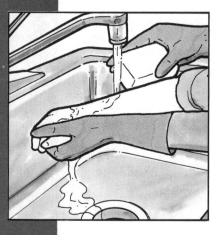

2. Wash the bite well with soap and water. Rinse well. (If the wound is bleeding heavily, quickly wash it. Then control the bleeding. Make sure EMS has been called.)

3. To control bleeding, apply pressure with gauze or a clean cloth. Elevate the wound unless you suspect the child has a broken bone. Maintain pressure and elevation until the bleeding stops. Then cover the wound with a clean bandage.

Information

- Wash your hands before and after giving first aid. If possible, wear disposable gloves when handling bites that have broken the skin.
- A sterile gauze pad makes the best pressure dressing.
- Bites need thorough cleansing because they can become infected easily. Until the bite heals, check for signs of infection, such as redness, tenderness, pus, or skin heat. Advise the child's parent to get medical help if the bite looks as if it is infected.
- Remind the child's parent to check if the child needs a tetanus shot.
- If the bite comes from an unknown or wild animal, call the police or animal control authorities to capture the animal.

Bites and Stings, Insect *(bees, yellow jackets, hornets, etc.)*

Important

Insect bites and stings can be life threatening to children who suffer severe allergic reactions like those described below.

What to Do

1. Follow the emergency action principles. Phone EMS or get medical help immediately if the child shows signs of an allergic reaction. Signs of allergic reaction include hives; very pale or flushed skin; spreading itchy rash; nausea; swelling; tightness in the nose, throat, or chest; difficulty breathing; and coughing or wheezing. If you see any of the signs of allergic reaction listed above, watch the child carefully. If the child is not breathing normally, call EMS at once. Help the child into the most comfortable position for breathing. Monitor the child's ABCs (airway, breathing, and circulation) until EMS arrives.

2. If there is a stinger, remove it by scraping it away with a stiff object, such as a credit card or your fingernail. You can use tweezers if you pull the stinger out in the same direction as it entered the skin.

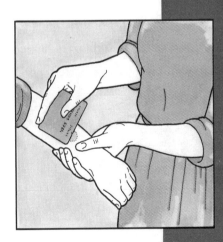

3. Wash the area with soap and water. Cover the area to keep it clean.

4. Apply a cold compress to reduce swelling and pain.

5. Stay alert for signs of allergic reaction.

Information

- Do not use baking soda, lotions, creams, sprays, antiseptics, or disinfectants.
- Always place a cloth between a cold compress and the skin to prevent skin damage.

Bites, Tick

What to Do

1. Follow the emergency action principles.

2. Remove the tick gently with tweezers. Wear gloves, if possible. Grasp the tick as close to the child's skin as possible and pull slowly to avoid breaking the tick. If you cannot remove the tick, or if parts of the tick remain in the skin, get medical help. If you do not have tweezers, use a glove, plastic wrap, or a piece of paper to protect your fingers. If you must use your bare fingers, wash your hands immediately afterward.

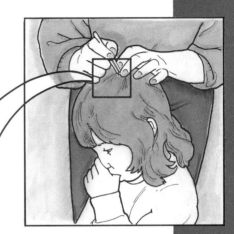

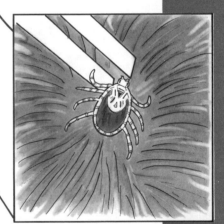

3. Wash the bite area with soap and water.

Important
- If the child feels ill, get medical help without delay.
- Be sure to tell the parent that the child has had a tick bite.

Bites, Poisonous Spider and Snake

What to Do

Spider Bite

1. Follow the emergency action principles. Phone EMS or the Poison Control Center, or get medical help immediately.

2. Wash the wound with soap and water. Keep the injured part still. Cover it to keep it clean. Apply ice or a cold compress to reduce pain and swelling. Place a cloth between the child's skin and the ice or cold compress to avoid skin damage. Remove any jewelry because the injured part might swell.

What to Do

Snakebite

1. Follow the emergency action principles. Phone EMS or the Poison Control Center, or get medical help immediately.

2. Wash the wound. **Do not apply ice or a cold compress to a snakebite.**

3. Keep the child quiet and calm. Keep the bitten body part still and keep it lower than the heart if possible.

4. When you take the child to medical help, carry the child or have him or her walk slowly.

Information

- If possible, note the color, size, shape, or any distinguishing marks on the spider or snake so you can describe it to EMS or the Poison Control Center.

Bleeding, Cuts

Open wounds in the skin or deep tissue can bleed heavily.
Blood vessels, muscles, tendons, and nerves may be damaged.

What to Do

1. Follow the emergency action principles. Phone EMS or get medical help immediately if the wound is large or deep or bleeding cannot be controlled.

2. Apply direct pressure with a clean cloth. Elevate the wound unless you suspect the child has a broken bone. You can help keep pressure on the wound by snugly wrapping a bandage around the injured area. Maintain pressure and elevation until the bleeding stops.

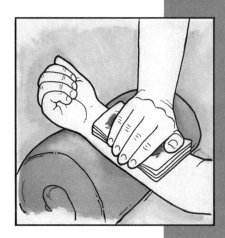

3. If bleeding soaks the cloth and/or bandage, apply another cloth without removing the first.

4. If bleeding is not severe, wash the wound with soap and water. Rinse well.

5. Place a sterile dressing or a clean cloth over the wound. Apply direct pressure for a few minutes to control any bleeding.

(Continued)

6. When bleeding has stopped, remove the dressing. Apply a new sterile dressing. Hold it in place with a bandage or tape.

7. Prevent or care for shock.

Information

- Wash your hands before and after giving first aid. If possible, wear disposable gloves for handling cuts. Avoid getting blood in your eyes, nose, or mouth.
- A sterile gauze pad or dressing makes the best pressure dressing.
- Do not use antiseptics or disinfectants.
- Cuts on the head may bleed heavily, but bleeding will stop with pressure and elevation.
- A cut may need stitches if—
  - It is longer than half an inch.
  - It is deeper than a quarter of an inch.
  - It continues to bleed.
  - The edges won't stay together.
- Cuts can usually be stitched safely for up to 6 hours after injury. The longer the wound stays open before stitches, the greater the risk of infection.
- Do not use a tourniquet or apply heat to a cut.
- To stop bleeding for cuts on the tongue, lips, or gums, have the child suck on a frozen juice bar or ice cube.
- Wrap in a plastic bag any item of the child's that may have come in contact with blood. Give the bag to the parent. Always wash hands after cleaning up blood, even if wearing gloves.
- Put any disposable bloody items in a plastic bag before discarding them.
- Wash and sanitize any bloody surfaces.
- Remind the child's parents to check if the child needs a tetanus shot.
- Tell the child's parents if you suspect a cut may become infected.

Bleeding, Scrapes

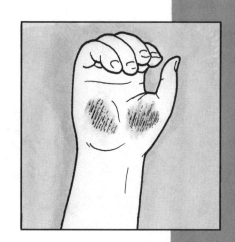

What to Do

1. Follow the emergency action principles. Phone EMS or get medical help to clean a large wound or a wound with deeply embedded materials, or if embedded materials remain after cleaning.

2. If the wound is not bleeding severely, wash it gently, but well, with soap and water. Rinse well.

3. To control any bleeding, apply pressure with a clean cloth. Elevate the wound unless you suspect the child has a broken bone. Maintain pressure and elevation until the bleeding stops.

4. When the bleeding has stopped, remove the cloth. If bleeding starts again, repeat pressure and elevation.

5. Apply a clean, dry dressing (nonstick, sterile). Hold the dressing in place with a bandage or tape.

Information

- A sterile gauze pad or dressing makes the best pressure dressing.
- Do not use antiseptics or disinfectants.

Bruises

What to Do

1. Follow the emergency action principles.

2. Apply pressure with a cold compress to reduce pain and swelling. Be sure to put a cloth between the cold compress and the skin to prevent injury to the skin.

3. Elevate the injured area unless you suspect the child has a broken bone.

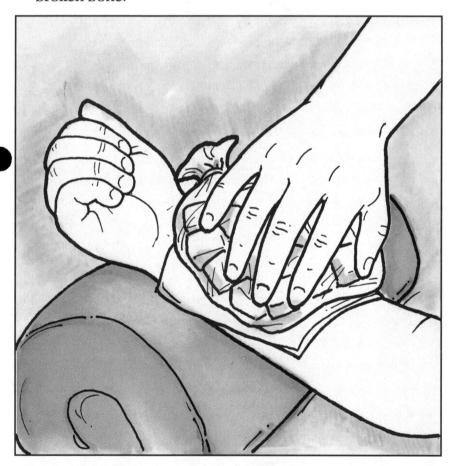

Important

Crushing injuries (from wringers, bicycle spokes, doors, etc.) or blunt injuries can cause internal damage. Phone EMS or get medical help immediately.

Burns, Chemical

What to Do

1. Follow the emergency action principles. Phone EMS or the

   Poison Control Center, or get medical help immediately.

(Continued)

2. Flush the chemical from the burned area with lots of cool, running water (at least one gallon) until medical help arrives. Remove any clothing that has the chemical on it, if possible.

If an eye is burned by a chemical, flush the eye with water until medical help arrives.

3. Prevent or care for shock.

Information

- Many household cleaning and garden supplies and workshop products are chemicals and can burn the skin.
- The deeper the burn, the more severe it is.
- The most serious burns—those on the face, hands, feet, and genitals—need medical attention immediately.
- Use a barrier between your own skin and the chemical, if possible.

Burns, Electrical

What to Do

1. Follow the emergency action principles.

- If the child is still touching the power source, turn off the electricity before you touch the child. Never pull a child away from a power source with your bare hands or with any object.

(Continued)

- Check the ABCs (airway, breathing, and circulation) carefully and care for any life-threatening conditions. Electricity can cause a child to stop breathing or the child's heart to stop beating.
- Phone EMS or get medical help immediately. All electrical burns must be seen by a doctor.

2. If the child is breathing, do a secondary survey to check all body parts. Check for more than one burn.

3. Apply clean, loose bandages (nonstick, sterile).

4. Prevent or care for shock.

Information

Contact with power lines, sockets, or outlets may cause electrical burns. All electrical burns are serious.

Burns, Heat *(also see Sunburn)*

Important
- If the child's clothes are on fire, tell the child to *stop, drop* to the ground, and *roll* to put out flames. Smother the flames or put them out with water. Then *cool* the burn with water.
- Remove smoldering clothing.

What to Do

1. Follow the emergency action principles.

2. Cool the burned area by flushing with cool running water or by covering it with a towel soaked in cool water. Allow time for the burn to cool. Keep cooling the area if pain continues or if the edges of the burn continue to feel warm. When the burn is cool, cut or carefully pull clothing away from the burned area. Do not try to remove clothing that is sticking to the skin.

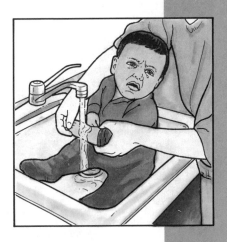

3. Cover the burned area with sterile dressings, if possible. Loosely bandage them in place.

4. Phone EMS or get medical help immediately for any burn on the face, hands, feet, or genitals; for burns on more than one part of the body; for burns that have blistered or have burned through the skin into the tissue below; or if the child is having difficulty breathing.

5. Prevent or care for shock.

(Continued)

Information

- Do not break blisters.
- Do not apply ointments, greases, powders, or medications without a doctor's approval.
- Give a conscious child fluids to drink.

Burns, Sunburn

What to Do

1. Follow the emergency action principles.

2. Get the child out of the sun.

3. Cool the skin with cool cloths or cool water.

4. Offer fluids to drink.

5. Keep the child out of the sun.

Important

- Get medical help for a sunburned infant; for a child with extensive sunburn on the face, hands, feet, genitals, or large areas of the body; or if a child's skin blisters.
- Get medical help if a child or infant has a fever as a result of a sunburn.

Information

- Do not apply sprays, creams, or ointments without a doctor's approval.

Choking (child)

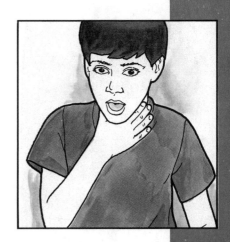

What to Do

For a conscious child—

1. Ask, "Are you choking?"

2. Tell the child you are going to help.

   Shout for help if a child—

   - Cannot cough, speak, or breathe.

   - Is coughing weakly.

   - Is making high-pitched noises.

3. Phone EMS for help.

Dial 911

(Continued)

4. Do abdominal thrusts as follows:

  • Stand or kneel behind the child. The child should be standing or sitting.

  • Wrap your arms around the child's waist.

  • Make a fist.

  • Place the thumb side of your fist against the middle of the child's abdomen just above the navel and well below the lower tip of the breastbone.

  • Grasp your fist with your other hand. Keep your elbows out and away from the child.

  • Press your fist into the child's abdomen with quick upward thrusts.

5. Repeat abdominal thrusts until the object comes out or the child becomes unconscious.

Important

The child should be taken to the hospital emergency department to be checked by a doctor even if he or she seems to be breathing well. The child may have breathing problems or internal injuries.

Information

• Do not raise a child's arms over the head. Do not pat a child on the back when the child is coughing or choking.
• If a child swallows a large object that does not cause choking but causes chest pain, see the first aid guide, Swallowed Objects.

(Continued)

If the child becomes unconscious, lower the child to the floor. Kneel beside the child.

1. Look for an object in the child's throat.

   • Grasp tongue and lower jaw and lift jaw.

   • If you can see an object in the throat, try to remove it with a finger sweep.

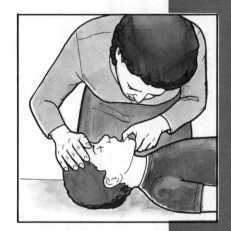

   • To do a finger sweep:

      • Slide finger down inside of cheek to base of tongue.

      • Sweep object out.

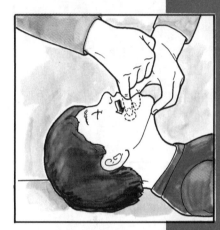

2. Open airway. Tilt head gently back and lift chin.

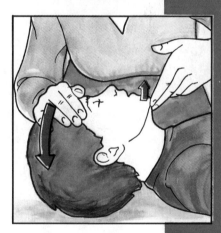

(Continued)

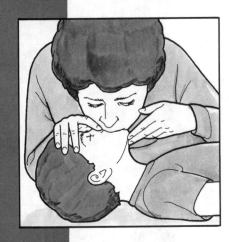

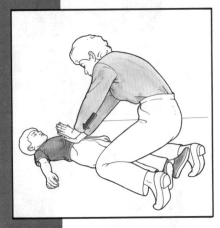

3. Give 2 slow breaths as follows:

- Keep head tilted back.

- Pinch nose shut.

- Seal your lips tightly around child's mouth.

- Give 2 slow breaths. Each breath should last 1 to 1½ seconds.

5 to 10

4. Do 6 to 10 abdominal thrusts.

If air won't go in—

- Kneel at the child's feet or straddle the child's legs.

- Place heel of one hand against middle of child's abdomen.

- Place other hand on top of first hand.

- Press into abdomen with quick upward thrusts.

5. Repeat steps 1, 2, 3, and 4 until airway is cleared or EMS personnel arrive and take over.

Important

The child should be taken to the hospital emergency department to be checked by a doctor even if he or she seems to be breathing well. The child may have breathing problems or internal injuries.

Information

- Do not raise a child's arms over the head. Do not pat a child on the back when the child is coughing or choking.
- If a child swallows a large object that does not cause choking but causes chest pain, see the first aid guide, Swallowed Objects.

Choking *(infant, birth to 1 year)*

What to Do

For a conscious infant—

1. Is the infant choking?

2. Shout for help if an infant—

   • Cannot cry, cough, or breathe.

   • Is coughing weakly.

   • Is making high-pitched noises.

3. Phone EMS for help.

4. Turn infant facedown.

   • Support infant's head and neck.

   • Turn infant facedown on your forearm.

   • Lower your forearm onto your thigh.

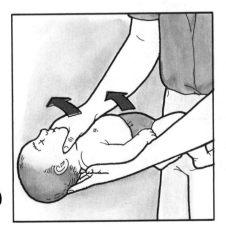 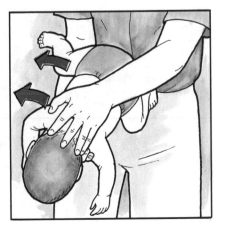

(Continued)

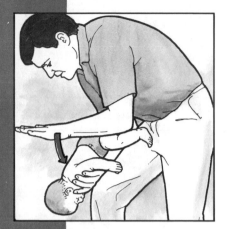

5. Give 5 back blows forcefully between infant's shoulder blades with heel of hand.

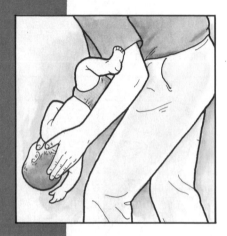

6. Turn infant onto back.

• Support back of infant's head and neck.

• Turn infant onto back.

• Lower your forearm onto your thigh.

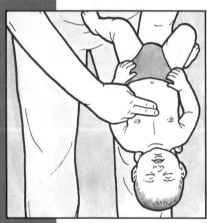

7. Give 5 chest thrusts.

• Place middle and index fingers on breastbone between nipple line and end of breastbone.

• Quickly compress breastbone 1/2 to 1 inch (1.3 to 2.5 centimeters) with each thrust.

8. Repeat steps 5, 6, and 7 until object is coughed up, infant starts to cry, cough, or breathe, or EMS personnel arrive and take over.

Important

The infant should be taken to the hospital emergency room to be checked by a doctor even if he or she seems to be breathing well. The infant may have breathing problems or internal injuries.

Information

Never raise an infant's arms over the head. Never pat an infant on the back when the infant is coughing or choking. (Continued)

If infant becomes unconscious, place infant on a firm, flat surface.

1. Look for an object in the infant's throat.

- Grasp tongue and lower jaw and lift jaw.

- If you can see an object in the throat, try to remove it with a finger sweep.

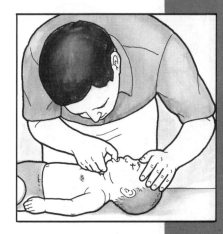

- To do a finger sweep:

  - Slide finger down inside of cheek to base of tongue.

  - Sweep object out.

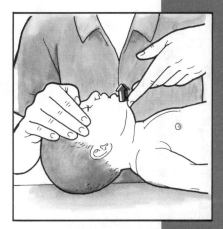

2. Open the airway.

- Tilt head gently back and lift chin.

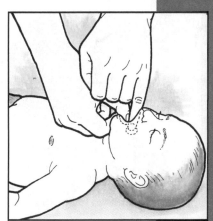

3. Give 2 slow breaths as follows:

- Keep head tilted.

- Seal your lips tight around infant's nose and mouth.

- Give 2 slow breaths for 1 to 1½ seconds each.

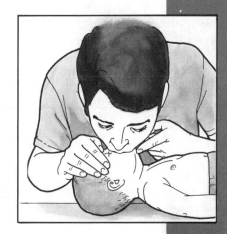

(Continued)

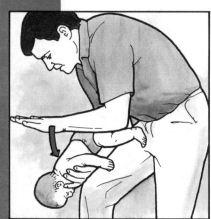

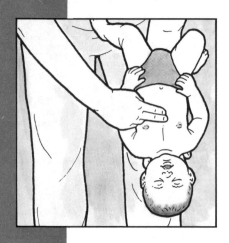

4. Give 5 back blows.

5. Give 5 chest thrusts.

6. Repeat steps 1, 2, 3, 4, and 5 until airway is cleared or EMS personnel arrive and take over.

Important

The infant should be taken to the hospital emergency room to be checked by a doctor even if he or she seems to be breathing well. The infant may have breathing problems or internal injuries.

Information

Never raise an infant's arms over the head. Never pat an infant on the back when the infant is coughing or choking.

Cold Emergencies

Frostbite

The nose, ears, chin, cheeks, fingers, and toes are the body parts affected most often by frostbite. Frostbite may result when a child has been exposed to very cold temperatures. The skin in a frostbitten area of the body is cold to the touch and looks waxy and discolored. When injured by cold, the skin may appear flushed, white, yellow, or blue. The child may also complain of lack of feeling (numbness) in the affected area.

What to Do

1. Follow the emergency action principles.
2. Take the child to a warm place.
3. Remove any cold, wet clothing and replace with dry clothing.
4. Have the child drink warm fluids, such as broth or water.
5. Soak frostbitten body parts in warm (100–105 degrees) water, not hot water. Soak until the frostbitten area looks pink. Handle body parts gently. Do not rub or massage them. Do not apply heat such as a hot water bottle or electric blanket.
6. Bandage injured parts loosely with nonstick, dry, sterile dressings. Put cotton or gauze between toes and fingers after warming them.
7. Prevent refreezing of thawed parts and care for shock.
8. Get medical help as soon as possible.

(Continued)

Hypothermia

Hypothermia happens when exposure to cold makes the body's temperature go too low. Signs and symptoms of hypothermia include shivering, dizziness, numbness, confusion, weakness, impaired judgment, impaired vision, glassy stare, and drowsiness. Hypothermia can occur if a child has been outside in the cold, in a cold room, or in cold water or wet clothing for a long time.

What to Do

1. Follow the emergency action principles. Phone EMS or get medical immediately.
2. Take the child to a warm place.
3. Remove any cold, wet clothing.

4. Warm the child's body slowly. Put dry clothing on the child and wrap him or her in blankets or clothing.
5. If the child is conscious, offer warm fluids, but no food. Give nothing by mouth if the child is unconscious.
6. Keep checking the ABCs (airway, breathing, and circulation).

Drowning

What to Do

1. Bring the submerged child to the surface.

2. Quickly remove the child from the water.

3. Shout for help. Have someone phone EMS.

4. Position the child on his or her back.

5. Check the child's airway and breathing.

6. Give 2 breaths if the child is not breathing.

7. Check the child's pulse.

8. Give rescue breathing or CPR as appropriate, unless the airway is blocked.

9. If the airway is blocked, give abdominal thrusts followed by 2 slow breaths until the airway is cleared. (Give chest thrusts to an infant.)

10. Continue to provide care until EMS arrives and takes over.

Ear Injuries

What to Do

Object in the Ear

1. Follow the emergency action principles.

2. Turn the child's head with the affected ear pointing *down*. Then the object can fall out easily, or you can grasp the object easily. Do not try to pull out difficult-to-remove objects. Get medical help.

Insect in the Ear

1. Follow the emergency action principles.

2. Turn the child's head so that the affected ear points *up*. Then the insect can fly or crawl out. If the insect does not come out, get medical help.

Bleeding From the Ear

1. Follow the emergency action principles. Phone EMS or get medical help if there is bleeding or drainage from inside the ear.

2. Do not stop bleeding from inside the ear. If the child has a head injury, see the first aid guide, Head and Spine Injuries.

3. If the bleeding is from a cut or tear on the outside part of the ear, apply direct pressure to control the bleeding. Then, clean the wound and cover it with a dry, sterile dressing. Get medical help if the ear tissue is torn.

Information

Never put anything in a child's ear.

Eye Injuries

Important

- Seek medical attention for any injury to the eye. There may be damage inside the eye that you cannot see.
- Do not apply pressure to any injury that involves the eye itself.

What to Do

Small Floating Object in the Eye

1. Follow the emergency action principles.

2. Hold the upper lid down and slightly away from the eye by the lashes. Always be very careful when touching or handling the eye or eye area. Tell the child to keep blinking to flush the eye with tears.

3. Try flushing the eye with cool water running from the inside corner of the eye outward if the object is still there.

4. If the object does not come out, close the lid over the injured eye. Cover the eye with an eye pad or guaze bandage. Do not bandage both eyes if only one eye is injured. If both eyes are injured, bandage them only if the child calmly accepts being unable to see.

5. Do not press on an injured eye. Do not apply medication.

6. Call EMS or get medical help if the object does not come out or eye problems persist.

(Continued)

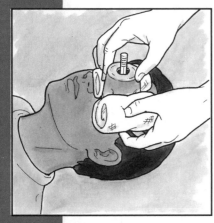

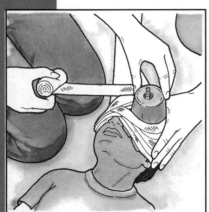

What to Do

Piercing Object in the Eyeball

1. Follow the emergency action principles. Phone EMS or get medical help.

2. Place the child on his or her back.

3. Do not try to remove the object.

4. Place a sterile dressing around the object.

5. Keep the object in place as best you can. You can do this by using a paper cup to support the object. Cut a hole in the cup if necessary.

6. Carefully bandage the cup in place. Cover the other eye to keep blood, fluid, and dirt out.

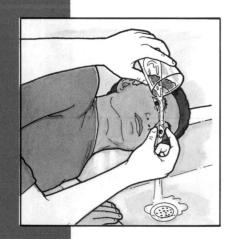

Chemicals in the Eye

1. Follow the emergency action principles. Phone EMS or get medical help.

2. Flush the eye with running water from the inside corner of the eye outward. Keep flushing until EMS arrives.

3. Do not use drops or ointment.

Blunt Blows to the Eye

1. Follow the emergency action principles. Phone EMS or get medical help immediately.

2. Keep the child lying down until the ambulance arrives.

3. Make the child comfortable.

Information

Wash your hands, if possible, before caring for an eye injury.

Fainting *(loss of consciousness)*

What to Do

1. Follow the emergency action principles.

2. Lay the child down.

3. Loosen any tight clothing. Keep the child's airway open. Check breathing and circulation.

4. Elevate the child's legs 8 to 12 inches above the body until the child fully recovers. Have the child sit up slowly and remain seated for 5 minutes before standing.

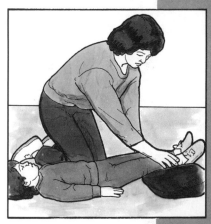

5. Call EMS or get medical help unless the child is known to have fainting spells and he or she recovers in less than 5 minutes.

6. Record the time, symptoms, and responses of the child and give these to the medical personnel who care for the child.

Information

- Fainting is a temporary loss of consciousness resulting from reduced blood supply to the brain. The child looks pale and sweaty. The skin is cool and moist. The child may feel dizzy or nauseous. Fainting may be caused by emotional stress, a sudden change in position (from lying down to sitting up, for example), standing up too long, or other situations in which too little blood reaches the brain.
- Do not use smelling salts or other stimulants. Do not pour cold water over the child's head.
- Offer nothing to drink until the child recovers completely.
- Parents should seek medical advice if the child has repeated fainting episodes.

Fractures, Dislocations, and Sprains

It is often difficult to tell the difference between fractures, dislocations, and sprains. Care for them all in the same way. Signs of these injuries include pain, swelling, deformity, changes in skin color around the injury, and inability to move the injured part normally. The body part also may look deformed. For example, the body part may be bent at an unusual angle.

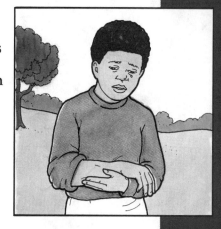

What to Do

1. Follow the emergency action principles. Phone EMS or get medical help if—

   - The injury involves a life-threatening emergency.
   - You suspect an injury to the head, neck, or spine.
   - The injury affects walking or breathing.
   - You cannot properly splint the injury to transport the child comfortably.
   - You suspect more than one injury.

2. Help the child rest in a comfortable position. Leave the child lying flat if you suspect a head, neck, or spine injury.

3. Control bleeding by applying light pressure.

4. Apply ice or a cold compress if the skin is not broken. Place a cloth between the ice or cold compress and the skin to prevent skin damage.

5. If possible, elevate the injured area above the level of the heart. Splint a part you suspect is fractured before elevating it.

6. Do not move the child or the injured part if EMS is on its way.

7. If you must move the child before help arrives, splint the injured part in the position in which you found it and in a position that is comfortable for the child.

8. Prevent or care for shock.

(Continued)

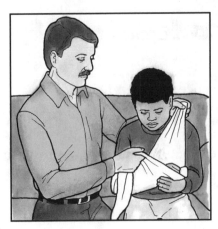

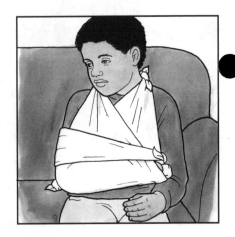

To splint a fracture, dislocation, or sprain

1. Use a stiff material such as wood or rolled-up newspaper as a splint. The splint must extend beyond the joints above and below the injury.

   • Tie the splint to the limb making sure that it supports the joints above and below the injury.

   • Use tape, a roll of gauze, or cloth to hold the splint against the injured part. Do not tie a bandage over the injury.

   • If you are splinting an arm, support the arm in a sling. Tie the sling over the uninjured shoulder. The hand should be higher than the elbow. Secure the arm to the chest with another bandage.

2. Or splint the injured part to another body part (for example, arm to chest, leg to leg).

3. Check fingers or toes for color and warmth to be sure the splint is not too tight.

4. If you must move the child, do so carefully and slowly.

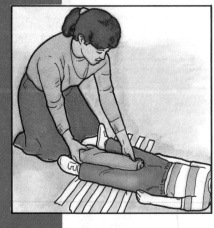

Head and Spine Injuries

Head injuries are often minor. However, you should suspect a serious injury to the head or spine if the child fell and hit his or her head and is unconscious, or if the child had a severe blow to the head or the body.

What to Do

1. Follow the emergency action principles. Phone EMS or get medical help if the child—

   • Is unconscious.

   • Does not recognize familiar people, does not know where he or she is, or behaves abnormally.

   • Cannot move normally.

   • Is dizzy or unusually sleepy.

   • Vomits repeatedly.

   • Has a severe headache that lasts longer than 1 hour.

   • Has blood or watery fluid in the ears or nose.

   • Has convulsions or seizures.

   • Has severe pain in the head or spine.

   • Has bruising around the eyes or behind the ears.

(Continued)

47

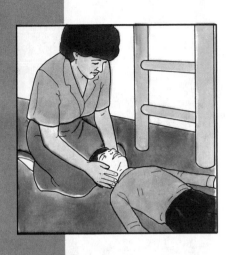

2. Keep the child as still as possible until EMS arrives. Keep the child's head and neck in the position in which you found them. Place your hands along both sides of the head to keep the head from turning.

3. If the child vomits, roll him or her as a unit onto one side to prevent choking and to allow breathing. Ask someone else to help you roll the child while you support the head and neck to keep them as still as possible.

4. Stay with the child until medical help arrives.

5. Make sure the child has an open airway, and keep checking that the child is breathing. Give rescue breathing if the child stops breathing.

6. Observe the child's level of consciousness.

7. Control external bleeding with dressings, direct pressure, and bandages.

8. Prevent or care for shock.

Important

For neck or spinal injuries, phone EMS or get medical help immediately. Keep the child's head and neck in the position in which you found them by placing your hands along both sides of the head. If the child vomits, roll the child as a unit onto one side to prevent choking and to allow breathing. Stay with the child until medical help arrives.

Information

Minor cuts on the head may bleed heavily, but bleeding can be controlled with direct pressure. Press gently on the wound because the skull may be fractured. If you feel a depression, a spongy area, or bone fragments, do not put direct pressure on the wound. Call EMS. Attempt to control bleeding with pressure on the area around the wound. After you have controlled the bleeding, apply dressings, and hold them in place with your hand. Secure the dressings with a bandage, if possible.

Heat Emergencies *(heat cramps, heat exhaustion, or heat stroke)*

Heat emergencies may occur when a child spends too much time in the heat. Heat cramps are the least severe heat emergency, but if not cared for, they may lead to heat exhaustion and heat stroke.

Heat Cramps

Muscle spasms in the arms, legs, or abdomen.

What to Do

1. Follow the emergency action principles.

2. Rest the child in a cool place.

3. Give water to drink (1/2 glass every 15 minutes).

(Continued)

Heat Exhaustion

Signs and symptoms are excessive fatigue and thirst, flushed skin, reduced sweating, headache, weakness and dizziness, and nausea and vomiting. The child may have an above-normal body temperature.

What to Do

1. Follow the emergency action principles.
2. Get the child out of the heat and into a cooler place immediately.

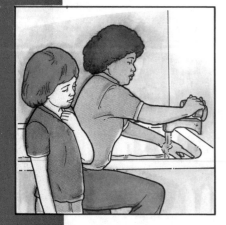

3. Prevent or care for shock. Lay the child on his or her back and elevate the legs.
4. Remove or loosen clothing.
5. Take the child's temperature. If it is elevated, cool the child by soaking the child in cool water or by wrapping in cool cloths. Then place the child in front of a fan, if possible. This will increase evaporation. Keep the child's skin wet. Rewet the cloths if they begin to dry.
6. Have the child sip cool water (1/2 glass every 15 minutes).
7. Phone EMS or get help immediately if the child starts vomiting, if the child is not well in 15 minutes, or if the child has a temperature over 101 degrees Fahrenheit (38.3 degrees Centigrade).

(Continued)

Heat Stroke

This is a life-threatening condition marked by disorientation; loss of consciousness; hot, red or pale skin; dry skin; headache and vomiting; and very high body temperature.

What to Do

1. Follow the emergency action principles. Phone EMS or get medical help immediately.

2. Take the child's temperature. If it is elevated, cool the child quickly by soaking the child in a cool bath or by wrapping the child in cool cloths.

3. Prevent or care for shock. Offer no fluids or food.

Information

• Heat stroke happens when the body temperature goes up in high heat, high humidity, or from heavy work or exercise.
• A child who has not had enough to drink, is overweight, is sick, or is very young may be more likely to get ill from the heat.

Nosebleeds

1. Follow the emergency action principles.

2. Have the child sit down with the head forward.

3. Pinch the child's nostrils together for 5 to 10 minutes, or until bleeding stops. Keep the child quiet for half an hour, because activity, talking, and laughing can start the nosebleed again.

Information

- Get medical help if bleeding continues.
- Do not attempt to control bleeding if you suspect that the child has a head, neck, or spine injury.

Poisoning (see Eye Injuries for chemicals in the eye and Burns, Chemical, for chemicals on the skin)

Signs and symptoms may include nausea, vomiting, diarrhea, abnormal breathing, slow pulse, unusual breath or body odors, burns around the mouth, changes in the color of the skin, drowsiness, unconsciousness, or convulsions.

What to Do

Swallowed Poisons

1. Follow the emergency action principles. Check the child's ABC's (airway, breathing, and circulation) carefully and continue to check them until you get medical help or advice.

2. Call the Poison Control Center. Follow their instructions. If there is no Poison Control Center, call a hospital emergency department or phone EMS and follow instructions.

3. Do not make the child vomit without medical advice.

Important

• Keep syrup of ipecac in your first aid kit. Give it only if EMS or the Poison Control Center tells you to do so. Check the expiration date on the bottle, and replace the bottle of syrup of ipecac when necessary.

• *Note:* The telephone number for the Poison Control Center in your community is:_____.

(Continued)

What to Do

Poisons on the Skin

1. Follow the emergency action principles. Check the child's airway, breathing, and circulation carefully and continue to check them until you get medical help or advice.

2. Flush with lots of water immediately. Remove any clothing that has poison on it.

3. Call the Poison Control Center. Follow their instructions.

4. Prevent or care for shock.

Inhaled Poisons

1. Follow the emergency action principles. Approach the child if it is safe for you to do so. Check the child's ABCs (airway, breathing, and circulation) carefully and continue to check them until help arrives.

2. Take the child to fresh air.

3. Call the Poison Control Center, phone EMS, or get medical help immediately.

4. Do rescue breathing if necessary.

Puncture Wounds

Puncture wounds can be caused by a nail, splinter, or other sharp, narrow object. Puncture wounds generally bleed very little.

What to Do

1. Follow the emergency action principles. Phone EMS or get medical help immediately if the object is large or is embedded. Bandage large embedded objects in place.

2. Pull out an easy-to-remove small object, such as a splinter or staple, with clean tweezers. Soak the wound in soapy water, if possible, to make removal easier.

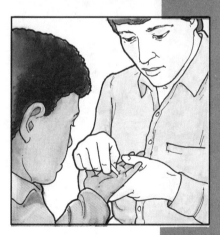

(Continued)

3. After removal, wash the wound well with soap and water; then rinse well. Try to soak the wound for at least 15 minutes, if possible.

4. Apply a loose bandage that will allow air to circulate while keeping the wound clean.

Information

- Do not use disinfectants or antiseptics without medical advice.
- Remind the child's parent to check whether the child needs a tetanus shot.

Rescue Breathing (child)

What to Do

1. Check for unresponsiveness.

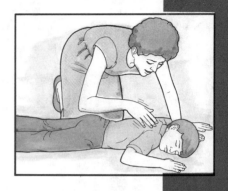

2. Shout for help if child is unresponsive.

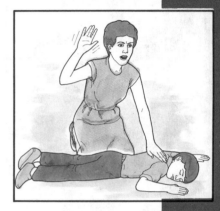

3. Position the child on his or her back.

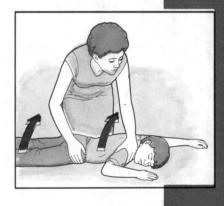

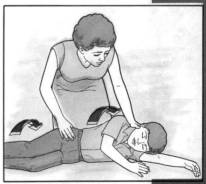

(Continued)

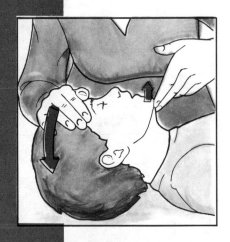

4. Open the airway. Tilt head gently back and lift chin.

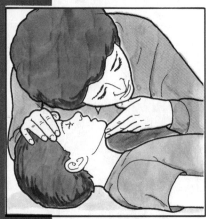

5. Look, listen, and feel for breathing for 3 to 5 seconds.

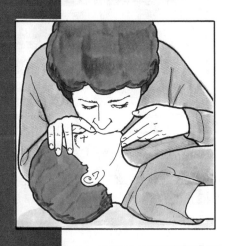

6. If child is not breathing, give 2 slow breaths as follows:

- Keep the airway open.

- Pinch the child's nose.

- Open your mouth wide and take a breath.

- Seal your lips tightly around the outside of the child's mouth.

- Give 2 slow breaths. Each breath should last 1 to 1½ seconds.

- Look for the child's chest to rise and fall. Listen and feel for air coming out of the child's nose and mouth.

- If air doesn't go into the lungs, gently tilt head farther back. Give 2 more breaths. (If air still does not go in, phone EMS and follow the procedure for choking.)

(Continued)

7. Check for pulse at the side of the neck for 5 to 10 seconds.

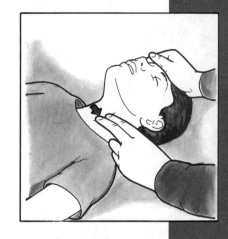

8. Phone EMS for help.

9. If the child is not breathing, but has a pulse, begin rescue breathing. (If the child has no pulse, begin CPR.)

- To give rescue breathing—
  - Keep airway open.
  - Give 1 breath every 3 seconds. Each breath should last 1 to 1½ seconds.

10. Recheck pulse after 1 minute (about 15 breaths).

- If child has a pulse, check for breathing for 3 to 5 seconds.
- If child is breathing, keep the airway open. Keep checking breathing and pulse closely. Cover the child. Keep the child warm and as quiet as possible.
- If child is not breathing, continue rescue breathing. Check the pulse once every minute.

Rescue Breathing (infant, birth to 1 year)

What to Do

1. Check for unresponsiveness

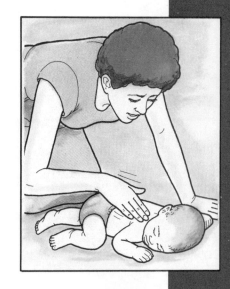

2. Shout for help if infant is unresponsive.

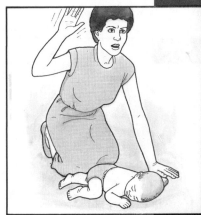

3. Position the infant on his or her back.

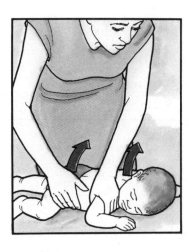

(Continued)

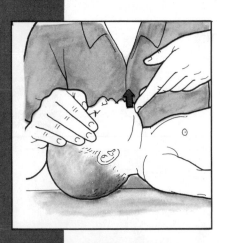

4. Open the airway. Tilt head gently back and lift chin.

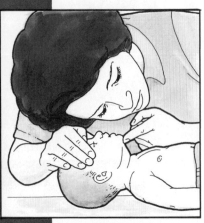

5. Look, listen, and feel for breathing for 3 to 5 seconds.

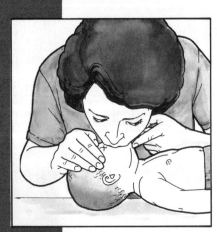

6. If infant is not breathing, give 2 slow breaths as follows:

- Keep the airway open.

- Open your mouth wide and take a breath. Seal your lips tightly around the infant's mouth and nose.

- Give 2 slow breaths. Each breath should last 1 to 1½ seconds.

- Look for the infant's chest to rise and fall. Listen and feel for air coming out of the infant's nose and mouth.

- If air doesn't go into the lungs, gently tilt head farther back. Give 2 more breaths. (If air still does not go in, phone EMS and follow the procedure for choking.)

(Continued)

7. Check for pulse in upper arm for 5 to 10 seconds.

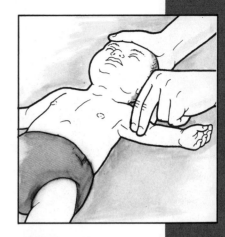

8. Phone EMS for help.

9. If the infant is not breathing, but has a pulse, begin rescue breathing. (If the infant has no pulse, begin CPR.)

- To give rescue breathing—
  - Keep the airway open.
  - Give 1 breath every 3 seconds. Each breath should last 1 to 1½ seconds.

10. Recheck pulse after 1 minute (about 20 breaths).

- If infant has a pulse, check for breathing for 3 to 5 seconds.
- If infant is breathing, keep the airway open. Keep checking breathing and pulse closely. Cover the infant. Keep the infant warm and as quiet as possible.
- If infant is not breathing, continue rescue breathing. Check the pulse once every minute.

Seizures

Signs of a seizure include uncontrollable muscle movements with brief blackouts, sudden falls, jerking, rigidity, and loss of consciousness. Drooling is common. Eyes may roll upward.

What to Do

1. Follow the emergency action principles. Call EMS for help if the child has not had a seizure before or if the seizure lasts more than 15 minutes.

2. Lay the child on the floor and keep the child clear of any objects. Roll the child onto his or her side to prevent the tongue, saliva, or vomit from blocking the airway.

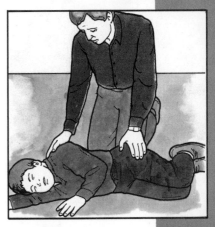

3. Do not hold or restrain the child or put anything between the child's teeth.

4. Loosen clothing, if possible.

5. Stay with the child.

6. Reassure the child.

(Continued)

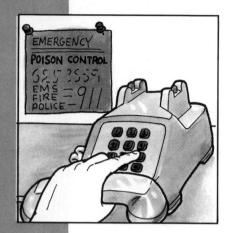

Important

Get medical help if this is the child's first seizure, if the seizure lasts more than 15 minutes, if the child hurts himself or herself, or if you have any other concerns.

Information

- Roll the child onto his or her side to prevent tongue, saliva, or vomit from blocking the airway.
- Note the time the seizure started and the time it ended.
- Note the types of movements the child made during the seizure.
- If the child has a fever, cool the child's body with lukewarm water.
- After a seizure, a child may be confused and/or drowsy.
- Seizures may be caused by a high fever in young children, infections of the brain, head injury, insulin shock in diabetics, poisons, or drug reactions.

Shock

Shock may be caused by any injury or illness, especially one that results in blood loss, allergic reactions, infections, or physical or emotional trauma. Signs of shock include pale, bluish or ashen, cool, moist skin; weakness; a fast, weak pulse; fast or irregular breathing; restlessness or anxiety; nausea and vomiting; or thirst.

What to Do

1. Follow the emergency action principles. Phone EMS immediately and give first aid for the injury or illness.

2. In all situations involving significant illness or injury—

   • Lay the child down.

   • Elevate the child's legs 8 to 12 inches above his or her body unless you suspect broken bones; a head, neck, or back injury; or the child is having difficulty breathing.

   • Control any external bleeding as soon as possible.

   • Keep the child's body at a comfortable temperature.

   • Reassure a conscious child.

   • Continue to check the ABCs (airway, breathing, and circulation).

   • If the child vomits, place him or her on one side to avoid blocking the airway.

   • Do not give the child anything to eat or drink.

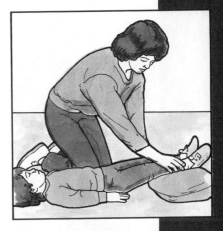

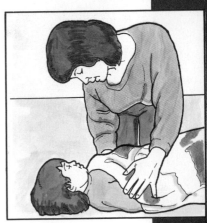

Important
Shock can be life threatening. If you see the signs of shock, give care immediately. You do not have to identify what is wrong before you give care for shock.

Swallowed Objects

If a child swallows an object and is having difficulty breathing, see the first aid guide, Choking. If the child can breathe without difficulty, follow the directions below.

What to Do

1. Follow the emergency action principles.

2. Offer water to help reduce pain if the child is not having difficulty breathing.

3. Get medical help if the discomfort or pain continues or if the swallowed object was not food.

Important

A very small object, such as a swallowed tooth, usually causes no problems; however, a coin or a toy may stop hurting but may still be stuck. Get medical advice any time a child swallows an object that is not food.

Tooth Injuries

What to Do

Knocked-out Permanent Tooth

1. Follow the emergency action principles.

2. Pick the tooth up by the chewing edge (crown), not the root. Do not rub or handle the root part of the tooth. Do not rinse or try to clean the tooth.

3. If possible, place the tooth back in the socket in the same position it was in.

4. Have the child bite down gently and/or hold the tooth in place with a sterile gauze pad, a tissue, or a clean cloth.

5. Take the child to a dentist as soon as possible.

If you cannot put the tooth back in its socket, do the following:

1. Put the tooth in a container of cool milk. Put it in water if milk is not available.

2. Place a sterile dressing or clean cloth in the space left by the tooth. Tell the child to gently bite down.

3. Take the child to the dentist as soon as possible. Be sure to bring the container with the tooth.

Important
The child should see a dentist within one hour If this is not possible, the child should still be seen by a dentist as soon as possible.

(Continued)

Knocked-out Baby Tooth

1. Follow the emergency action principles.

2. Place the tooth in a container of milk. Place it in water if milk is not available. Do not try to reinsert the tooth. Cover the container so that the contents will not spill.

3. Ask the parent to take the child to a dentist as soon as possible. Give the closed container with the tooth to the parent.

Tooth—Cracked, Broken, or Chipped

1. Follow the emergency action principles.

2. Rinse the mouth with warm water.

3. Apply a cold compress on the face in the area of the injury.

4. Locate and save teeth or any pieces of a tooth.

5. Ask the parent to take the child to a dentist.

First Aid Card for Special Conditions

For children with diabetes, asthma, reactions to insect stings, or other conditions that may require emergency management, ask the child's doctor to write out a first aid card for the problem. The card should follow the format below:

Child's Name: _____

Type of Problem: _____

Description: _____

_____

Causes: _____

_____

First Aid

- _____

  _____

  _____

  _____

- _____

  _____

  _____

  _____

- _____

  _____

  _____

  _____

- _____

  _____

  _____

MISSION OF THE AMERICAN RED CROSS

The American Red Cross, a humanitarian organization led by volunteers and guided by its Congressional Charter and the Fundamental Principles of the International Red Cross Movement, will provide relief to victims of disaster and help people prevent, prepare for, and respond to emergencies.

ABOUT THE AMERICAN RED CROSS

To support the mission of the American Red Cross, over 1.3 million paid and volunteer staff serve in some 1,600 chapters and blood centers throughout the United States and its territories and on military installations around the world. Supported by the resources of a national organization, they form the largest volunteer service and educational force in the nation. They serve families and communities through blood services, disaster relief and preparedness education, services to military family members in crisis, and health and safety education.

The American Red Cross provides consistent, reliable education and training in injury and illness prevention and emergency care, providing training to nearly 16 million people each year in first aid, CPR, swimming, water safety, and HIV/AIDS education.

All of these essential services are made possible by the voluntary services, blood and tissue donations, and financial support of the American people.

FUNDAMENTAL PRINCIPLES OF THE INTERNATIONAL RED CROSS AND RED CRESCENT MOVEMENT

HUMANITY

IMPARTIALITY

NEUTRALITY

INDEPENDENCE

VOLUNTARY SERVICE

UNITY

UNIVERSALITY

TEST BEST®

for Test Prep

Strategies for
- *Reading*
- *Vocabulary*
- *Math*
- *Listening*
- *Language*

STECK-VAUGHN
BERRENT

A Harcourt Company

www.steck-vaughn.com

Test Best® for Test Prep
Level G

Contents

Credits

Project Editor: Amy Losi
Cover Design: Steven Coleman

Test Best® is a registered trademark of Steck-Vaughn Company.

Test Best® for Test Prep — Level G

ISBN 0-8172-5830-2

Published by © Steck-Vaughn/Berrent Publications, a division of Steck-Vaughn Company.

5 6 7 8 9   03 02

The following strategies will help you do your best on standardized reading tests. These three strategies will assist you in organizing the information needed to successfully answer the questions.

STRATEGY 1

The CHECK AND SEE Strategy

This strategy can be used when a question asks for a fact from the story. The answer to the question is right there in the story. It is not hidden. Some of the same words may be in the story and in the question.

 Check and See will help you answer *remembering information* questions.

This is the Check and See Strategy

1.   READ: **Read** the question.

2.   FIND: **Find** the words you need in the story.

3.   DECIDE: **Decide** which strategy to use.
     Check and See: Put a **check** next to the sentence
                where you can **see** the words you need
                to answer the question.

4.   ANSWER: Choose the best **answer**.

STRATEGY 2

The PUZZLE PIECE Strategy

This strategy can be used when a question asks you what something means. Sometimes there does not seem to be an answer. It is not stated in the story.

 Puzzle Piece is the strategy to use when you must fit facts together to get the answer. This is like putting a puzzle together. Puzzles are made up of many pieces. You cannot look at one piece and know what the picture is. Only when you put the pieces together can you see the whole picture.

This is the Puzzle Piece Strategy

1. READ: **Read** the question.

2. FIND: **Find** the facts you need in the story.

3. DECIDE: **Decide** which strategy to use.
    Write: **Write** the facts in puzzle pieces.
    Put Together: **Put** the puzzle pieces **together** to see the picture.

4. ANSWER: Choose the best **answer**.

STRATEGY 3

The WHAT LIGHTS UP Strategy

This is another strategy you can use when an answer is not in the story. To answer the question you need to add your own ideas to the story. This added information can come from your own experiences.

 What Lights Up can help you see if something is true, real, useful, or a fact. It can help you see what would happen if the story had a different ending.

You can use the **What Lights Up Strategy** to answer the hardest type of question. This is when you are asked to read and think of your own ideas. These questions are called *evaluating* and *extending meaning* questions.

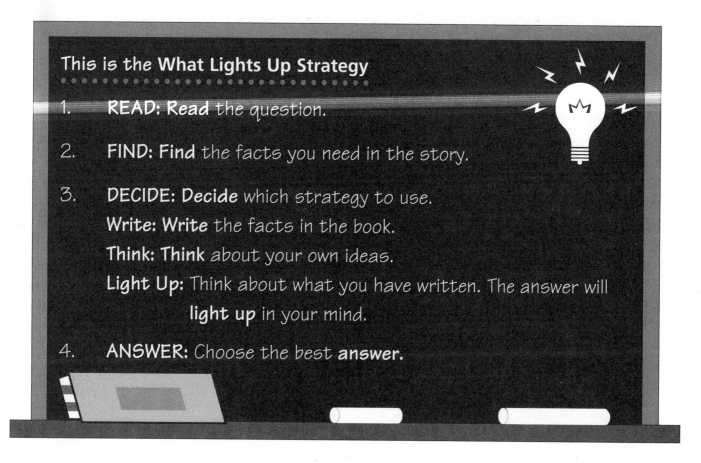

This is the What Lights Up Strategy

1. **READ: Read** the question.

2. **FIND: Find** the facts you need in the story.

3. **DECIDE: Decide** which strategy to use.
    Write: Write the facts in the book.
    Think: Think about your own ideas.
    Light Up: Think about what you have written. The answer will **light up** in your mind.

4. **ANSWER:** Choose the best **answer.**

5

Specific Objectives

Objective 1: Determining word meanings
Prefixes and suffixes, context clues, technical words, and words with multiple meanings

Objective 2: Identifying supporting ideas
Recalling facts and details, sequential order, following directions, and describing settings

Objective 3: Summarizing main ideas
Stated and implied main ideas, and identifying summaries

Objective 4: Perceiving relationships and recognizing outcomes
Cause-and-effect and making predictions

Objective 5: Making inferences and generalizations
Interpreting graphs and diagrams, inferring information, drawing conclusions, making judgments, and evaluating plot

Objective 6: Recognizing points of view, facts, and opinions
Author's purpose, persuasive language, and discerning facts and points of view

Modeled Instruction

Directions: Read each passage carefully. Darken the circle for the correct answer, or write your answer in the space provided.

Objective 1: Determining Word Meanings

Prefixes and suffixes are parts of some words. A *prefix* appears at the beginning of a word. A *suffix* appears at the end of a word. Both prefixes and suffixes affect the meaning of the word. Readers can use them to help figure out the meaning of a word.

Both of the teenagers had a problem with their mother. They were good students, helped around the house, and did their own laundry. But she remained hypercritical.

1   In this selection, the word **hypercritical** means —

A   hysterical.

B   underactive.

C   overly critical.

D   under pressure.

Hint: "Hyper-" is a prefix that means too much.

Bob went to look at the apartment with the realtor. The neighborhood looked nice enough, and there were lots of stores within walking distance. They walked up a flight of stairs outside; it was the first apartment on the right. When they opened the door, Bob could not believe how spacious the rooms were.

2   In this paragraph, the word **spacious** means —

F   large.

G   crowded.

H   dirty.

J   sparkling.

Hint: The suffix "-ious" means characterized by.

He had said some pretty bad things to the teacher when he saw her after school. Maybe he had just had enough of being called upon in class when he was unprepared. In retrospect, however, he was sorry he had lost his temper. He vowed to meet with his teacher the next morning to make things right.

3   In this paragraph, what does the word **retrospect** mean?

_____

_____

_____

_____

_____

_____

_____

Hint: "Retro-" is a prefix that means backwards.

GO ON

Answers
1 Ⓐ Ⓑ Ⓒ Ⓓ   2 Ⓕ Ⓖ Ⓗ Ⓙ

Objective 1: Determining Word Meanings

Sometimes you can figure out the meaning of a new word by using the words around it as clues.

A woman in Australia and a woman in England were pen pals for a long time. Their correspondence lasted over 75 years.

1 **In this paragraph, the word correspondence means —**

   A letter writing.

   B friends.

   C phone calls.

   D mailbox.

   Hint: You get a clue as to what the word correspondence means in the first sentence.

At the beach, there is a contest for building castles from the sand. Some of the castles are very elaborate. They have towers, windows, and even bridges.

2 **In this paragraph, the word elaborate means —**

   F sandy.

   G short.

   H plain.

   J fancy.

   Hint: You get a clue as to what the word elaborate means by reading the description of the castles in the last sentence.

Animals that live in the desert are well protected. Their small bodies help them escape the heat that scorches the ground. Some animals stay in tunnels when the hot sun beats down.

3 **In this paragraph, the word scorches means —**

   _____

   _____

   _____

   _____

   _____

   _____

   Hint: You get a clue as to what scorches means by the numerous references to heat.

GO ON

Objective 1: Determining Word Meanings

Specialized or technical words are words used in specific subjects, such as science and social studies. Readers can use all the other information in the text to help determine the meaning of such words.

In 1902, a man asked a woman to marry him. She said, "Yes." They decided to wait a few years before they got married. They finally got around to matrimony in 1969.

1   **In this paragraph, the word matrimony means —**

   A   talking.

   B   trying.

   C   marrying.

   D   dying.

   Hint: You get a clue as to what the word matrimony means by reading the many references to marriage throughout.

In 1980, someone threw a grape more than three hundred feet. A man caught the grape in his mouth. The site of this event was a football field in Louisiana.

2   **In this paragraph, the word site means –**

   F   toss.

   G   place.

   H   time.

   J   game.

   Hint: Site is a technical word. You get a clue as to what it means in the sentence in which it appears.

Pepper was once very rare. Armies seized it when they took over a city. In the fifth century, the Romans had to give three thousand pounds of it to enemies. Besides pepper, the winners also took gold, silver, and silk as part of their booty.

3   **In this paragraph, the word booty means —**

   _____

   _____

   _____

   _____

   _____

   _____

   _____

   Hint: Booty is a technical word. You get a clue as to what it means from reading the entire paragraph.

▶GO ON▶

Answers

1 Ⓐ Ⓑ Ⓒ Ⓓ   2 Ⓕ Ⓖ Ⓗ Ⓙ

Objective 1: Determining Word Meanings

A word can have different meanings depending on when and how you use it. Readers can figure out the correct meaning of a word by reading the entire passage.

No one could call him dishonest. If he found a wallet with $100 in it, he would return it to its owner. He was a <u>just</u> man.

1   In this passage, the word <u>just</u> means —

    A rich.

    B phony.

    C only.

    D righteous.

Hint: Read the whole passage to determine what kind of man he was.

Wanda came into the room looking for Rochelle. I told her that Rochelle had <u>just</u> left.

2   In this passage, the word <u>just</u> means —

    F only.

    G a very short time ago.

    H never.

    J a very long time ago.

Hint: You must read the whole selection to determine the meaning.

As we walked through it, I saw how beautiful the estate of the foreign diplomat was. Each building within the <u>compound</u> was more beautiful than the last.

3   In this passage, the word <u>compound</u> means —

    A combination of elements.

    B enclosed space containing buildings.

    C architectural drawing.

    D painting.

Hint: Read both sentences to determine the meaning.

The chemist invented a new <u>compound</u>. He hoped this mixture would give him the recognition he deserved.

4   In this passage, the word <u>compound</u> means —

    F combination of elements.

    G enclosed space.

    H architectural drawing.

    J painting.

Hint: You must read both sentences to determine the meaning.

STOP

Answers

1 Ⓐ Ⓑ © Ⓓ   2 Ⓕ Ⓖ Ⓗ Ⓙ   3 Ⓐ Ⓑ © Ⓓ   4 Ⓕ Ⓖ Ⓗ Ⓙ

Objective 2: Identifying Supporting Ideas

Some facts and details are important. By noticing and remembering them, you will better understand what the passage is about.

Many hundreds of years ago, a monk from India traveled to China. He began teaching people special movements to train the mind and body. His students learned to sit very still for a long time, breathing slowly. They learned shadowboxing and hand movements. All these movements came to be called *kung fu*.

When a Japanese army invaded a Chinese island, kung fu experts came to the rescue. They turned back the spears of the Japanese with their bare hands. The amazed Japanese called this weapon *kara* (empty) *te* (hand). Some Japanese then learned karate themselves, keeping it a secret for centuries. But after World War II, American soldiers discovered karate. The secret was no longer a secret. Teachers opened schools for people wanting to learn this ancient art. Today, karate schools are all over the world.

1 **A monk came from India to —**

A China.

B Japan.

C America.

D an island.

Hint: Look at the first sentence.

2 **Now karate schools are —**

F for fighters.

G in Japan.

H for strong hands.

J all over the world.

Hint: Look at the last sentence in the second paragraph.

3 **How did Chinese kung fu experts turn back the Japanese?**

_____

_____

_____

_____

_____

_____

_____

Hint: Look at the second sentence in the second paragraph.

▶ GO ON ▶

Answers

1 (A) (B) (C) (D)   2 (F) (G) (H) (J)

Objective 2: Identifying Supporting Ideas

Sometimes it is helpful to arrange events in the order they happened. This may help you to understand the passage better.

The Mohawks once lived in Canada, but they grew weary of battling with the Algonquins there. So they moved south and settled on the banks of the Hudson River. Occasionally, however, some made short trips back to their old home. On one trip, enemies captured the Mohawk chief and his oldest son. The chief's wife and younger son grieved deeply. "I will find my father and brother and return with them," declared the boy. "Every night, Mother, build a fire on this cliff. The light will guide us home."

The woman built a fire every night. Years went by, and she continued to wait. Every night she sat by the fire in sorrow, and her tears tumbled down the cliff. Finally, one night, her younger son climbed the cliff, carrying the bones of his father and brother. He and his mother wept together. Then Manitou, the Great Spirit, sent lightning to carry them to his home in the sky. That same bolt of lightning transformed the woman's tears to crystal, and today her crystal tears still glisten on Diamond Rock.

1 **Which of these happened first in the story?**

   A The Mohawks moved south to the Hudson River.

   B A chief and his son traveled back to their old home.

   C Enemies captured the Mohawk chief and his son.

   D The chief's wife and younger son grieved.

Hint: Read the beginning to find what happened first.

2 **When did the younger son and his mother weep?**

   F before the son went in search of his father and brother

   G on a trip down the Hudson River

   H after the son returned with the bones of his father and brother

   J when the son built a fire on the cliff

Hint: Read sentences 4 and 5 in the second paragraph.

3 **When did the younger son leave home?**

_____

_____

_____

_____

_____

_____

_____

Hint: Read sentences 4 and 6 in the first paragraph.

Answers
1 Ⓐ Ⓑ Ⓒ Ⓓ   2 Ⓕ Ⓖ Ⓗ Ⓙ

Objective 2: Identifying Supporting Ideas

Written directions tell the reader how to do something. To follow them means to do them in the same order in which they are given.

It seemed simple enough, so Peter did not know why his mother was making such a big deal out of it. The college coach had called and asked him to send him a copy of his football schedule and high school transcript. They were considering giving him an athletic scholarship.

Peter went to the guidance office and got a copy of the transcript and walked to the post office to mail it. When he got there, he realized he had left the football schedule at home, so he went home and got that. Back at the post office, he realized that he needed an envelope and also that he should make copies of each item so that he would have them to send to other colleges that might call. So he left the post office again and went to the stationery store to make copies and buy envelopes. Luckily, he met his friend Tom, so that he could borrow a dollar to make copies.

Carrying the growing number of items in hand, Peter went back to the post office and started to address the envelope. Where was it going? He knew the coach's name, but not his address. So he called his sister from the pay phone in the lobby and asked her to read the return address of the school from the envelope on the kitchen counter. Finally, he folded the transcript and schedule in thirds, put them in the envelope, put a stamp on it (after waiting in line to buy one), and put it in the out-of-town slot in the lobby. Big deal.

1   **What was the first thing that Peter did?**

   A got a copy of his high school transcript

   B got a copy of his football schedule

   C had copies of his transcript made

   D went to the guidance office and asked about what he needed

Hint: Read the start of the passage until you come to the answer.

2   **Before he spoke with Tom, Peter had realized all but one of the following —**

   F   that he needed the football schedule.

   G that he needed an envelope.

   H that he needed to make copies.

   J that he needed the coach's address.

Hint: Make a list of what Tom realized before he met his friend.

3   **What did Peter do after he made the copies?**

   _____

   _____

   _____

   _____

   _____

   _____

   _____

Hint: Read the part when Peter makes copies.

▶ GO ON ▶

Answers

1 Ⓐ Ⓑ Ⓒ Ⓓ   2 Ⓕ Ⓖ Ⓗ Ⓙ

Objective 2: Identifying Supporting Ideas

The setting of a story lets the reader know when and where it is taking place.

It was a gray November day in 1963. A fishing boat rocked in the Atlantic Ocean off the southern coast of Iceland. Suddenly, a great black cloud burst from the water. Loud noises rumbled from the ocean, too. The ship's captain sent out a radio call. Something very unusual was happening!

During the next three hours, many scientists and reporters arrived at the scene. By now the cloud was 12,000 feet high. Huge explosions sent ash, dust, and hot rocks into the air. The watchers could see something just under the water's surface. A fiery island was growing in the Atlantic. It was caused by a volcano in the ocean.

1   **The fiery island started growing in the year —**

    A   1993.

    B   1936.

    C   1963.

    D   1863.

Hint: This asks about when the story takes place.

2   **The fishing boat was off the coast of —**

    F   Ireland.

    G   Greenland.

    H   Iceland.

    J   November.

Hint: This asks about where the story takes place.

3   **During what season did the volcano erupt?**

    _____

    _____

    _____

    _____

    _____

    _____

    _____

Hint: This asks about when the story takes place.

STOP

Answers

1 (A) (B) (C) (D)   2 (F) (G) (H) (J)

Objective 3: Summarizing Main Ideas

The main idea is the overall meaning of a piece of writing. Often the main idea is written in the passage.

Allied soldiers in World War II were trapped at Dunkirk, France, and they could not escape because the shallow water kept rescue ships from landing. But hundreds of people in England took rowboats, tugs, and barges across the English Channel. For eight days, this odd navy carried soldiers from the beaches to the large ships. More than 300,000 soldiers were taken to safety.

1 What is the main idea of this passage?

  A Small ships are better than big ships.

  B Many soldiers were saved.

  C Soldiers were rescued from Dunkirk by the English.

  D The big ships could not get into shallow water.

Hint: What does the whole story talk about?

Sharks have a number of "tools" that help them find food. They have a keen sense of hearing and can smell blood from almost 2,000 yards away. They also have a special system of channels in their skin that helps them feel the vibrations of a struggling swimmer. We know that in clear water, sharks can see their prey from about fifty feet away.

2 What is the main idea of this selection?

  F Sharks hear well.

  G Sharks have poor vision.

  H Sharks sense food in a special way.

  J Sharks like struggling swimmers.

Hint: What does the entire passage talk about?

Every year, hungry deer do millions of dollars' worth of damage to young pine trees. But scientists in Washington have found a way to protect the trees using a substance called *selenium*. Selenium produces a bad smell when dissolved. A bit of this element is put in the ground near trees. Rain dissolves the selenium, and the tree absorbs it. The bad smell keeps the deer away until the tree is fully grown.

3 What is the main idea of this passage?

_____

_____

_____

_____

_____

_____

_____

Hint: What is most of the passage about?

> GO ON

Answers

1 Ⓐ Ⓑ Ⓒ Ⓓ   2 Ⓕ Ⓖ Ⓗ Ⓙ

Objective 3: Summarizing Main Ideas

Often the main idea is not given in the text. Sometimes the reader needs to figure it out by putting the facts together.

The spots on a fawn's coat let it hide in shady areas without being seen. The viceroy butterfly looks like the bad-tasting monarch, so birds avoid both. The hognose snake hisses when it fears another animal. When the opossum is attacked, it plays dead. Distressed turtles hide in their shells until they're sure it's safe to come out again.

1   The main idea of the passage is —

   A   each species has a unique way of preserving itself.

   B   some harmless animals look dangerous.

   C   spots and stripes can make animals less visible.

   D   birds don't like monarch butterflies.

   Hint: What is the entire paragraph trying to suggest?

Alfred Nobel invented dynamite to help builders. But it was used for war, which made him feel very guilty. He was a rich man, so he set up a $9 million fund. Today the fund is used to reward people who have improved human life. Nobel prizes are awarded in six fields including peace, medicine, and chemistry.

2   What is the main idea implied in the passage?

   F   Nobel wanted to have a positive impact on society.

   G   Nobel was afraid of failure.

   H   Nobel wanted his invention used for more purposes.

   J   Nobel's invention proved useless for building purposes.

   Hint: Read the entire paragraph to determine the main idea suggested.

One hundred viruses placed side by side would be no wider than a human hair. But these germs cause more than fifty diseases. Chicken pox, colds, and rabies are all caused by viruses. More than 21 million people have died from the flu caused by these tiny germs. Scientists are seeking ways to get rid of these tiny killers.

3   What is the main idea of this passage?

   _____

   _____

   _____

   _____

   _____

   _____

   _____

   Hint: What is suggested, but not stated, in the passage?

▶GO ON▶

Answers
1 Ⓐ Ⓑ Ⓒ Ⓓ   2 Ⓕ Ⓖ Ⓗ Ⓙ

Objective 3: Summarizing Main Ideas

A summary contains the main idea of a passage. A summary is brief, yet it covers the main points.

Aluminum once was a very expensive metal. It cost more than $500 a pound. But in 1886, two scientists discovered a way to make the metal more cheaply. Two years later, another scientist refined the process even more. Then the price of the metal was less than 30¢ a pound. Today aluminum is so cheap that it is often thrown away.

1 **What is the best summary of this passage?**

A Aluminum used to cost a lot of money.

B The price of aluminum has lowered over the years.

C Scientists have refined the process of making aluminum foil.

D Aluminum is a strong metal.

Hint: Look for the statement that sums up the passage.

Product codes are the bars and numbers on a product label. The first numbers tell which company made the item. The last numbers identify the product and size. A laser reads the bars at the checkout. The computer finds the price for that product and prints the price on the cash register receipt. Store owners can change prices of items simply by changing the computer. The records stored in the computer also help stores to determine which items sell well.

2 **What is this passage mostly about?**

F Product codes were developed to ensure customer safety.

G A product code system is an efficient way of pricing goods.

H A machine can read numbers and bars.

J Numbers are assigned to companies.

Hint: Which statement best describes the passage as a whole?

No part of this document may be reproduced without the written permission of the publisher.

Answers

1 Ⓐ Ⓑ Ⓒ Ⓓ   **2** Ⓕ Ⓖ Ⓗ Ⓙ

GO ON

17

In 1815, Mount Tambora in Indonesia blew its top. The huge blast cut 4,000 feet off its peak, and it killed 12,000 people. The dust from the explosion spread around the world. It blocked the sunlight. Europe and America were very cold the following year. In June, ten inches of snow fell in New England. The year 1816 was called the year without any summer.

3   **What is this story mostly about?**

A   Many people died because of Mount Tambora.

B   A volcanic explosion in 1815 had a major impact.

C   People gave an unusual name to the year 1816.

D   Ten inches of snow fell in New England in June.

Hint: You need to read the entire passage to determine the best summary.

Air plants, such as mosses and lichens, grow on buildings and stones and get their food and water from the air around them. Plants that grow on trees, such as mistletoe, get their food and water from the trees they live on. Sometimes, the trees die if the plants growing on them take away too much food or water.

4   **What is this story mostly about?**

F   Some kinds of plants grow on buildings.

G   Mistletoe sometimes kills trees.

H   Some plants don't have to live in soil to survive.

J   Mosses and lichens get food and water in various ways.

Hint: Pick the choice that best covers the main point of the passage.

STOP

Answers
3 Ⓐ Ⓑ Ⓒ Ⓓ   **4** Ⓕ Ⓖ Ⓗ Ⓙ

Objective 4: Perceiving Relationships and Recognizing Outcomes

Often when we read, we need to see cause-and-effect relationships. Knowing what happened and what made it happen will help us to better understand what we read.

Rodney bragged to his friends that he could find his way around anywhere. One day, though, Rodney was delivering pizza in a strange part of town. Though he searched for half an hour, he could not locate the address he needed. Finally he had to stop to ask for directions. His face turned red, and he began to stutter as he asked how to find the place.

1 **What happened when Rodney got embarrassed?**

   A He got overheated.

   B He got lost.

   C His face got red and he stuttered.

   D He started bragging.

   Hint: Getting embarrassed is the cause. What happened as a result of this?

Over the years Jason and his dog, Flash, had shared many good times and great adventures. They played together, and sometimes they even slept together. But Flash got old, and his eyesight and hearing began to fade. He even started snapping at children, so Jason knew the time had come to put Flash to sleep. Although the idea of taking Flash to the vet made Jason very sad, he knew it was for the best.

2 **What made Jason know the time had come to put Flash to sleep?**

   F Jason loved his dog Flash.

   G Jason knew the vet needed business.

   H Flash began to snap at children.

   J Jason was very sad.

   Hint: Knowing the time had come to put Flash to sleep is the effect. What made this happen?

Angela did not like to go to the park any more. She used to spend her springtime afternoons there, enjoying the flowers and the fresh air. But now she saw more and more old people in the park, sitting alone on the benches. They seemed so sad and lonely that Angela wished she never had to grow old.

3 **What caused Angela to dislike going to the park?**

   A Her fear that she would become allergic to the flowers.

   B Seeing too many lonely old people.

   C She was afraid that she may be robbed.

   D The change of seasons made it less comfortable.

   Hint: Not going to the park is the effect. Pick the choice that made this happen.

The young man wouldn't listen to anyone. He was too sure of himself and felt he could handle any situation. Others had warned him not to camp alone in the freezing weather, but he did not listen to them. When he fell into icy water, he could not build a fire to warm himself. No one was there to help him.

4 **What caused the young man to get into trouble?**

   _____

   _____

   _____

   _____

   _____

   _____

   _____

   Hint: Getting into trouble is the effect. What made this happen?

GO ON

Answers
1 Ⓐ Ⓑ Ⓒ Ⓓ   **2** Ⓕ Ⓖ Ⓗ Ⓙ   **3** Ⓐ Ⓑ Ⓒ Ⓓ

19

Objective 4: Perceiving Relationships and Recognizing Outcomes

Often, the reader can predict, or tell in advance, what is probably going to happen next. The reader must think about what would make sense if the story were to continue.

High school had not been an easy time for Diane. Her friends seemed to have so much more time for fun than she did. That just made today even more special. As she walked up the steps in her black cap and gown, she felt a real sense of pride. Glancing over at her parents, she saw her mother wipe a tear from her cheek.

1 What will probably happen next?

A Diane will go to the library to study.

B Diane will receive her diploma.

C The family will go to dinner together.

D Diane will give her mother a handkerchief.

Hint: Once you figure out what Diane is doing, you will know the answer.

May's parents were having guests for dinner. Her mother asked May to help set the table. She noticed that May was trying to carry too many dishes at one time. May loaded down a tray with ten crystal glasses and had trouble lifting the heavy tray. Her mother had warned her, but May paid no attention.

2 What will May probably do next?

F drop the tray

G set the table

H serve the guests

J stop listening to her mother

Hint: Think about what the passage seems to be leading toward.

It was Jonathan's first day at his new school. Before school, groups of students gathered in front of the building. It seemed as if everyone but Jonathan was with a group of friends. They were all talking and laughing together. He walked over to a bench and sat down to read. Then he noticed someone coming toward him. It was Paul, a boy he had met last summer at the local pool.

3 What will Jonathan probably do next?

A get up and leave

B go over to the group of students

C say hello to Paul as he comes closer

D ask Paul if he wants to go to the pool with him again

Hint: Based on the other sentences, what seems most likely to happen next?

To Sheila, the alarm clock seemed to go off especially early that morning. She forced herself out of bed and put on her running clothes. Once she was outside, the cold air helped her wake up. It was just a few days before the race, and she wanted to be in top condition.

4 What will Sheila probably do next?

_____

_____

_____

_____

_____

_____

_____

_____

Hint: You need to look at all the facts in the story. What is most likely to happen next?

Answers

1 Ⓐ Ⓑ Ⓒ Ⓓ   **2** Ⓕ Ⓖ Ⓗ Ⓙ   **3** Ⓐ Ⓑ Ⓒ Ⓓ

20

Objective 5: Making Inferences and Generalizations

Often texts come with graphs or diagrams. They help the reader better understand the passage.

Temperature and Humidity for Ten Days in May

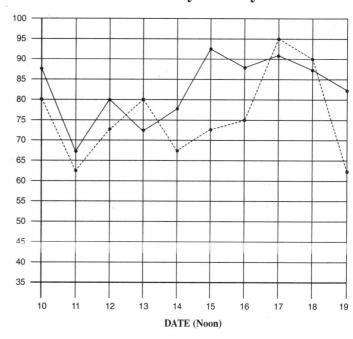

KEY

———— Temperature in Degrees

------------ Humidity in Percent

The weather in Florida varies somewhat, but it always seems that there is a lot of humidity in May. Both the temperature and humidity vary considerably. Low humidity with warm temperatures is the perfect type of weather for the beach. The discomfort and perspiration index seem to rise as the humidity rises.

1 **On which day did both the humidity and temperature drop about twenty percent?**

A May 11

B May 13

C May 15

D May 16

Hint: Check the "Temperature" and "Humidity" lines for each of the dates in the choices.

2 **According to the graph, which would be the worst beach day? Why?**

_____

_____

_____

_____

_____

_____

_____

_____

Hint: First decide what would make up the worst beach day, according to the author.

➤ GO ON ➤

Answers

1 Ⓐ Ⓑ Ⓒ Ⓓ

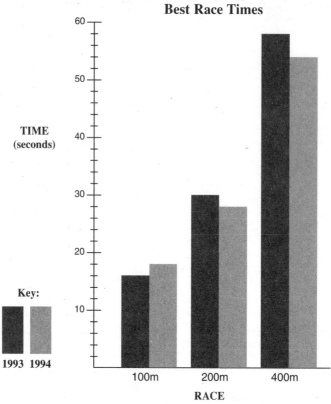

John F. Kennedy High School's Best Race Times

TIME (seconds)

Key:
1993 1994

RACE
100m   200m   400m

John F. Kennedy High School's track team has won its second 200m race championship. It finished both the 100m and 400m in second place. Although Kennedy has a good team, Wedgewood High School had an outstanding year. They edged Kennedy in both the 100m and 400m but were not able to beat them in the 200m.

3 In the 1994 championship 200m race, the time it took Wedgewood High to run the race could have been —

F 32 seconds.

G 28 seconds.

H 26 seconds.

J 24 seconds.

Hint: Look at the bars on the graph that show Kennedy High's 200m time.

4 In which race did the Kennedy High team's performance get worse from 1993 to 1994?

_____

_____

_____

_____

_____

_____

_____

_____

Hint: Read both the graph and the key that accompanies it.

GO ON

Answers
3 Ⓕ Ⓖ Ⓗ Ⓙ

Objective 5: Making Inferences and Generalizations

When a reader makes an inference, it means that the information in the passage has told the reader something indirectly.

El Santo was a famous fellow in Mexico. He was successful as a wrestler, but he was also a top movie star. In his movies, he played a masked wrestler who helped catch criminals and monsters. His best film was *The Mummies of Guanajuato.* El Santo died in 1984.

1   What conclusion can you draw after reading this passage?

    A   The wrestler performed good deeds.

    B   El Santo hated wrestling.

    C   The Mexican people like wrestling.

    D   El Santo died at the hands of a criminal.

Hint: First eliminate the choices that you think cannot be right.

When people began to grow crops, they needed to know when to plant their seeds. They noticed that the best time to plant came at the same time each year. The early Egyptians counted the number of full moons between planting times. The times between moons were called months of the year. The Egyptians then noticed a bright star in the sky at planting time. They counted 365 days between the appearances of this star. Then they divided these days by 12 months to invent the first year.

2   What can you conclude after reading this?

    F   Egyptians invented the first calendar.

    G   The Egyptians invented time.

    H   The Egyptians were astronomers.

    J   The Egyptians counted one day every time the star appeared.

Hint: Although never stated, the selection is describing the invention of something.

The ancient Greeks made up stories to explain their world. They thought that many gods and goddesses controlled the universe. The greatest Greek god was Zeus, who controlled the weather. When a storm raged with thunder and lightning, Zeus was at work. The Greeks believed that the natural world was alive and that it should be treated with respect.

3   What is inferred by this passage?

    A   The Greeks did not understand science.

    B   The Greeks thought Zeus controlled the universe.

    C   The ancient Greeks weren't smart.

    D   The Greeks thought Zeus was the least powerful god.

Hint: Look for the choice that is not written in the passage, but implied.

Charlene awoke with a shriek. Her pajamas were soaked with sweat, and she could feel herself trembling. The night was dark and still, and the furniture in her room loomed like shadowy monsters. Charlene closed her eyes and tried to fall asleep again. But the night was too quiet, and her eyes popped open. Suddenly, Charlene heard a scratching noise at her window. She buried her head under her pillow, wishing the night was over.

4   What can you infer after reading this?

_____

_____

_____

_____

_____

_____

_____

Hint: Think about this happening to you.

▶ **GO ON**

Objective 5: Making Inferences and Generalizations

Sometimes a reader needs to generalize. This means to come up with a general statement about something in the text.

The special material in our body that makes us who we are is called DNA. Except for identical twins, everybody has different DNA. Since DNA is everywhere in the body, scientists believe that DNA patterns are better than fingerprints for identifying people.

1   From this story you can make the generalization that —

A   DNA may become a commonly used way of identifying people.

B   identical twins have the same fingerprints.

C   fingerprints are the best way for the police to fight crime.

D   DNA patterns for identical twins are similar.

Hint: Read the whole paragraph. Generalize what might happen in the future.

A comet is like a dirty ball of snow. It is made of frozen gases, frozen water, and dust. As a comet approaches the sun, the icy center gets hot and evaporates. The gases made by the evaporation form the tail of the comet. The dust left behind in the process forms meteor showers.

2   From this paragraph you can guess that —

F   comets are made of snow.

G   throwing a ball of snow can turn it into a comet.

H   without the sun, a comet would look different to us.

J   meteor showers are visible with a telescope.

Hint: Which choice is the best "guess"?

Nations fight wars for many reasons. In the 1880s, a war between the United States and Great Britain almost started because of a pig. The trouble took place on an island off the coast of Washington state. An American shot a pig owned by a British man. Tempers flared, and troops were sent to the island. The dispute, known as the Pig War, was soon settled without any fighting.

3   The story suggests that —

A   many soldiers were injured in the war.

B   the war was fought in Europe.

C   the pig was cooked when the war ended.

D   in the 1880s, the Americans and British did not get along well.

Hint: Which choice is a general statement rather than a specific one?

Mongooses are small Asian mammals that kill poisonous snakes and, sometimes, rats. In the 1890s, sugar planters in Hawaii imported mongooses to control the rats there. But the planters made a big mistake. They learned too late that mongooses roam by day, while rats roam by night. Now mongooses are a problem in Hawaii.

4   How did the sugar planters make their problems worse?

_____

_____

_____

_____

_____

_____

Hint: What is the general idea of this passage?

GO ON

Answers

1 Ⓐ Ⓑ Ⓒ Ⓓ   2 Ⓕ Ⓖ Ⓗ Ⓙ   3 Ⓐ Ⓑ Ⓒ Ⓓ

Objective 5: Making Inferences and Generalizations

A good reader will evaluate what he or she reads and make his or her own judgment about the text. Often things are implied in a text, rather than stated directly.

Tom Evans was on a field trip in Big Bend National Park in Texas. He and his college classmates had come from Chicago to hunt for fossils. As he was searching, Evans spotted something sticking out of a dirt mound. It turned out to be a major discovery. Evans had found the complete skull of a dinosaur. The four-foot-long skull came from a chasmosaurus, which resembled a rhinoceros. The skull had been buried for about eighty million years.

1   What does this passage tell you about Tom Evans?

A   He was a straight-A student.

B   He flew from Chicago to Big Bend National Park.

C   He was an observant person.

D   He enjoyed gardening.

Hint: Review the facts. Think about what they say about Tom.

Longfellow wrote a poem that made Paul Revere famous for his ride to Concord to warn people that the British were coming. Actually, Revere never made it to Concord, nor was he alone. Two other riders, William Dawes and Dr. Samuel Prescott, went with him. It was Dr. Prescott who warned Concord about the British.

2   From the paragraph, you can tell that —

F   the people of Concord weren't warned.

G   Paul Revere had a friend named William Dawes.

H   Longfellow was famous for his poetry.

J   because of a well-known poem, people are misinformed about historical facts.

Hint: You need to read the entire paragraph and evaluate the information before making a choice.

The Agriculture Department inspects packages from foreign countries. It makes sure that plant diseases aren't brought into the country. Dogs are trained to sniff for food. When the dogs smell food, they sit down by the passenger carrying it.

3   From the passage, you can tell that —

A   the Agriculture Department provides us with an important safeguard.

B   dogs bring a lot of disease into North America.

C   it is not good to alert officials to food packages.

D   food should be grown in North America and not imported.

Hint: None of the choices are stated in the passage, but one of them is a conclusion that the reader can determine after reading the text.

When men sip drinks from cups, they usually look into them. Women usually look above the rim. Men often examine their nails with their palms facing upward and their fingers curled. But women extend their fingers with their palms facing downward to view their nails.

4   What judgment can you make about men and women after reading this paragraph?

_____

_____

_____

_____

_____

_____

Hint: Read the entire paragraph. Think about the point that is being made.

▶ GO ON

Answers

1 Ⓐ Ⓑ Ⓒ Ⓓ   2 Ⓕ Ⓖ Ⓗ Ⓙ   3 Ⓐ Ⓑ Ⓒ Ⓓ

Objective 5: Making Inferences and Generalizations

The setting is the when and where of a story. The characters are the people or people-like figures in the story. The plot is the sequence of events that makes up the core of the story.

Ilse Bing was a photographer in the 1930s. She was one of the first photographers to use a camera to make works of art. Cameras had been around since the late 1800s. However, most photographers used them to take pictures of news events or famous people. Bing took photos of people who were dressed beautifully or oddly.

At about the same time, Laura Gilpin was working in the American Southwest. She took pictures as she hiked through the desert. One of Gilpin's most famous pictures is called "Shiprock, New Mexico." It shows a gigantic rock standing alone in a valley. Gilpin made many of her prints on a special soft paper. The special paper made her prints look cloudy and gray, like old paintings.

1   Ilse Bing was a photographer in the —

    A nineteenth century.

    B twentieth century.

    C eighteenth century.

    D twenty-first century.

Hint: Read the first sentence.

2   Laura Gilpin was working in —

    F the east.

    G the midwest.

    H the southwest.

    J the west.

Hint: Read the paragraph about Gilpin.

3   How were their photographs different?

_____

_____

_____

_____

Hint: Read about both women's photos.

Louise and her mother were driving home one evening. They had been visiting Louise's aunt. Louise soon noticed that her mother was slowing down. It was getting impossible to see the road. For the next hour, their car crept slowly along the road. Headlights would suddenly appear in front of them, and they would move as far to the right of the road as they could. Both women were praying that they would get home safely.

4   What is the setting of this passage?

    A It was a bright night.

    B It was dark and foggy.

    C It was a poorly paved road.

    D There were large potholes in the road.

Hint: Picture the scene in your mind. Which choice seems most like that picture?

5   What conclusion can you draw about the characters' mood in this passage?

_____

_____

_____

_____

_____

_____

Hint: Think about how you might feel in the same situation.

STOP

Answers
1 Ⓐ Ⓑ Ⓒ Ⓓ   **2** Ⓕ Ⓖ Ⓗ Ⓙ   **4** Ⓐ Ⓑ Ⓒ Ⓓ

Objective 6: Recognizing Points of View, Facts, and Opinions

The author's point of view is what he or she thinks or feels about what he or she is writing. Opinions express points of view.

The National Park System costs $1.2 billion to operate. Of that amount, $900,000 is spent on costs associated with visitors. The system has 368 locations, including major parks, such as the Grand Canyon, and small, specialized parks that feature one thing. We need to reexamine the type and quality of parks paid for by federal dollars. An independent commission could review the parks and determine whether or not they all should be kept open and what level of fees should be charged to park users. Currently, the people who use parks pay less than ten percent of the costs of operating them.

1   What is the author suggesting?

A   A commission should start closing the smaller parks.

B   The government should pay a larger portion of the costs of running the national parks.

C   There is a need to reexamine the current parks to be sure we want to keep them and see if we need them all.

D   The National Park System will be fine if we just eliminate some of the smaller specialized parks.

Hint: In this passage, the author's point of view is clearly stated in sentences 4 and 5.

2   The author would agree with which of the following?

F   The National Park System should continue as it is.

G   Government systems waste time and money.

H   It is good to reevaluate things as time goes on.

J   The park system should be shut down.

Hint: Think about the author's point of view regarding the National Park System and figure out what he or she would most likely think about the choices given.

3   Should some national parks be closed because they are too expensive to run? Explain your answer.

_____

_____

_____

_____

_____

_____

_____

Hint: Use the information in the paragraph to form your opinion.

GO ON

Answers
1 Ⓐ Ⓑ Ⓒ Ⓓ   2 Ⓕ Ⓖ Ⓗ Ⓙ

27

No part of this document may be reproduced without the written permission of the publisher.

People are concerned that irradiated food will lead to an increase in cancer. But what about the benefits of reduced toxins, food decontamination, and a longer shelf life? Have x-rays caused people to become radioactive? Irradiation eliminates poisonous toxins and microorganisms. Scientists have found more of a chemical reaction in frozen and canned food than in food that has been irradiated. Sixty-seven percent of consumers would be willing to pay more for chicken that has significantly fewer toxins, according to a recent survey.

4   With which statement would this author most likely agree?

   A   Frozen foods are safer than irradiated foods.

   B   X-rays cause people to become radioactive.

   C   People are foolish to worry about cancer.

   D   Irradiation reduces the risks of contamination.

Hint: The answer is stated in the passage.

5   What is the author's purpose in writing this selection?

   F   to convince people that x-rays are unsafe

   G   to convince people that x-rays are safe

   H   to convince supermarkets to raise their prices

   J   to convince people that irradiated food is safe

Hint: Read the last sentence.

6   List the benefits of irradiation that the author mentions in this paragraph.

_____

_____

_____

_____

_____

_____

_____

Hint: Read the entire paragraph.

GO ON

Answers
4 Ⓐ Ⓑ Ⓒ Ⓓ   5 Ⓕ Ⓖ Ⓗ Ⓙ

Objective 6: Recognizing Points of View, Facts, and Opinions

When an author wants to convince the reader of something, he or she uses language that backs up his or her point of view. Often the language is very descriptive and emotional.

The money spent on political campaigns is paltry when compared to expenditures for commercial advertising. If we limited campaign spending, the incumbents would have an unfair advantage. Limiting campaign spending is like limiting free speech, which is embodied in the First Amendment of the Constitution. Maybe we should reform political campaigns, but not limit spending on them. What we really need to ensure is that all candidates who wish to can afford to campaign effectively.

1   **The author is saying that —**

    A   campaigns cost too much.

    B   campaign spending should not be limited.

    C   there should be an amendment to the Constitution.

    D   we should limit campaign spending.

Hint: Read the entire paragraph.

2   **When the author writes, "Limiting campaign spending is like limiting free speech," he is saying that —**

    F   we should limit free speech.

    G   political campaigns should be free.

    H   since free speech is limited, we should limit campaign spending.

    J   limiting campaign spending is unconstitutional.

Hint: Read the entire sentence.

National service can teach the values of hard work, self-sacrifice, and learning to live with different people. It can put our youth back to work. It can teach them job skills and instill the values of discipline, responsibility, and civic obligation. It can also provide long-term investment in the education and skills of our citizens. National service can also bring us together as a nation. We need to move back to a central core of beliefs.

3   **What is the author promoting?**

    A   making long-term investments

    B   writing a central core of beliefs

    C   living with different people

    D   starting a national service program

Hint: Read the entire paragraph.

4   **When the author writes, "It can also provide long-term investment in the education and skills of our citizens," she is trying to convince the reader that —**

    F   the benefits of national service can last a lifetime.

    G   education is important to the citizens of this country.

    H   national service is a long-term program.

    J   education is more important than national service.

Hint: Reread the sentence in context.

GO ON

Answers
1 (A) (B) (C) (D)   2 (F) (G) (H) (J)   3 (A) (B) (C) (D)   4 (F) (G) (H) (J)

Objective 6: Recognizing Points of View, Facts, and Opinions

It is important to recognize the difference between fact and opinion. A fact is real and true. An opinion states a point of view. Words that describe are used to offer opinions.

Basketball is the only major sport that is a totally American game. Jim Naismith started it all. During the 1880s, Naismith taught athletics at a college in Massachusetts.

In the fall, Naismith's students spent long, exciting hours on the football field. But when winter came, the students moved indoors and did exercises. Most students soon grew bored. They kept asking for an indoor game that was as exciting as football.

Naismith began to think about a new kind of ball game that could be played safely in a small gym. He decided that players shouldn't use bats or run while holding the ball. Players would use only their hands to pass or throw the ball to other players. Naismith still had one big question. How would players score points? He went to the college store room and pulled out two peach baskets!

There was a balcony all around the gym. It was exactly ten feet above the floor. Naismith hung one peach basket on the balcony at each end of the gym. Then he divided the class into two teams of nine players each. The first basketball game began when he threw a soccer ball up between the team captains.

The players dashed up and down the gym, yelling with excitement as they tried to throw the ball into the peach baskets. The game stopped for a while when a player sank the ball. Someone climbed a ladder to get it out. After all, there is no hole in the bottom of a peach basket; but that was the only pause in the first basketball game. The final score was 1-0.

As basketball became popular at other colleges, teams made up their own rules. However, a set of rules was developed within a few years. A special ball and an open hoop took the place of the soccer ball and peach baskets. The game of basketball had begun.

1 **Which of the following is a fact about Jim Naismith?**

   A   He was a good teacher.

   B   He taught athletics.

   C   He preferred indoor sports to outdoor sports.

   D   Basketball players are overpaid because of him.

   Hint: A fact is real and true. What is actually said in the story?

2 **Which of the following is a fact?**

   F   Basketball is as exciting as football.

   G   College basketball is more exciting than high school basketball.

   H   Basketball would be a better game if the baskets were lowered.

   J   The game of basketball has a set of rules.

   Hint: Facts have to be true all the time. What is said in the story?

3 **Which of the following is NOT a fact from the story?**

   A   The balcony was ten feet above the gym floor.

   B   Each team had nine players.

   C   Basketball is the only major sport that is totally American.

   D   Naismith taught athletics at a college in the 1980s.

   Hint: Three of the statements can be found in the story. One is not true.

GO ON ▶

Answers

1 Ⓐ Ⓑ Ⓒ Ⓓ   2 Ⓕ Ⓖ Ⓗ Ⓙ   3 Ⓐ Ⓑ Ⓒ Ⓓ

Ending World Hunger

In some parts of the world, food shortages cause many people to starve. No one should have to be hungry. Somehow people must find a way to increase the world's food crop.

To do this, governments should grant more money to scientists who are studying little-known, edible plants. There are currently about 20,000 kinds of edible plants. Only about 100 of them are grown as food crops. People should take advantage of natural foods. It is unfair to allow people to starve while plants are available for them to eat.

A sensible solution to world hunger would be to direct government funds toward scientists. Spending money to end hunger in this way should be a goal for all governments.

4   **Which of the following is a fact from the selection?**

F   governments should grant money to scientists

G   there are about 20,000 kinds of edible plants

H   people should take advantage of natural foods

J   it is unfair to allow people to starve

Hint: Read the second paragraph

5   **The author's purpose in writing this selection is to—**

A   persuade people to eat more plants

B   describe the work of scientists

C   explain the causes of world hunger

D   propose a possible solution to food shortages

Hint: Read the last paragraph.

6   **What is the author's solution to world hunger?**

_____

_____

_____

_____

_____

_____

_____

Hint: Read the entire story.

Answers

4 Ⓕ Ⓖ Ⓗ Ⓙ   **5** Ⓐ Ⓑ Ⓒ Ⓓ

Directions: Read the selection carefully. Darken the circle for the correct answer, or write your answer in the space provided.

> **TRY THIS**
>
> More than one answer choice may sound correct. Choose the answer that goes best with the story.

Sample A   **Answering an Ad**

Josh had always wanted a pen pal. Therefore, he was excited to see the ad in his magazine guaranteeing to match people as pen pals. He followed the directions in the ad, and sent $5.00 and a brief letter describing himself to the address in the ad.

What did Josh hope to receive by following the directions in the ad?

A   a pen

B $5.00

C   a pen pal

D   a magazine

> **THINK IT THROUGH**
>
> The correct answer is <u>C</u>. Josh wanted a pen pal, and the second sentence states that the ad guaranteed to match pen pals.

STOP

Adopting a Junior High School

Several schools in the southeastern part of our country were damaged or destroyed by a hurricane. These schools need help rebuilding in order to open by the beginning of October. The schools have asked for donations of school supplies.

Our school has adopted Jackson Junior High School in southern Florida. We will hold a school-supply drive to help the students of this school. The kinds of supplies needed include gym bags, locks for lockers, art boxes, scissors, pens and pencils, folders, and rulers. The school also needs books to help rebuild their school library.

The drive will begin on Monday, September 7 and end Friday, September 25. Please bring your donations to the school gym before or after school. Students wishing to volunteer to sort and pack items and label boxes, please contact the principal. I would like to take this opportunity to thank all donators and volunteers in advance for your support of this drive.

1   **Why was a school-supply drive being held for Jackson Junior High School?**

A   The school had burned down.

B   The school had hurricane damage.

C   The students were very poor.

D   Supplies were ruined by a flood.

2   **Besides making donations, what else does the school want students to do?**

_____

_____

_____

_____

_____

_____

GO ON

Answers
SA Ⓐ Ⓑ Ⓒ Ⓓ   1 Ⓐ Ⓑ Ⓒ Ⓓ

Hiking in a National Park

Emily pulled her jacket closer and looked into the campfire. The night was cold and clear, and even though it was too dark to see them, Emily could smell the pine trees that surrounded the campsite. Thousands of stars sparkled like tiny diamonds in the night sky. It was beautiful! Emily couldn't believe she was actually there in the national park. Just that morning when she woke up in her own bed she thought, "Another hot, humid, boring day, just like every other day this summer."

But then she remembered! Today was different. Her favorite aunt and uncle, Melissa and John, had invited her to join them on a backpacking trip. They had picked her up at 8:00 a.m. and had driven most of the day to get to the national park. They just had time to pitch their tents, build the fire, and cook dinner before it got dark. Emily had gone into the forest to gather firewood. Then she had helped Melissa make hamburger patties. She hadn't realized how hungry she was until she smelled them cooking. Everything tasted better when you were outside, she decided.

"Well, it's too dark to do anything else tonight," Uncle John said. "We might as well go to bed now so that we can get up at sunrise. I want to get an early start on the trail. Be sure to zip your tent, Emily. You wouldn't want to wake up with a rattlesnake in your sleeping bag!"

Emily couldn't decide whether he was teasing her or not. She made sure she zipped the tent tight, just in case. She crawled into her sleeping bag and wiggled around, trying to get comfortable. It had been a long day, but she was too excited to sleep. She wished she had brought a flashlight and a book. She wondered what adventures the next day would bring.

Emily woke up to the sounds of pots clanging. She crawled out of her tent and opened her backpack. "Look at this!" she exclaimed in dismay. Some small creature had chewed a hole in her bag of trail mix and eaten the whole thing. "Well, some little field mouse had a great breakfast!" Melissa said, "Never mind, I brought plenty of snacks for all of us."

After breakfast, Emily's uncle helped her adjust her backpack. It was heavier than she expected it to be. Then they took off on the trail. The three hikers followed a river for a while, then they crossed it. Emily was *apprehensive*. She held her breath as she walked on the narrow log that served as a bridge. She didn't want to fall into the icy water.

The trail led back into the forest. Melissa walked in front, and Emily and John followed. Suddenly all three heard a terrifying sound—a loud, close rattle! Melissa jumped forward. Emily jumped backward and bumped into her uncle. About a foot to the right of the trail, they saw what was making the sound—a five-foot-long rattlesnake! The snake continued rattling its tail. They noticed something peculiar about the snake. Its mouth was wide open, and it was eating a field mouse. Apparently the snake was in the middle of its lunch.

John relaxed as soon as he realized what was happening. He explained that snakes' teeth point inward. It's very difficult for them to spit something out once they have begun eating. The rattlesnake couldn't harm them as long as it had something in its mouth. Melissa got her camera. They sat a short distance away and took pictures while they observed the rattlesnake. The snake continued to rattle but didn't move away. John told Emily that snakes only eat every ten days or so. It takes them a long time to swallow and digest their prey.

After a while, they left the snake and began hiking again. Emily's heart was still beating fast. She decided that Uncle John hadn't been teasing when he told her to zip up her tent. He wouldn't have to remind her about that tonight!

3 This selection is mainly about—

F summer vacations.

G the danger of rattlesnakes.

H getting along with relatives.

J hiking in a national park.

4 At the beginning of the selection Emily feels —

A angry and disappointed.

B worried and nervous.

C excited and happy.

D lonely and sad.

5 What is the last thing Emily did before she went to sleep?

F She wiggled around, trying to get comfortable.

G She zipped up the tent.

H She helped Melissa make hamburger patties.

J She went looking for rattlesnakes.

6 What did the snake most likely do after the three hikers left?

_____

_____

_____

_____

_____

_____

7 What happened to Emily's bag of trail mix?

A Emily ate it.

B Her Uncle John ate it.

C It fell out of Emily's backpack.

D A small animal ate it.

8 The word *apprehensive* means—

F amused.

G fearful.

H excited.

J careless.

9 Uncle John told the others that—

A rattlesnakes have a good sense of smell.

B rattlesnakes cannot hear.

C snakes have teeth that point inward.

D coyotes and foxes eat rattlesnakes.

10 What lesson did Emily learn by the second night?

_____

_____

_____

_____

_____

_____

_____

Notice for Eighth-Grade Students and Their Parents!

As you may know, all eighth-grade students are invited to participate in an outdoor education program. This program will once again be held at Fullersburg Outdoor Education Center, which is approximately 90 miles from our school.

Students will leave school the morning of the first day, travel by school bus to Fullersburg, sleep over three nights, and return the evening of the fourth day. All meals will be provided by the center. The school PTA has agreed to pay for the cost of room and board for each student. The school district will pay for the remaining costs, including the program and the bus transportation.

Participation in this program is open to all students who are able and willing to behave appropriately on an outing in which cooperation, respect for others, and following directions is expected. School behavior will be used to help determine the participants. Students who do not participate in the outdoor education program will attend classes at school.

All eighth-grade teachers and the principal will also attend the program as chaperons. The staff at Fullersburg will provide the instructional program.

Reservations for the trip must be made by completing the attached reservation form and returning it to the school by March 15.

The Fullersburg Outdoor Education Center

Fullersburg Outdoor Education Center contains several hundred acres of wooded land along the Salt River. There are a variety of trees, a swamp area, and a dry creek bed. During the Great Depression the Civilian Conservation Corps planted trees and built shelters throughout the center.

The heated lodge at the center was completed in 1981. The lodge consists of a large classroom, a kitchen, a glassed-in dining area with a breathtaking view of the woods and river, a nature museum, two bunk rooms with bathrooms, and private sleeping quarters for chaperons.

The daily schedule for students at Fullersburg includes breakfast and clean-up, an outdoor activity with an instructional follow-up, lunch and clean-up, an outdoor activity with an instructional follow-up, supper and clean-up. After supper there are recreational activities. Before bedtime there are treats, an evening program, and then showers.

Some of the outdoor activities that students can choose include archery, horseback riding, hiking, orienteering, animal tracking, bird watching, fishing, and canoeing. If there is enough snow on the ground, students may choose cross-country skiing, sledding, or snowshoeing as an activity. If the river is frozen, students may play broom hockey or ice skate.

11 According to the flyer, the outdoor education program—

F has never been held at Fullersburg before.

G is usually held at the school.

H has been held at Fullersburg in the past.

J is held at different places each year.

12 According to the flyer, who is invited to participate in the outdoor education program?

A all seventh- and eighth-grade students

B eighth-grade students who are on the honor roll

C eighth-grade students and their parents

D all eighth-grade students who can behave properly

13 Costs for the outdoor education program will be paid for by—

F the PTA and the school district.

G the students.

H the parents.

J the teachers and community businesses.

14 Where would this notice most likely be found?

_____

_____

_____

_____

_____

_____

_____

15 According to the flyer, which of these statements is true?

A Fullersburg is located several hundred miles from the school.

B The students will need to provide their own transportation to the center.

C Students who do not participate in the outdoor program will attend classes taught by the principal at the school.

D The staff at Fullersburg will provide the instructional program.

16 Which of these statements is an *opinion* in the flyer?

F The outdoor education center is located along the Salt River.

G The heated lodge at the center was completed in 1981.

H Students are expected to clean up after themselves.

J The dining area has a breathtaking view of the woods and river.

17 According to the selection, the students can play broom hockey—

A in the bunk rooms.

B in the glassed-in dining room.

C on the river if it is frozen.

D in the large classroom.

18 What might be the author's purpose in writing this flyer?

_____

_____

_____

_____

_____

_____

_____

▶ GO ON

The Sport of In-line Skating

Most people are familiar with roller-skating. In-line skating, however, is one of the fastest-growing sports in the world. In 1984 there were 20,000 in-line skaters. By 1992 there were more than three million in-line skaters.

In-line skates have a single row of polyurethane rollers attached to the bottom of a padded boot. The number of rollers on a skate can vary from three to five. At the rear of the skate is a heel stop.

I bought my first pair of in-line skates with money that I had saved from birthdays and from baby-sitting jobs. I bought a pair of four-wheeled skates for $65.00. I also decided to buy the safety equipment—gloves, helmet, kneepads, elbow pads, wrist guards—recommended by friends who are in-line skaters. I left the store broke, but *exhilarated.*

As soon as I got home I wanted to start skating. A friend who is a member of the International In-line Skating Association suggested that I learn to stop before I started to skate. She suggested that I practice on a safe grassy area. So I walked to a nearby park. I spent about an hour practicing to stop. When I felt comfortable stopping, I found an empty tennis court and I practiced skating strokes. I fell several times. Each time I fell, I was grateful that I was wearing the safety equipment. I'll never forget that day. My body was in pain, but my spirit was lifted by the thrill of gliding across cement.

It has been three years since I bought my first in-line skates. My friends and I belong to an in-line skating club. Our local YMCA allows us to use their rink, and the health club allows in-line skating an hour every day in the gym. I believe that my skills at in-line skating are good enough for me to become a professional skater.

GO ON

19   In this selection, the word *exhilarated* means—

F   exhausted.

G   excited.

H   excluded.

J   expanded.

20   The selection implies that roller-skating is—

A   as popular as in-line skating.

B   more difficult than in-line skating.

C   a sport of the past.

D   not as safe as in-line skating.

21   What is at the rear of an in-line skate?

F   a heel stop

G   a polyurethane roller

H   a safety guard

J   a distance meter

22   Which of these is an *opinion* in the selection?

A   In-line skating is one of the fastest-growing sports in the world.

B   My skills at in-line skating are good enough for me to become a professional skater.

C   In-line skates can have three, four, or five wheels.

D   Safety equipment for in-line skating includes gloves, a helmet, kneepads, elbow pads, and wrist guards.

23   What should you do if you were asked to skim this selection?

F   carefully reread the selection

G   recall the main idea of the selection

H   quickly look through the selection

J   review your notes about the selection

24   The web shows some important ideas in the selection. Fill in the empty boxes with the missing information.

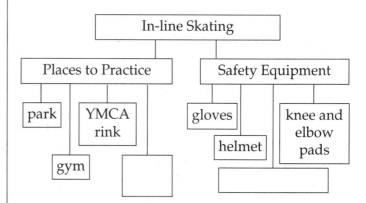

25   Describe the author's first day on in-line skates.

_____

_____

_____

_____

_____

_____

_____

_____

Answers

19 Ⓕ Ⓖ Ⓗ Ⓙ   **21** Ⓕ Ⓖ Ⓗ Ⓙ   **23** Ⓕ Ⓖ Ⓗ Ⓙ

20 Ⓐ Ⓑ Ⓒ Ⓓ   **22** Ⓐ Ⓑ Ⓒ Ⓓ

Schedule for Jefferson County Fair				
FRI.	11:00–12:00	1:00	2:00	3:00
	Judging of 4-H craft projects	Footraces $\longrightarrow$		
		Toddlers	4-5 year olds	6-8 year olds
SAT.	Pet parade	Footraces $\longrightarrow$		
	Judging of 4-H farming projects	9-10 year-olds	11-12 year olds	13-14 year olds
			Teddy bear picnic	
SUN.	Baby contest	Crowning of 4-H king and queen	Marching band contest	
	Judging of 4-H livestock projects			

26 When is the marching band contest scheduled to take place?

A Sunday at 11:00

B Saturday at 2:00

C Sunday at 2:00

D Saturday at 11:00

27 How many events are scheduled for Sunday?

F 2

G 3

H 4

J 5

28 For a 4-H project, Kyle raised a pig named Rufus and entered it in the fair. When would Kyle learn if Rufus won a prize?

_____

_____

_____

_____

_____

_____

_____

29 What event will be missed by the 11-12 year olds who participate in the footraces?

A Pet parade

B Crowning of king and queen

C Teddy bear picnic

D Baby contest

30 If 11-year-old Carole and 12-year-old Rachel entered the footraces, when would their race take place?

F Friday at 1:30

G Friday at 3:00

H Saturday at 1:30

J Saturday at 2:00

31 Where would you most likely find this schedule?

_____

_____

_____

_____

_____

_____

_____

Answers

26 Ⓐ Ⓑ Ⓒ Ⓓ   **27** Ⓕ Ⓖ Ⓗ Ⓙ   **29** Ⓐ Ⓑ Ⓒ Ⓓ   **30** Ⓕ Ⓖ Ⓗ Ⓙ

Sample A

Going Camping

Jen is very excited about going camping with her cousins Bill and Mindy. The cousins are good friends. The campers plan to travel to the Grand Canyon where they will stay for two weeks.

On their trip the three cousins most likely will—

A be very bored

B fight and argue continually

C have an enjoyable time

D ignore one another

For questions 1–35 carefully read each selection and the questions that follow. Then darken the circle for the correct answer, or write your answer in the space provided.

Visiting a High-Altitude City

A visitor to a city in Bolivia such as La Paz might find the following recommendations in a brochure in the hotel room:

If it is your first day here in our lovely city, you must take it easy and rest. We recommend that you not walk for even short distances. You must not climb stairs.

These recommendations are posted in hotel rooms to help warn visitors of the potential hazards of being at a high altitude. You see, La Paz is located at a high altitude in the Andes Mountains. People who are not used to living at such altitudes can contract *sorojche*, or altitude sickness. Nausea, headaches, and tired muscles are some of the symptoms of this illness. These symptoms are caused by lack of oxygen from the thin air at high altitudes.

People who rent cars in La Paz are given containers of water to take with them. Car radiators quickly boil over in high altitudes because water boils at a lower temperature in high altitudes than in low altitudes. Water needs to be replaced often in radiators of cars driven at high altitudes.

1 How do people get *sorojche*?

A by driving too fast

B from resting the day they arrive in a city

C by buying it in a local store

D from too much activity the first few days in a high-altitude location

2 This article was written mainly to—

F explain the hazards of a high altitude.

G describe things to see in La Paz.

H welcome visitors to Bolivia.

J help you take care of rental cars.

3 Why should people who rent cars take containers of water with them?

_____

_____

_____

_____

_____

_____

_____

Answers

SA Ⓐ Ⓑ Ⓒ Ⓓ   **1** Ⓐ Ⓑ Ⓒ Ⓓ   **2** Ⓕ Ⓖ Ⓗ Ⓙ

VISIONEAR

The latest ALL-IN-ONE ENTERTAINMENT CENTER includes:

- 27-inch television
- video recorder and player
- speaker phone
- CD player
- fax machine
- color printer
- personal computer

Other features include: remote control, 195 TV channels, and a superior sound system.

• •

This Entertainment Center is the latest innovation in sight and sound. IT DOES EVERYTHING except pop your popcorn! You can actually cruise the Internet and talk to your friends on the speaker phone while you watch your favorite television program.

Many people already enjoy the convenience of *VISIONEAR*. You should be part of the "VISION" crowd and own one too! Imagine how people will look up to you because you were smart enough to be one of the FIRST people to own this superior Entertainment Center.

VISIONEAR is a quality product that everyone wants to own. We back this product with our 100% money-back guarantee, good for 40 days. NO IFS, ANDS, or BUTS. If you don't want it, we'll take it back. There is a small charge for restocking the product.

GO ON ➡

4 This ad suggests that the Visionear—

    A has advanced technology.

    B has a popcorn popper.

    C is inexpensive to purchase.

    D is too heavy for one person to carry.

5 This ad was written mainly to tell about—

    F the company that produces Visionear.

    G the uses of a fax machine.

    H a new home entertainment center.

    J the cheapest television set for sale.

6 Which of these is an *opinion* in the ad?

    A Other features include: remote control...

    B You can actually cruise the Internet...

    C Visionear is a quality product...

    D There is a small charge for...

7 If you were asked to rename the Visionear, what would you call it? Why?

_____

_____

_____

_____

_____

_____

8 The ad tries to appeal to your desire to—

    F save the environment.

    G be one of the first people to own the product.

    H get good grades in school.

    J travel to other countries and see new places.

9 There is enough information in this ad to show that Visionear—

    A is a fairly new product.

    B has been tested by a government agency.

    C is not expensive.

    D has an automatic shut-off system.

10 The Visionear has a money-back guarantee for—

    F 30 days.

    G 40 days.

    H 90 days.

    J 100 days.

11 What else would you like to add to the Visionear?

_____

_____

_____

_____

_____

_____

_____

GO ON

Answers

4 Ⓐ Ⓑ Ⓒ Ⓓ   **6** Ⓐ Ⓑ Ⓒ Ⓓ   **9** Ⓐ Ⓑ Ⓒ Ⓓ

5 Ⓕ Ⓖ Ⓗ Ⓙ   **8** Ⓕ Ⓖ Ⓗ Ⓙ   **10** Ⓕ Ⓖ Ⓗ Ⓙ

Sally Ride Makes History in Space

On June 18, 1983, Sally Ride became the first American woman to travel in space. She helped place three satellites over different parts of the world and conducted science experiments. But just as important as the scientific duties she performed, Ride showed a generation of girls that they could reach for the stars. The fields of science and space exploration were now open to women as well as men.

Sally Ride was born on May 26, 1951, in California. As a child her two favorite activities were sports and reading. She loved to play softball, football, and soccer. When she was about ten years old, she began to play tennis. She became one of the top junior tennis players in the country and was offered a tennis scholarship at a private high school in Los Angeles. It was there that she became truly interested in the field of science.

In college Sally Ride continued to play tennis and to study science. Her favorite subjects were astronomy and physics, and, after a few years, Sally also started taking English courses. She especially liked learning about Shakespeare. Sally Ride graduated from Stanford University in 1973 with degrees in English and physics. She continued graduate school at Stanford, combining her interests in physics and astronomy, and received a doctorate in *astrophysics.*

One day while Sally was looking for a job, she saw an advertisement from NASA (National Aeronautics and Space Administration) in the Stanford school paper. NASA was seeking applicants for a new space shuttle program. They were looking for engineers, scientists, and doctors to train as part of a group of astronauts, so Sally completed the forms and became one of the 208 finalists. The finalists were sent to the Johnson Space Center in Houston, Texas, where they were asked many questions. They were tested on how they would perform in an emergency situation. They also had to show that they were in good physical condition. Sally was thankful that she had always been physically active.

In January 1978, Sally Ride was selected to be one of the 35 astronaut candidates. The candidates moved to Houston for one year of training. If they successfully completed the training, they would have the opportunity to become astronauts. Sally's future husband, Steven Hawley, was also in this group. In 1979 both Ride and Hawley became astronauts.

In April 1982, Ride called her family and announced that she had been chosen as one of the astronauts for the seventh shuttle flight! The five astronauts worked closely together in a large office for the next year. They trained for the flight and learned to work together as a team.

On the day the space shuttle was to lift off, crowds of onlookers gathered along the Florida beaches to witness the launch. The mission went very smoothly and satellites were launched over Canada, Indonesia, and Germany. The flight lasted six days and made 98 orbits around the earth. When it touched down, Sally Ride had made history.

GO ON

12   **Sally Ride became famous as the first—**

A   astronaut in space.

B   woman in space.

C   scientist in space.

D   American woman in space.

13   **Which of the following is an *opinion*?**

F   Sally Ride liked playing sports.

G   Sally Ride became a valuable role model for girls.

H   Sally Ride studied science in college.

J   Sally Ride graduated from Stanford University in 1973.

14   **In this selection the word *astrophysics* means—**

A   the study of marketing and advertising.

B   the study of the way people lived in the past.

C   the study of the physical and chemical nature of stars.

D   the study of the human mind.

15   **What was the first step Sally Ride took in becoming the first American woman to travel in space?**

_____

_____

_____

_____

_____

_____

_____

16   **This article would most likely be found in a book titled—**

F   *Famous Soccer Players.*

G   *People Who Love Shakespeare.*

H   *American Women in Space.*

J   *Scientific Experiments in Space.*

17   **How did Sally Ride's love of sports help her become an astronaut?**

A   Astronauts should play tennis well if they want to be successful.

B   Participating in sports kept her in top physical condition.

C   Only people who are very coordinated can become astronauts.

D   All astronauts love sports.

18   **Why did the five astronauts who were chosen for the seventh shuttle flight work together in one large office?**

F   NASA wanted all of the astronauts in the same room for security reasons.

G   They needed to learn to work together.

H   NASA didn't have much office space.

J   They were all good friends and did not want separate offices.

19   **If the author added a paragraph at the end of this selection, what would it include?**

_____

_____

_____

_____

_____

_____

_____

_____

▶**GO ON**

Answers

12 Ⓐ Ⓑ Ⓒ Ⓓ	**14** Ⓐ Ⓑ Ⓒ Ⓓ	**17** Ⓐ Ⓑ Ⓒ Ⓓ
13 Ⓕ Ⓖ Ⓗ Ⓙ	**16** Ⓕ Ⓖ Ⓗ Ⓙ	**18** Ⓕ Ⓖ Ⓗ Ⓙ

Suffering from Allergies

Do you suffer from allergies? Did you know that more than forty million people in the United States have allergy problems? You may have heard the word *allergy* many times without knowing exactly what it means. An allergy is an unusual reaction to something that is harmless to most people. For example, if you have a ragweed allergy, you probably start sneezing whenever you are near ragweed. If you have a shellfish allergy, you might develop a rash if you eat lobster, shrimp, or crayfish.

People have probably had allergies throughout history. The paintings on the wall of an Egyptian ruler's tomb show that he died after being stung by a bee. This was a violent allergic reaction! Around A.D. 200 a Greek physician wrote about people sneezing when they were exposed to certain plants. Although allergies have existed for thousands of years, it was not until the mid-1800s that the medical community began to understand the causes and characteristics of allergies. At that time an English physician, W. R. Kirkman, collected the yellow dust called pollen from grasses he had grown. When he began to sneeze, he realized that he had discovered the cause of hay fever.

About the same time, another English doctor, Charles Blackley, developed an allergy test. He scratched one of his arms and put rye grass pollen on the cut. The scratch itched, swelled, and turned red. Blackley then scratched his other arm without adding pollen to the cut. Nothing happened. Blackley had the proof that he was allergic to rye grass. This test is called a scratch test, and it is still used today.

Our bodies protect us from germs and viruses by making substances called *antibodies*. Antibodies fight the germs and viruses that cause illness. An allergic reaction is really a mistake—the body mistakes something that is usually harmless, such as pollen, for a harmful invader. Special antibodies are produced and then the body releases a chemical that causes a runny nose, itchy skin, and sometimes, wheezing.

The material that produces an allergic reaction is called an allergen. Many allergens, such as mold, pollen, and mites, are present in the air. Mold is a small plant that grows in wet places. Mold spores are carried by the wind. Many grasses, weeds, and trees produce pollen that is carried by the wind. Mites are insects that are so small they cannot be seen. If you sneeze when the wind blows, you may be allergic to one of these things.

People can be allergic to many different things. Some people are allergic to certain foods. Their allergic reactions to these foods often include upset stomach, rashes, or breathing problems. Some foods that can cause allergic reactions are dairy products, wheat, corn, nuts, seafood, eggs, chocolate, and oranges.

Some people are allergic to drugs such as aspirin and penicillin, and other people are allergic to certain chemicals present in soaps and paints. Some people have allergic reactions when they are stung by bees or bitten by ants or mosquitoes. Doctors can help the allergy sufferer by prescribing pills, sprays, or nose drops. If these don't provide relief, doctors sometimes suggest allergy shots.

GO ON

20 This selection would *most* likely be found in—

   A a travel guide to Greece.

   B an economics textbook.

   C a health magazine.

   D a world history textbook.

21 In an allergic reaction, the body mistakes an allergen for—

   F pollen.

   G an antibody.

   H a blood cell.

   J a harmful invader.

22 The third paragraph tells about—

   A the history of allergies.

   B the causes of allergies.

   C the development of the scratch test.

   D how to avoid allergies.

23 In the fourth paragraph, the word *antibodies* means—

   F germs blown in the wind.

   G viruses that attack the body.

   H substances the body makes to fight illness.

   J medicine given to allergy sufferers.

24 How do we know that people had allergies thousands of years ago?

_____

_____

_____

_____

_____

_____

25 All of the following phrases describe mold *except*—

   A it grows in wet places.

   B it protects us from viruses.

   C it is a small plant.

   D its spores are carried by the wind.

26 If you have hay fever, you will probably—

   F avoid fields when grasses are producing pollen.

   G use special soap to avoid getting a rash.

   H produce allergens.

   J avoid eating any dairy products.

27 If you sneeze when the wind blows you may be allergic to—

   A aspirin and penicillin.

   B mold, pollen, or mites.

   C chocolate or shellfish.

   D ants and bees.

28 Why do you think the author wrote this article?

_____

_____

_____

_____

_____

_____

_____

A Visit to the Rain Forest

"I can't believe that you and I are both winners in the Amazon Rain Forest Adventure!" shouted Jess to her friend and fellow environmentalist.

"It is highly unusual for the government to choose two students from the same school for this educational journey. But we both worked hard on our science experiments, and our essays about why we wanted to go on this trip were chosen first and second in the state. Also, Mr. Hancock recommended both of us to the selection committee," Winnie responded with enthusiasm.

Jess and Winnie were both members of the school's Environmental Impact Committee (EIC). They made posters explaining the importance of the rain forests and how they provide Earth with forty percent of its oxygen supply by converting carbon dioxide into oxygen. Jess and Winnie also contacted speakers from the local university. These speakers conducted a school assembly showing the kinds of animals and plants that live in the rain forests and are in danger of becoming *extinct* as the rain forests disappear.

The girls' two-week trip to Brazil's Amazon Rain Forest started in Macapá, a city located at the mouth of the Amazon River. There were eight other students in their group. Four adults guided the students on a boat trip down the Amazon. During their journey they saw piranha (fish with razor-sharp teeth), alligators, monkeys, passion-fruit trees, and gorgeous flowers in every color imaginable. When the group reached Manaus they made themselves comfortable in a cabin near the river.

"The first night in the cabin was the most unforgettable. All night long I could hear the cries of animals in the rain forest, but of course I could see nothing because there were no lights near our cabin. I was nervous and afraid to sleep," said Winnie in her talk with her peers upon returning home from Brazil.

"I was so tired that first night from the exhaustion of canoeing for six hours that I slept very well," explained Jess.

"I was impressed with the difficult life of the people who live in the rain forest. They have none of the conveniences that we take for granted. They love the environment, though, and do not abuse it. I think this is partly because they are very dependent on their environment for the things they need to live," said Winnie.

"While I was in the rain forest enjoying its beauty and unique ecosystem, I thought about what I could do to help save this special place," said Jess. "I've decided to design a reusable container for use in grocery stores instead of grocery bags. This will lessen the number of trees cut down to make the bags. I hope to sell the bags to consumers and use the profits to buy as many acres of rain forest as possible," explained Jess.

GO ON

29 The description of the trip along the Amazon River helps you understand—

  F the work done by the university researchers.

  G the environment of a rain forest.

  H the enthusiasm the girls felt for their trip.

  J the rain forest at night.

30 In this selection, the word *extinct* means—

  A no longer existing.

  B no longer active.

  C no longer burning.

  D no longer being used.

31 The device the author uses in the first two paragraphs is—

  F suspense.

  G dialogue.

  H repetition.

  J flashback.

32 This selection would most likely be found in a book titled—

  A *Science Experiments*.

  B *School Assembly*.

  C *Educational Adventures*.

  D *The History of Recycling*.

33 Winnie explained why she was afraid the first night in the cabin so that—

  F her fellow students would understand how she felt.

  G Jess would admit that she too was afraid at night.

  H people would know why she did not like her trip.

  J her friends would be afraid to visit the rain forest.

34 Toward the end of the selection, how does Winnie feel about the people of the rain forest?

_____

_____

_____

_____

_____

_____

_____

35 What does Jess decide to do to save the rain forest?

_____

_____

_____

_____

_____

_____

_____

STOP

Answers

29 Ⓕ Ⓖ Ⓗ Ⓙ   **31** Ⓕ Ⓖ Ⓗ Ⓙ   **33** Ⓕ Ⓖ Ⓗ Ⓙ

30 Ⓐ Ⓑ Ⓒ Ⓓ   **32** Ⓐ Ⓑ Ⓒ Ⓓ

48

Determining Word Meanings

Directions: Darken the circle for the word or group of words that has the same or almost the same meaning as the underlined word.

TRY THIS

Choose your answer carefully. The other choices may seem correct. Be sure to think about the meaning of the underlined word.

Sample A

To <u>link</u> means to—

A separate

C clap

B join

D wash

THINK IT THROUGH

The correct answer is <u>B</u>, **join**. **Link** means "join." **Link** does not mean separate, clap, or wash.

STOP

1 To <u>amend</u> something is to—

A repeat it

C correct it

B copy it

D save it

2 To <u>meddle</u> is to—

F ignore

H knit

G interfere

J avoid

3 <u>Permanent</u> means—

A lasting

C pleasant

B annoying

D temporary

4 Something that is <u>witty</u> is—

F foolish

H boring

G serious

J clever

5 To <u>infuriate</u> is to make very—

A frightened

C safe

B happy

D angry

6 To <u>comply</u> is to—

F obey

H pretend

G suspect

J admire

7 An <u>intermission</u> is a kind of—

A pamphlet

C recess

B errand

D competition

8 A <u>hoax</u> is a kind of—

F box

H trick

G candy

J rope

9 To <u>cite</u> is to—

A look over

C speak for

B find out

D refer to

10 Something that is <u>profound</u> is—

F deep

H easy

G stupid

J shallow

STOP

Answers

SA Ⓐ ● Ⓒ Ⓓ   3 ● Ⓑ Ⓒ Ⓓ   6 ● Ⓖ Ⓗ Ⓙ   9 Ⓐ Ⓑ Ⓒ ●

1 Ⓐ Ⓑ ● Ⓓ   4 Ⓕ Ⓖ Ⓗ ●   7 Ⓐ Ⓑ ● Ⓓ   10 ● Ⓖ Ⓗ Ⓙ

2 Ⓕ ● Ⓗ Ⓙ   5 Ⓐ Ⓑ Ⓒ ●   8 Ⓕ Ⓖ ● Ⓙ

49

Matching Words with More Than One Meaning

Directions: Darken the circle for the sentence that uses the underlined word in the same way as the sentence in the box.

TRY THIS	Read the sentence in the box. Decide what the underlined word means. Then find the answer choice in which the underlined word has the same meaning.

Sample A

> We made a <u>fast</u> exit from the crowded gym.

In which sentence does <u>fast</u> have the same meaning as it does in the sentence above?

A The <u>fast</u> current washed the pier away.

B The clock in the hall is running <u>fast</u>.

C The baby was <u>fast</u> asleep in a crib.

D You must <u>fast</u> before medical tests.

THINK IT THROUGH	The correct answer is <u>A</u>. In choice <u>A</u> and in the sentence in the box, <u>fast</u> means "moving quickly."

1

> Our team won first <u>place</u> in the race.

In which sentence does <u>place</u> have the same meaning as it does in the sentence above?

A <u>Place</u> the bowl carefully on the table.

B The beach is a quiet <u>place</u> to relax.

C Which <u>place</u> at the table is yours?

D Don't worry if you finish in last <u>place</u>.

2

> The actor forgot his opening <u>line</u>.

In which sentence does <u>line</u> have the same meaning as it does in the sentence above?

F Don't cross the yellow <u>line</u> on a highway.

G We had to stand in <u>line</u> to get movie tickets.

H Can you rewrite the last <u>line</u>?

J The children will <u>line</u> up to go outside.

3

> We'll all do our <u>part</u> on the project.

In which sentence does <u>part</u> have the same meaning as it does in the sentence above?

A Which <u>part</u> of the city is the oldest?

B Ben wants a <u>part</u> in the school play.

C I replaced a broken <u>part</u> on my car.

D Isabel won't <u>part</u> with her hat.

4

> Small <u>craft</u> are in danger in storms.

In which sentence does <u>craft</u> have the same meaning as it does in the sentence above?

F The cat showed great <u>craft</u> in catching the mouse.

G Sam can <u>craft</u> many things from wood.

H Sailing <u>craft</u> of all types filled the harbor.

J Weaving is an ancient <u>craft</u>.

Answers

SA Ⓐ Ⓑ Ⓒ Ⓓ   **1** Ⓐ Ⓑ Ⓒ Ⓓ   **2** Ⓕ Ⓖ Ⓗ Ⓙ   **3** Ⓐ Ⓑ Ⓒ Ⓓ   **4** Ⓕ Ⓖ Ⓗ Ⓙ

Using Context Clues

Directions: Darken the circle for the word or words that give the meaning of the underlined word, or write your answer in the space provided.

> **TRY THIS**
>
> Read the first sentence carefully. Look for clue words in the sentence. Then use each answer choice in place of the underlined word. Be sure that your answer and the underlined word have the same meaning.

Sample A

The <u>dismal</u> weather has been cold and rainy for days. <u>Dismal</u> means—

A bright   C windy

B gloomy   D changeable

> **THINK IT THROUGH**
>
> The correct answer is B. <u>Dismal</u> means "gloomy." The clue words are "cold" and "rainy." All four choices have something to do with weather. But only <u>gloomy</u> has the same meaning as <u>dismal</u>.

---

1 Miriam was <u>dubious</u> about her chances of winning. <u>Dubious</u> means—

A positive   C doubtful

B hopeful   D happy

2 The <u>sapling</u> had to be watered twice a day. A <u>sapling</u> is a—

F large bush   H species of tropical bird

G young tree   J type of rose

4 The stream <u>receded</u> after the rains stopped. <u>Receded</u> means—

A withdrew   C overflowed

B flowed   D flooded

3 The baby sitter tried to quiet the <u>boisterous</u> children. <u>Boisterous</u> means—

_____

_____

_____

_____

5 The student included many details and gave an <u>accurate</u> summary of the story. <u>Accurate</u> means—

F exaggerated   H poor

G exact   J partial

6 Painting is a <u>tedious</u> task because you must work slowly and carefully. <u>Tedious</u> means—

A painful   C boring

B creative   D interesting

7 The patient suffered <u>acute</u> pain from his injuries. <u>Acute</u> means—

F frequent   H intense

G slight   J mild

8 The charity had a fund-raiser to <u>generate</u> money for its projects. <u>Generate</u> means—

_____

_____

_____

_____

Answers

SA Ⓐ Ⓑ Ⓒ Ⓓ   2 Ⓕ Ⓖ Ⓗ Ⓙ   5 Ⓕ Ⓖ Ⓗ Ⓙ   7 Ⓕ Ⓖ Ⓗ Ⓙ

1 Ⓐ Ⓑ Ⓒ Ⓓ   4 Ⓐ Ⓑ Ⓒ Ⓓ   6 Ⓐ Ⓑ Ⓒ Ⓓ

Test

Sample A

To <u>motivate</u> is to—

A discourage

B work

C accept

D inspire

For questions 1–9, darken the circle for the word or group of words that has the same or almost the same meaning as the underlined word.

1 A <u>boulevard</u> is a kind of—

A building

B watch

C street

D museum

2 An <u>abyss</u> is a—

F crater

G movie

H kind of dress

J fruit

3 <u>Vacant</u> means—

A colorful

B fresh

C occupied

D empty

4 A <u>jaunt</u> is—

F an experience

G an outing

H a problem

J an opportunity

5 To <u>convey</u> is to—

A build

B transport

C examine

D memorize

6 A <u>boutique</u> is a kind of—

F store

G designer

H show

J florist

7 To <u>recollect</u> is to—

A remember

B watch

C forget

D bargain

8 Someone who is <u>optimistic</u> is—

F discouraged

G hopeful

H sad

J funny

9 To <u>collapse</u> means to—

A fall down

B go around

C sell out

D blow up

Answers

SA Ⓐ Ⓑ Ⓒ ⬤   2 ⬤ Ⓖ Ⓗ Ⓙ   4 Ⓕ ⬤ Ⓗ Ⓙ   6 ⬤ Ⓖ Ⓗ Ⓙ   8 Ⓕ ⬤ Ⓗ Ⓙ
1 Ⓐ Ⓑ ⬤ Ⓓ   3 Ⓐ Ⓑ Ⓒ ⬤   5 Ⓐ ⬤ Ⓒ Ⓓ   7 ⬤ Ⓑ Ⓒ Ⓓ   9 ⬤ Ⓑ Ⓒ Ⓓ

52

Sample B

There are costumes in the old trunk.

In which sentence does trunk have the same meaning as it does in the sentence above?

A   The baby elephant raised its trunk.

B   Two squirrels ran down the tree trunk.

C   Put these boxes in the trunk of my car.

D   Grandmother's trunk is in the basement.

 STOP

For questions 10–13, darken the circle for the sentence in which the underlined word means the same as it does in the sentence in the box.

10

Will the town recover from the storm damage?

In which sentence does recover have the same meaning as it does in the sentence above?

F   Jill got some fabric to recover the cushion.

G   I will recover from the accident soon.

H   Will the police recover the stolen property?

J   Those recyling companies recover steel from old appliances.

11

Does Matt exercise to stay fit?

In which sentence does fit have the same meaning as it does in the sentence above?

A   My clothes don't fit since I've grown.

B   Will that table fit here?

C   You need to be fit to enter that race.

D   Shoes that don't fit properly can hurt.

12

A flood can sweep away everything in its path.

In which sentence does sweep have the same meaning as it does in the sentence above?

F   Our track team will sweep all the events.

G   Can you sweep aside your doubts?

H   Karl will sweep the gym floors.

J   The famous actress likes to sweep into a room.

13

Her clothes were in a mess on the floor.

In which sentence does mess have the same meaning as it does in the sentence above?

A   I'll clean up this mess before I leave.

B   Please don't mess with my things!

C   She'll mess this up if she is in a hurry.

D   The soldiers met in the mess tent.

14

Dad will hang the painting for me.

Write a new sentence in which hang has the same meaning as it does in the sentence above.

_____

_____

_____

_____

_____

_____

_____

➤ GO ON

Answers
SB Ⓐ Ⓑ Ⓒ Ⓓ   10 Ⓕ Ⓖ Ⓗ Ⓙ   11 Ⓐ Ⓑ Ⓒ Ⓓ   12 Ⓕ Ⓖ Ⓗ Ⓙ   13 Ⓐ Ⓑ Ⓒ Ⓓ

53

Sample C

We camped in the grotto under the cliffs. A grotto is—

A   a group of trees

B   a small cave

C   a simple hut

D   a forest preserve

For questions 15–20, darken the circle for the word or words that give the meaning of the underlined word.

15   It has been an extremely brutal winter with very cold temperatures. Brutal means—

A   harsh

B   windy

C   gentle

D   pleasant

16   Brass is an alloy of copper and zinc. An alloy is—

F   a type of plastic

G   a mixture of metals

H   a kind of sword

J   a kind of ore

17   The two interstate highways run in different directions, but they intersect in Atlanta. Intersect means—

A   end

B   run parallel

C   cross each other

D   begin

18   She offered a feeble excuse for her tardiness, but she could tell we didn't believe it. Feeble means—

F   truthful

G   excellent

H   exaggerated

J   weak

19   That sofa was manufactured in our new furniture factory. Manufactured means—

A   sold

B   designed

C   made

D   used

20   Brad took Jana's arm and escorted her down the runway. Escorted means—

F   accompanied

G   led

H   followed

J   carried

Write the following meanings:

21   Because Gerardo is organized and efficient, he is a capable office manager. Capable means—

_____

_____

_____

_____

22   Marta smiled when she heard the joyful clamor coming from the playroom. Clamor means—

_____

_____

_____

_____

Math Problem-Solving Strategies

Overview

The Problem-Solving Plan

When solving math problems follow these steps:

STEP 1: WHAT IS THE QUESTION/GOAL?

Read the problem. Decide what must be found. This is sometimes in the form of a question.

STEP 2: FIND THE FACTS

Locate the factual information in three different ways:

  A. KEY FACTS...the facts you need to solve the problem.

  B. FACTS YOU DON'T NEED...those facts which are not necessary for solving the problem.

  C. ARE MORE FACTS NEEDED?...decide if you have enough information to solve the problem.

STEP 3: SELECT A STRATEGY

Decide what strategies you might use, how you will use them, and then estimate what your answer will be. If one strategy doesn't help you to solve the problem, try another.

STEP 4: SOLVE

Apply the strategy according to your plan. Use an operation if necessary, and clearly indicate your answer.

STEP 5: DOES YOUR RESPONSE MAKE SENSE?

Write your answer in a complete sentence. Read the problem again. Check to see that your answer makes sense. Use estimation to check calculations.

PROBLEM/QUESTION:

Justine drives to her company's main office every day, Monday through Thursday. The trip is 20 miles one way. On Friday, she drives to the regional office. This trip is 50 miles one way. How many miles does Justine drive in three weeks?

STEP 1: WHAT IS THE QUESTION/GOAL?

STEP 2: FIND THE FACTS

STEP 3: SELECT A STRATEGY

STEP 4: SOLVE

STEP 5: DOES YOUR RESPONSE MAKE SENSE?

Problem 2

PROBLEM/QUESTION:

Ian began the week with $48. On Monday, he spent half of it. On Tuesday, he spent one-third of the amount he still had. On Wednesday, he spent one fourth of the money he still had. On Thursday, he spent one-sixth of the amount he still had. On what day did he spend the most money?

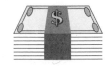

STEP 1: WHAT IS THE QUESTION/GOAL?

STEP 2: FIND THE FACTS

STEP 3: SELECT A STRATEGY

STEP 4: SOLVE

STEP 5: DOES YOUR RESPONSE MAKE SENSE?

Understanding Number Relationships

Directions: Darken the circle for the correct answer, or write in the answer.

> **TRY THIS** Read each problem carefully. Make sure you understand the question that is being asked. Then choose the best method to solve the problem.

Sample A

Which fraction is smallest in value?

A $\frac{1}{8}$ C $\frac{3}{5}$

B $\frac{1}{5}$ D $\frac{3}{8}$

> **THINK IT THROUGH** The correct answer is <u>A</u>. The fraction $\frac{1}{8}$ is smaller than the other fractions listed. Using the common denominator 40, $\frac{1}{8}$ becomes $\frac{5}{40}$, and the other fractions become $\frac{8}{40}$, $\frac{24}{40}$, and $\frac{15}{40}$.

STOP

---

1 What is the value of point X on the number line?

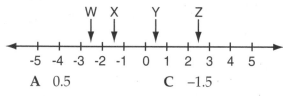

A 0.5   C −1.5

B 2.5   D −2.5

2 Each ▢ represents 0.01.

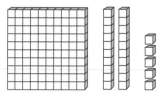

Which decimal is shown by the figure above?

F 1.25

G 12.5

H 0.0125

J 120.5

3 After picking berries, 4 friends compared the amounts of berries in their buckets. Juan's bucket was $\frac{2}{3}$ full, Jamie's bucket was $\frac{4}{5}$ full, Lenny's bucket was $\frac{3}{4}$ full, and Hazel's bucket was $\frac{3}{8}$ full. How would these amounts be arranged in order from greatest to least?

A $\frac{4}{5}, \frac{3}{4}, \frac{2}{3}, \frac{3}{8}$ C $\frac{3}{8}, \frac{3}{4}, \frac{4}{5}, \frac{2}{3}$

B $\frac{2}{3}, \frac{3}{4}, \frac{3}{8}, \frac{4}{5}$ D $\frac{3}{8}, \frac{2}{3}, \frac{4}{5}, \frac{3}{4}$

4 The thermometer shows the reading early this morning. By noon, the temperature had increased 15° from the early morning reading. What is the new reading?

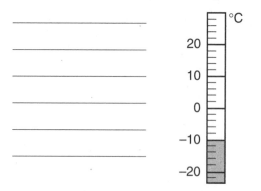

STOP

Answers
SA Ⓐ Ⓑ Ⓒ Ⓓ   1 Ⓐ Ⓑ Ⓒ Ⓓ   2 Ⓕ Ⓖ Ⓗ Ⓙ   3 Ⓐ Ⓑ Ⓒ Ⓓ

Understanding Number Theory

Directions: Darken the circle for the correct answer, or write in the answer.

Read the question twice before choosing your answer. Make sure you understand the question that is being asked. Think about which numbers stand for ones, tens, hundreds, and so on.

Sample A

The call number on this library catalog card is 612.48. What is the value of the 8 in this number?

A 8 ten-thousandths

B 8 thousandths

C 8 hundredths

D 8 tenths

612.48	Remembering Vietnam/Quy Luong
L	Luong, Quy
	Illustrations by Thuy Dang
	San Francisco: Freedom Rings Press,
	1990
	147 p. : ill. ; 23 cm.
	1. Vietnam. I. Luong, Quy. II. Title

THINK IT THROUGH

The correct answer is C. In the number 612.48, the 8 is in the hundredths place, so its value is 8 hundredths. The 4 is in the tenths place.

1 Which of these means the same as 5^3?

A 15

B 125

C 8

D 243

2 One estimate for the distance from Earth to the Andromeda Galaxy is 2,300,000 light years. What is this distance expressed in scientific notation?

F 2.3×10^5

G 23×10^5

H 2.3×10^6

J $2^3 \times 10^7$

3 How would the product $3 \times 3 \times 7 \times 5 \times 5$ be expressed in exponential notation?

A $3^3 \times 7 \times 5^5$

B 2^3

C $3^2 \times 7 \times 5^2$

D 10^5

4 Look at the factor tree shown here. Notice the number of branches in the factor tree.

How many branches will the number 17 have in its completed factor tree?

_____

_____

_____

Answers

SA Ⓐ Ⓑ Ⓒ Ⓓ   1 Ⓐ Ⓑ Ⓒ Ⓓ   2 Ⓕ Ⓖ Ⓗ Ⓙ   3 Ⓐ Ⓑ Ⓒ Ⓓ

Working with Algebra

Directions: Darken the circle for the correct answer, or write in your answer.

Sample A

Which value of x makes the equation $x - 12 = 40$ correct?

A 60   C 45

B 52   D 38

THINK IT THROUGH

The correct answer is <u>B</u>, <u>52</u>. Because the unknown number minus 12 equals 40, it is necessary to add 40 and 12 to find the unknown.

---

1 Meg baked a chocolate cake. She knows that the cake contains 2,700 calories. She has cut the cake into 12 equal-sized pieces. If c represents the number of calories in one piece, which equation can she use to find the number of calories in each piece?

A $12 + c = 2{,}700$

B $12 \div c = 2{,}700$

C $12c = 2{,}700$

D $2700 - c = 12$

2 What is another way to write $6\,(a + 7)$?

F $(6 + a) \times (6 + 7)$

G $6a + 7$

H $7 \times (6 + a)$

J $(6 \times a) + (6 \times 7)$

3 It took Gene three times as long to paint one side of the fence as it took David to paint the other side. If h is the number of hours David painted, which expression shows the time spent by Gene painting?

A $3 \times h$

B $3 - h$

C $3 + h$

D $3 \div h$

4 Which of the following problems could be solved by the equation $2x = 36 + 52$?

F Greg has 36 trading cards. Harry has twice as many. How many cards does Harry have?

G Class A has 36 students, and Class B has twice as many students. How many more students are in Class B?

H The first plant is 36 inches tall, and the second plant is 52 inches tall. If their heights were doubled, how tall would they each be?

J Tank A has 36 fish, and Tank B has 52 fish. If the fish are divided equally between both tanks, how many fish will be in each tank?

5 Clara's pay from her paper route is based on the expression $\$15 + \$0.10p$, where p is the number of papers she delivers during the week. What would her weekly pay be if she delivers 315 papers each week?

_____

_____

_____

_____

Answers

SA Ⓐ Ⓑ Ⓒ Ⓓ   **1** Ⓐ Ⓑ Ⓒ Ⓓ   **2** Ⓕ Ⓖ Ⓗ Ⓙ   **3** Ⓐ Ⓑ Ⓒ Ⓓ   **4** Ⓕ Ⓖ Ⓗ Ⓙ

Understanding Patterns and Functions

Directions: Darken the circle for the correct answer, or write in the answer.

Sample A

Look at the pattern shown here. Which number is missing?

101, 105, 109, ☐, 117

A   113   C   110

B   112   D   107

THINK IT THROUGH

The correct answer is A. The pattern shows that each number increases by 4. Therefore, to find the missing number, add 109 and 4 to get the answer, 113.

🛑 STOP

---

1   A special machine changes numbers according to a certain rule. The *out* number in the table shows the result when the rule is applied to the *in* number.

In	5	45	20
Out	1	9	4

What number will 30 be changed to?

A   150

B   35

C   25

D   6

2   In a basketball free-throw contest held at the high school, Rudy made 4 out of 5 free throws. At this rate, how many free throws could he expect to make in 25 tries?

_____

_____

_____

_____

_____

_____

3   Fran bought 6 yards of blue tapestry material. She used it to upholster 3 chairs. How much of the material would she need to upholster 7 chairs?

F   21 yards

G   16 yards

H   14 yards

J   10 yards

4   Shown here are the first three figures in a pattern. How many stars would be in the seventh figure of the pattern?

★ ★   ★ ★ ★   ★ ★ ★ ★
  ★   ★ ★   ★ ★ ★
★ ★   ★ ★ ★   ★ ★ ★ ★

A   20

B   23

C   26

D   28

🛑 STOP

Answers

SA Ⓐ Ⓑ Ⓒ Ⓓ   **1** Ⓐ Ⓑ Ⓒ Ⓓ   **3** Ⓕ Ⓖ Ⓗ Ⓙ   **4** Ⓐ Ⓑ Ⓒ Ⓓ

Working with Probability and Statistics

Directions: Darken the circle for the correct answer, or write in the answer.

Sample A

Two pennies are tossed into the air. What is the probability they will match either heads-heads or tails-tails when they land?

A $\frac{1}{1}$ C $\frac{1}{4}$

B $\frac{1}{2}$ D $\frac{1}{8}$

THINK IT THROUGH

The correct answer is <u>B</u>. There are four possible outcomes: heads-heads, tails-tails, heads-tails, and tails-heads. Two of these four possibilities will match. That makes the correct answer a probability of $\frac{2}{4}$, or $\frac{1}{2}$.

---

1 Two six-sided number cubes, each numbered 1 through 6, are rolled together. What is the probability that they will land with the numbers on the top face having a sum greater than 10?

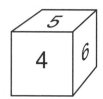

A 1 out of 6

B 1 out of 12

C 2 out of 36

D 10 out of 30

2 These are Yung's bowling scores for the past month.

192	148	192
150	175	202
269	225	240
148	121	192

What is Yung's bowling average?

_____

_____

3 According to this graph, which two energy sources together account for nearly one half?

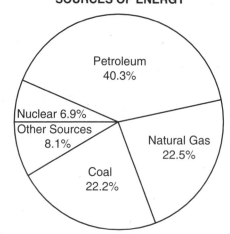

SOURCES OF ENERGY

F Nuclear and natural gas

G Coal and other sources

H Petroleum and coal

J Natural gas and coal

4 Helen has a choice of 3 colors of paint, 4 kinds of curtains, and 2 colors of carpet to decorate her apartment. How many different combinations of paint, curtains, and carpets can she use?

A 9   C 24

B 18   D 36

Miguel earned $20 at his part-time job. The following graph shows how he spent the money. Study the graph. Then answer questions 5 and 6.

Miguel's Earnings

5   What percent of his money did Miguel spend on lunch and magazines combined?

F   50%   H   20%

G   30%   J   25%

6   Which tally chart shows the data in the circle graph?

A

Lunch	⋕⋕ ⋕⋕ ⋕⋕ ⋕⋕
Magazines	⋕⋕ ⋕⋕ ⋕⋕ ⋕⋕ ⋕⋕ ⋕⋕
Owed	⋕⋕
Savings	⋕⋕ ⋕⋕ ⋕⋕ ⋕⋕ ⋕⋕ ⋕⋕ ⋕⋕ ⋕⋕ ⋕⋕

B

Lunch	⋕⋕ ⋕⋕ ⋕⋕ ⋕⋕ ⋕⋕
Magazines	⋕⋕ ⋕⋕ ⋕⋕ ⋕⋕
Owed	⋕⋕
Savings	⋕⋕ ⋕⋕ ⋕⋕ ⋕⋕ ⋕⋕ ⋕⋕ ⋕⋕ ⋕⋕ ⋕⋕

C

Lunch	⋕⋕ ⋕⋕ ⋕⋕
Magazines	⋕⋕ ⋕⋕
Owed	⋕⋕
Savings	⋕⋕ ⋕⋕ ⋕⋕ ⋕⋕ ⋕⋕

D

Lunch	⋕⋕ ⋕⋕ ⋕⋕ ⋕⋕
Magazines	⋕⋕ ⋕⋕ ⋕⋕ ⋕⋕ ⋕⋕
Owed	⋕⋕
Savings	⋕⋕ ⋕⋕ ⋕⋕ ⋕⋕ ⋕⋕

The graph below shows the prices of two stocks over a period of time. Use the graph to answer questions 7–9.

Stock Values During a 12-month Period

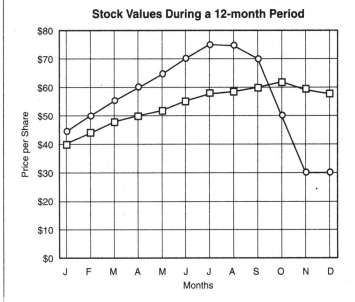

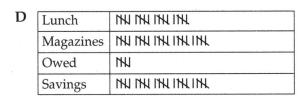

7   What was the greatest price difference between Abbott and Claney stock during the period shown on the graph?

F $30   H $19

G $27   J $15

8   Ella bought 20 shares of Claney stock in April and sold them in October at the current price at that time. About how much profit did she make?

A   About $100

B   About $220

C   About $285

D   About $325

9   If Larry bought 12 shares of Abbott stock on May 4, what did he pay for the stock?

_____

_____

_____

_____

STOP

Understanding Geometry

Directions: Darken the circle for the correct answer, or write in the answer.

TRY THIS

Read each question carefully. Look for key words such as area, volume, radius, and diameter. Use the objects shown or named to help you answer each question.

Sample A

Uncle Tony's vegetable garden is in the shape of a square. What is the area of his garden?

A   14 sq ft

B   28 sq ft

C   56 sq ft

D   196 sq ft

14 ft

THINK IT THROUGH

The correct answer is D, 196 sq ft. To determine the area of a square, multiply side by side:

$A = s2$. So, $14 \times 14 = 196$.

---

1   Michiko's mother stores buttons in the box shown here. What is the volume of the box? (Use $V = l \times w \times h$.)

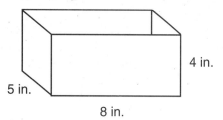

4 in.

5 in.

8 in.

A   160 cu in.

B   80 cu in.

C   73 cu in.

D   17 cu in.

2   An ice-skating rink is shown here. What is the area of the rink? (Use $A = lw$.)

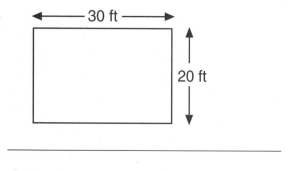

30 ft

20 ft

---

3   Rectangle FGDE is similar to rectangle ECBA. Which line segments are perpendicular?

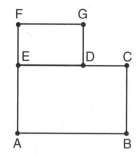

F $\overline{FG}$ and $\overline{DC}$

G $\overline{AB}$ and $\overline{ED}$

H $\overline{EA}$ and $\overline{AB}$

J $\overline{CB}$ and $\overline{FE}$

4   An apple pie has a diameter of 9 inches. What is its circumference rounded to the nearest whole number? (Use $C = \pi d$ and $\pi = 3.14$.)

A   14 inches

B   28 inches

C   36 inches

D   57 inches

GO ON

Answers

SA Ⓐ Ⓑ Ⓒ Ⓓ   **1** Ⓐ Ⓑ Ⓒ Ⓓ   **3** Ⓕ Ⓖ Ⓗ Ⓙ   **4** Ⓐ Ⓑ Ⓒ Ⓓ

5 Which of these angles appears to be an obtuse angle?

F

G

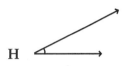
H

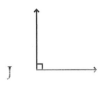
J

6 Which transformation moves the figure from position A to position B?

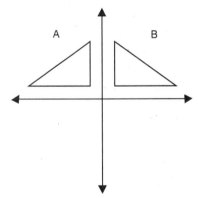

A Rotation

B Translation

C Reflection

D Extension

7 The diameter of this circle is represented by which line segment?

F $\overline{XA}$

G $\overline{XC}$

H $\overline{BX}$

J $\overline{AC}$

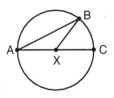

8 Which of these pattern pieces would not form a cube if folded along the dotted lines?

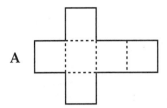
A

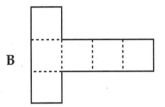
B

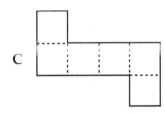
C

D

9 The distance from the edge to the center of a circle is called the

_____

_____

_____

_____

_____

_____

STOP

Answers

5 Ⓕ Ⓖ Ⓗ Ⓙ   **6** Ⓐ Ⓑ Ⓒ Ⓓ   **7** Ⓕ Ⓖ Ⓗ Ⓙ   **8** Ⓐ Ⓑ Ⓒ Ⓓ

Working with Measurement

Directions: Darken the circle for the correct answer, or write in the answer.

TRY THIS

Read the question carefully. Study the answer choices. Sometimes more than one answer looks correct. Use the objects shown or named to help you answer each question.

Sample A

Which of these units is used to measure length on a ruler?

A degrees

B kilograms

C centimeters

D liters

THINK IT THROUGH

The correct answer is <u>C</u>. Degrees are used to measure temperature, kilograms are used to measure mass, liters are used to measure capacity, and <u>centimeters</u> are used to measure length.

---

1 Mr. Baker cooked $4\frac{1}{2}$ quarts of rice. How many 1-cup servings did this make?

A $5\frac{1}{2}$ cups

B 9 cups

C 10 cups

D 18 cups

2 The scale model shown here represents a rectangular parking lot.

Scale: 1cm represents 15m

Use your centimeter ruler to help answer this question. What is the actual length of each of the 2 long sides of the parking lot?

F 4 meters

G 15 meters

H 60 meters

J 90 meters

3 Use your inch ruler to help answer this question. What is the approximate length of one side of this toy block?

$\frac{1}{2}$ inch = 2 inches

_____

_____

_____

_____

4 Tammy caught a catfish that was $2\frac{2}{3}$ feet long. How many inches long was it?

A 16 inches

B 26 inches

C 29 inches

D 32 inches

Answers
SA Ⓐ Ⓑ Ⓒ Ⓓ   1 Ⓐ Ⓑ Ⓒ Ⓓ   2 Ⓕ Ⓖ Ⓗ Ⓙ   4 Ⓐ Ⓑ Ⓒ Ⓓ

5 How high off the ground is the kite?

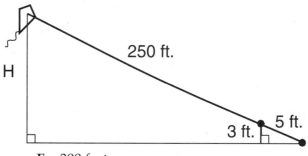

- **F** 300 feet
- **G** 245 feet
- **H** 150 feet
- **J** 145 feet

6 The testing session began at 8:45 A.M. The time limit on the first test was 35 minutes and the time limit on the second test was 40 minutes. There was a 10-minute break between the tests. At what time did the session end?

- **A** 10:00 A.M.
- **B** 10:10 A.M.
- **C** 10:25 A.M.
- **D** 11:05 A.M.

7 Gino and Claire went to see a movie last night. The movie began at 7:30 P.M. It lasted $1\frac{3}{4}$ hours. What time did the movie end?

- **F** 9:15 P.M.
- **G** 9:20 P.M.
- **H** 9:30 P.M.
- **J** 9:45 P.M.

8 On a map of a cross-country ski area, 1 inch represents 3 miles. What is the distance between two turn-around areas 4 inches apart on the map?

- **A** 3 miles
- **B** 4 miles
- **C** 7 miles
- **D** 12 miles

9 The picture shows that Miyoshi is standing 6 yards from the tree. How many feet is that?

six yards between girl and tree

_____

_____

_____

_____

_____

_____

10 Marty's soccer team starts its practice at 4:30 P.M. It ends at 5:15 P.M. How long does Marty's soccer team practice?

_____

_____

_____

_____

_____

_____

Answers

5 Ⓕ Ⓖ Ⓗ Ⓙ   **6** Ⓐ Ⓑ Ⓒ Ⓓ   **7** Ⓕ Ⓖ Ⓗ Ⓙ   **8** Ⓐ Ⓑ Ⓒ Ⓓ

Using Problem-Solving Strategies

Directions: Darken the circle for the correct answer, or write in the answer.

TRY THIS

Study each problem carefully. Think about what each problem is asking, then decide on the best strategy to find the answer.

Sample A

A local factory produces tuners for car radios. Of the 400 tuners produced each hour, 30 are damaged. How many undamaged tuners does the factory produce in an 8-hour day?

A 370

B 430

C 2,960

D 3,440

THINK IT THROUGH

The correct answer is <u>C</u>, <u>2,960</u>. If 30 out of 400 produced each hour are damaged, then 370 are undamaged. To find how many undamaged tuners are produced in 8 hours, multiply 370 times 8 to get 2,960.

---

1 Joyce decorated a tree in her yard with popcorn for birds to eat. On the first branch, she hung a string with 4 pieces of popcorn. On the second branch, she hung a string with 8 pieces of popcorn, and on the third branch a string with 16 pieces of popcorn. If she continued this pattern, how many pieces of popcorn would be on the string that she hung on the fifth branch?

A 18

B 24

C 32

D 64

2 During the first three hours at the car wash, 15 fewer cars were washed during the first hour than during the third hour. During the second hour, 5 more cars were washed than during the first hour. During the third hour, 40 cars were washed. How many cars were washed during the second hour?

_____

_____

_____

_____

3 Frances wants to provide each of her students with 5 strips of leather for an art project. She buys the leather strips at a craft store for $0.89 each. What other information is needed to learn how much Frances pays for the leather strips?

F the length of each strip

G the number of students in her class

H the number of strips in a package

J the colors of strips available

Use the figure shown here to answer question 4.

					12	Row 1
				14	16	Row 2
			18	20	22	Row 3
		24	26	28	30	Row 4
	32	34	36	38	40	Row 5
						Row 6

4 Fill in the numbers to complete Row 6.

Using Estimation

Directions: Darken the circle for the correct answer, or write in the answer.

TRY THIS — Round numbers when you estimate. For some problems, there are no exact answers. Then you should take your best guess. You can check your answer by using the numbers given in the problem.

Sample A

Lucas bought 3 magazines: one for $3.25, one for $2.75, and one for $4.57. With tax included, about how much did Lucas spend?

A $9

B $11

C $13

D $15

THINK IT THROUGH — The correct answer is <u>B</u>, <u>$11.00</u>. Round $3.25 to $3.00, $2.75 to $3.00, and $4.57 to $5.00. The sum of these estimates is $11.00, which would include about $0.80 in tax. Check by adding $3.25, $2.75, $4.57 and $0.80. The sum is $11.37.

---

1 Terri is working on a class project. She cut a pine board into 12 equal parts. She used 9 of the pieces to build some shelves. About what percent of the board is left?

A 6%

B 9%

C 12%

D 25%

2 Mr. Petrovich has 11,200 coins in his collection. He plans to add another 1,500 to his collection this year. What is the best estimate of the number of coins Mr. Petrovich will have at the end of this year?

F 11,000 coins

G 12,000 coins

H 13,000 coins

J 14,000 coins

3 Ellen enjoys exercise. It usually takes her 9 minutes to jog a mile. What is a reasonable estimate of the time it would take Ellen to jog 5 miles?

A less than 30 minutes

B between 30 and 40 minutes

C between 40 and 50 minutes

D more than 50 minutes

4 On Liz's vacation she planned to travel $297\frac{3}{4}$ kilometers on a train. If the train had traveled $74\frac{1}{2}$ kilometers, what is the best estimate of the number of kilometers she had left to travel?

F $120\frac{1}{4}$ kilometers

G 225 kilometers

H 270 kilometers

J 370 kilometers

5 This chart shows some of the rivers in Africa.

River	Length
Nile River	4,145 miles
Limpopo River	1,100 miles
Niger River	2,600 miles
Orange River	1,300 miles
Zambezi River	1,650 miles

About how much shorter is the Orange River than the Nile River?

_____

_____

_____

Answers
SA Ⓐ Ⓑ Ⓒ Ⓓ   1 Ⓐ Ⓑ Ⓒ Ⓓ   2 Ⓕ Ⓖ Ⓗ Ⓙ   3 Ⓐ Ⓑ Ⓒ Ⓓ   4 Ⓕ Ⓖ Ⓗ Ⓙ

Test

Sample A

Which fraction is greatest in value?

$$\frac{2}{12} \qquad \frac{2}{4} \qquad \frac{2}{2} \qquad \frac{2}{6}$$

A $\frac{2}{12}$ C $\frac{2}{2}$

B $\frac{2}{4}$ D $\frac{2}{6}$

STOP

For questions 1–38, darken the circle for the correct answer, or write in the answer.

1 The stock number on an item is 54.763. What is the value of the 3 in 54.763?

  A 3 ten-thousandths

  B 3 thousandths

  C 3 hundredths

  D 3 tenths

2 Light travels at a speed of 186,282 miles per second. How could this number be expressed in scientific notation?

  F $1,862.82 \times 10^3$ H 1.86282×10^4

  G 1.86282×10^5 J 186.282×10^{-3}

3 What is the value of point B on the number line?

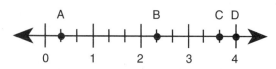

  A $2\frac{1}{3}$ C $3\frac{2}{3}$

  B $\frac{1}{3}$ D 4

4 Which fraction does not have the same value as the other fractions?

$$6\frac{2}{3} \qquad \frac{20}{3} \qquad 6\frac{9}{12} \qquad 6\frac{4}{6}$$

  F $6\frac{2}{3}$ H $6\frac{9}{12}$

  G $\frac{20}{3}$ J $6\frac{4}{6}$

5 Which problem could be solved by the equation $x = 0.3 \times 200$?

  A Three hamburgers cost $2. How much does one cost?

  B A theater holds 200 people. How many people would be able to attend 3 showings of a movie?

  C The regular fare of $200 for a plane ticket was just reduced by 30%. What would the savings be?

  D The temperature in an oven was 200 degrees. It was then increased by 0.3 degrees. What is the current oven temperature?

6 Which decimal shows the part of this figure that is shaded?

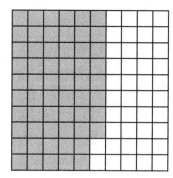

  F 5.8   H 0.058

  G 0.58   J 5.08

7 In what way are the numbers in the oval related?

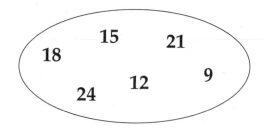

_____

_____

_____

_____

GO ON

Answers
SA Ⓐ Ⓑ Ⓒ Ⓓ   **2** Ⓕ Ⓖ Ⓗ Ⓙ   **4** Ⓕ Ⓖ Ⓗ Ⓙ   **6** Ⓕ Ⓖ Ⓗ Ⓙ
70   **1** Ⓐ Ⓑ Ⓒ Ⓓ   **3** Ⓐ Ⓑ Ⓒ Ⓓ   **5** Ⓐ Ⓑ Ⓒ Ⓓ

8   If 32 = 5*d* +7, what is the value of *d*?

A   2

B   4

C   5

D   8

9   Andy has the 2 cubes shown here. They have the numbers 1, 2, 3, 4, 5, and 6 on their faces. If he rolls the cubes together, what is the probability that the 2 numbers showing at the top of the cubes will total 6 when added together?

F $\frac{1}{4}$

G $\frac{5}{24}$

H $\frac{1}{6}$

J $\frac{5}{36}$

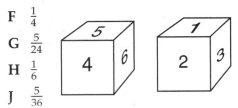

10   Ray uses 4 boards to build 1 step, 10 boards to build 2 steps, and 18 boards to build 3 steps. Following this pattern, how many boards would you expect Ray to use to build 5 steps?

_____

_____

_____

_____

_____

_____

11   At a recent marshmallow-eating contest, the winner ate 20 marshmallows in 5 minutes. At that rate, how many marshmallows would the winner eat if the contest has lasted 25 minutes?

A   120

B   100

C   40

D   25

12   Emma bought 2 pairs of socks for $2.95 each. She bought a pair of shoes that cost 8 times as much as a pair of socks. Which expression could be used to determine the cost of the shoes?

F   (8 − 2) + $2.95

G   ($2.95 × 2) + ($2.95 × 8)

H   (8 + 2) − $2.95

J $2.95 × 8

13   The average (mean) temperature for 4 days was 74 degrees. Which set of temperatures could reasonably show the exact temperatures for the 4 days?

A   74°, 75°, 76°, 77°

B   74°, 72°, 72°, 70°

C   78°, 75°, 74°, 74°

D   72°, 76°, 68°, 80°

14   The camera club is responsible for decorating one of the bulletin boards at school. They change the bulletin board every month. They have three colors of border trim, 5 background colors, and 2 styles of lettering to choose from. If they use 1 border, 1 background color, and 1 style of lettering at a time, how many months of bulletin-board combinations can they make?

F   30 months

G   15 months

H   10 months

J   6 months

GO ON

Answers

8   Ⓐ Ⓑ Ⓒ Ⓓ   11   Ⓐ Ⓑ Ⓒ Ⓓ   13   Ⓐ Ⓑ Ⓒ Ⓓ

9   Ⓕ Ⓖ Ⓗ Ⓙ   12   Ⓕ Ⓖ Ⓗ Ⓙ   14   Ⓕ Ⓖ Ⓗ Ⓙ

This table shows the prices of four different kinds of markers. Study the table. Then answer questions 15–17.

Markers		
Kind	Number in box	Price per box
Wide tip	6	$3.00
Narrow tip	10	$3.50
Pastel colors	7	$5.50
Neon colors	5	$5.75
Washable	12	$5.40

15 Becky spent $9.25 for markers. Which two kinds of markers did she buy?

   A wide tip and washable

   B pastel colors and wide tip

   C neon colors and narrow tip

   D washable and pastel colors

16 How many more washable markers are in a box than pastel colors?

   F 5

   G 6

   H 7

   J 19

17 Juan bought a box of markers for which the cost of one marker was the lowest priced of the five kinds. Which kind of marker did he buy?

_____

_____

_____

_____

_____

Study the following graph. Then answer questions 18–20.

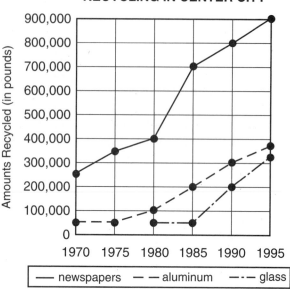

RECYCLING IN CENTER CITY

— newspapers — — aluminum —·— glass

18 In what year did the people of Center City begin to recycle glass?

   A 1970   **C** 1985

   B 1980   **D** 1990

19 In what year did the people of Center City recycle four times as much newspaper as glass?

   F 1975   **H** 1985

   G 1980   **J** 1990

20 Which of the following conclusions can be made about Center City?

   A Recycling is declining in Center City.

   B Center City residents need to build a new park.

   C Recycling has become important to the residents of Center City.

   D Center City residents will probably stop recycling newspapers.

> GO ON

21 Which edge of the cube shown here is parallel to edge CD?

F $\overline{CG}$

G $\overline{AE}$

H $\overline{EF}$

J $\overline{BD}$

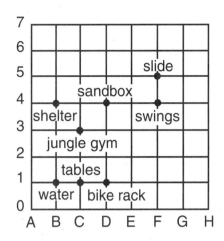

22 Wendy wanted to sew a new tablecloth for her round table. The radius of the table is 18 inches. What is the approximate circumference of the table? (Use C = πd and π = 3.14.)

A about 113 inches

B about 92 inches

C about 72 inches

D about 57 inches

23 There are 4 red beads, 8 yellow beads, and 2 pink beads in a bag. If one bead is picked at random from the bag, what is the probability that it will be red?

F $\frac{1}{2}$

G $\frac{2}{5}$

H $\frac{2}{7}$

J $\frac{1}{4}$

24 The diameter of this circle is represented by which line segment?

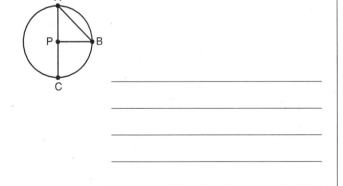

_____

_____

_____

_____

_____

25 Which ordered pair in the park represents the location of the jungle gym?

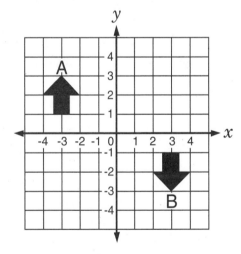

A (C, 2)

B (D, 3)

C (B, 4)

D (C, 3)

26 Which transformation moves the figure from position A to position B?

F reflection

G rotation

H translation

J extension

GO ON

Answers

21 Ⓕ Ⓖ Ⓗ Ⓙ   **22** Ⓐ Ⓑ Ⓒ Ⓓ   **23** Ⓕ Ⓖ Ⓗ Ⓙ   **25** Ⓐ Ⓑ Ⓒ Ⓓ   **26** Ⓕ Ⓖ Ⓗ Ⓙ

27 Joan's piano lesson begins at 3:35. It ends at 4:05. How many minutes long is the lesson?

A   45 minutes

B   40 minutes

C   35 minutes

D   30 minutes

28 The scale model shown here represents the circular foundation of an 18th-century lighthouse in southern England.

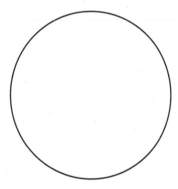

Scale: 1 inch represents 16 feet

Use your inch ruler to help answer this question. What is the actual diameter of the foundation of the lighthouse?

F   14 feet

G   20 feet

H   28 feet

J   36 feet

29 A commuter train left the Shady Grove depot at 6:53 A.M. for a trip to Pecan Gap that takes 1 hour and 16 minutes. At what time should the train arrive at its destination?

_____

_____

_____

_____

30 Juanita competes in races 4 times a year. It takes her between 30 and 35 minutes to run a $4\frac{1}{2}$-mile race. What would be a reasonable time for her to run a $2\frac{1}{4}$-mile race?

A   between $6\frac{3}{4}$ and 9 minutes

B   between 8 and 10 minutes

C   between 15 and 20 minutes

D   between 50 and 60 minutes

31 Swimming lessons at the local park district swimming pool cost $18.00 for 2 weeks of lessons. What is the best estimate of the total cost for 7 people to take swimming lessons at the pool?

F $30

G $70

H $90

J $140

32 Drew was leveling a table. One corner had to be raised $\frac{3}{4}$ inch. He had some pieces of wood $\frac{1}{16}$ inch thick. How many pieces of wood would he need to use for the corner to make the table level?

_____

_____

_____

_____

_____

_____

►GO ON

33 The temperature outside rose 41 degrees during a 12-hour period. If the temperature rose the same number of degrees every hour, what is a good estimate of the number of degrees the temperature rose each hour?

A 2 degrees

B 3 degrees

C 6 degrees

D 7 degrees

34 About how far is it from Belton to Trell on the map shown here?

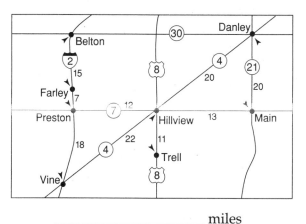

_____ miles

35 How many cubes are in this stack?

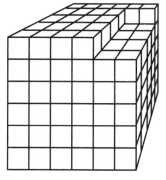

F 30

G 160

H 172

J 196

36 There are 24 parking spaces in each row in a parking lot. What information is needed to find the maximum number of parking spaces in the parking lot?

A the number of cars parked in each row

B the area of the parking lot

C the number of parking rows

D the number of empty parking spaces

37 Each square-shaped box in the pattern shown here decreases in length and width by $\frac{1}{2}$ unit each time. If Box 1 originally measured 12 by 12 units, what would be the dimensions of Box 9?

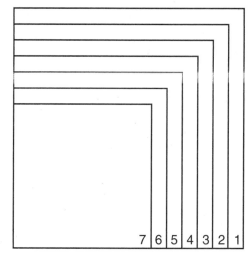

F 1 by 1 unit

G 4 by 4 units

H 5 by 5 units

J 10 by 10 units

38 Brand A laundry detergent costs more than Brand D. Brand D costs less than Brand X. Brand Z costs more than Brand A. Which of the following is most likely true?

A Brand Z costs more than Brand D.

B Brand X and Brand A cost the same.

C Brand Z costs less than Brand X.

D Brand A costs more than Brand X.

STOP

Math Procedures
Using Computation

Directions: Darken the circle for the correct answer. Darken the circle for *NH, Not Here,* if the correct answer is not given.

TRY THIS	Check the answer to a division problem by multiplying. Multiply your answer by the divisor in the problem. That answer should equal the larger number in the problem.

Sample A

$1.5\overline{)45}$

A 3
B 300
C 30
D 0.3
E NH

THINK IT THROUGH	The correct answer is <u>C</u>, <u>30</u>. First, move the decimal in 1.5 to 15. Next, move the decimal one place in 45 to 450, and write the decimal in the quotient. Then, divide as with whole numbers. Last, check the answer by multiplying 30 by 1.5.

STOP

1

$10\frac{1}{4} - 2\frac{3}{4} =$

A $8\frac{1}{2}$
B $8\frac{3}{4}$
C $7\frac{1}{4}$
D 13
E NH

2

$43\overline{)8285}$

F 190
G $192\frac{29}{43}$
H $191\frac{42}{43}$
J $192\frac{12}{43}$
K NH

3

852
× 29

A 24,708
B 24,372
C 24,608
D 14,708
E NH

4

$0.7\overline{)0.56}$

F 0.8
G 8
H 80
J 0.08
K NH

5

$3.84 \times 4.6 =$

A 3.840
B 17.664
C 176.64
D 27.664
E NH

6

$\frac{1}{5} \div \frac{1}{8} =$

F $\frac{1}{40}$
G $1\frac{3}{8}$
H $\frac{3}{5}$
J $1\frac{3}{5}$
K NH

STOP

Answers

SA Ⓐ Ⓑ Ⓒ Ⓓ Ⓔ   2 Ⓕ Ⓖ Ⓗ Ⓙ Ⓚ   4 Ⓕ Ⓖ Ⓗ Ⓙ Ⓚ   6 Ⓕ Ⓖ Ⓗ Ⓙ Ⓚ
1 Ⓐ Ⓑ Ⓒ Ⓓ Ⓔ   3 Ⓐ Ⓑ Ⓒ Ⓓ Ⓔ   5 Ⓐ Ⓑ Ⓒ Ⓓ Ⓔ

Using Computation in Context

Directions: Darken the circle for the correct answer. Darken the circle for *NH, Not Here,* if the correct answer is not given.

TRY THIS | Read the word problem carefully. Then set up the word problem as a computation problem. Solve the problem and compare it to the answer choices.

Sample A

Pat's rope measured 54 feet long, and Nick's rope was 65 feet long. What is the total length of the ropes?

A   100 feet

B   109 feet

C   119 feet

D   11 feet

E   NH

THINK IT THROUGH | The correct answer is <u>C</u>, <u>119</u> feet. To find the combined length of the two ropes, add 54 feet and 65 feet to get <u>119 feet</u>.

---

1   Mrs. Schultz's car has a gas tank that holds $12\frac{1}{2}$ gallons of gas. She used $\frac{1}{5}$ of a tank of gas. How many gallons did she use?

A $2\frac{1}{2}$ gallons

B $3\frac{1}{2}$ gallons

C   4 gallons

D $3\frac{3}{4}$ gallons

E   NH

2   Gwen was planting tomato plants in a row $6\frac{2}{3}$ yards long. She put the plants $\frac{2}{3}$ yard apart. How many plants were in the row?

F $8\frac{2}{3}$

G   9

H   10

J $7\frac{1}{3}$

K   NH

3   Alex spent $2.40 for cough medicine, $1.29 for cough drops, and $0.79 for tissues. What was the total cost of these items?

A $3.88

B $3.47

C $4.48

D $5.48

E   NH

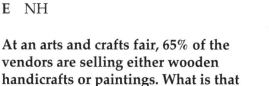

4   At an arts and crafts fair, 65% of the vendors are selling either wooden handicrafts or paintings. What is that percent rounded to a compatible fraction?

F $\frac{1}{3}$

G $\frac{1}{2}$

H $\frac{2}{3}$

J $\frac{3}{4}$

K   NH

Answers

SA Ⓐ Ⓑ Ⓒ Ⓓ Ⓔ   2 Ⓕ Ⓖ Ⓗ Ⓙ Ⓚ   4 Ⓕ Ⓖ Ⓗ Ⓙ Ⓚ

1 Ⓐ Ⓑ Ⓒ Ⓓ Ⓔ   3 Ⓐ Ⓑ Ⓒ Ⓓ Ⓔ

Test

Sample A

$\frac{2}{3} \div \frac{5}{6} =$

A $\frac{5}{9}$

B $\frac{3}{5}$

C $1\frac{1}{4}$

D $\frac{5}{6}$

E NH

STOP

Sample B

At the bowling alley Gina scored 133 in her first game, 146 in her second game, and 138 in her third game. What were Gina's total points for the 3 games?

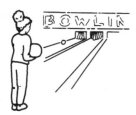

F 371

G 408

H 417

J 517

K NH

STOP

For questions 1–14, darken the circle for the correct answer. If the correct answer is not given, darken the circle for *NH, Not Here.* If no choices are given, write in the answer.

1

$8.4 \times 0.934 =$

A 78.456

B 7.8456

C 0.78456

D 784.56

E NH

2

$44\overline{)8085}$

F $183\frac{3}{4}$

G $183\frac{23}{44}$

H $182\frac{34}{44}$

J 183

K NH

3

$6.183 \times 2.4 =$

A 14.8392

B 1.48392

C 0.148392

D 148.392

E NH

4

$2\frac{1}{3}$
$+ 4\frac{5}{12}$

F $6\frac{2}{5}$

G $6\frac{1}{2}$

H $6\frac{3}{4}$

J $6\frac{5}{6}$

K NH

5

$8\frac{2}{5} - 3\frac{7}{10} =$

A $4\frac{7}{10}$

B $12\frac{1}{10}$

C $3\frac{7}{10}$

D $3\frac{2}{5}$

E NH

6

$0.8\overline{)0.72}$

F 9

G 90

H 0.9

J 0.09

K NH

7

648
$\times 33$

A 3888

B 20,384

C 21,384

D 21,284

E NH

8

706
$\times 285$

_____

_____

_____

GO ON

Answers

SA Ⓐ Ⓑ Ⓒ Ⓓ Ⓔ

SB Ⓕ Ⓖ Ⓗ Ⓙ Ⓚ

1 Ⓐ Ⓑ Ⓒ Ⓓ Ⓔ

2 Ⓕ Ⓖ Ⓗ Ⓙ Ⓚ

3 Ⓐ Ⓑ Ⓒ Ⓓ Ⓔ

4 Ⓕ Ⓖ Ⓗ Ⓙ Ⓚ

5 Ⓐ Ⓑ Ⓒ Ⓓ Ⓔ

6 Ⓕ Ⓖ Ⓗ Ⓙ Ⓚ

7 Ⓐ Ⓑ Ⓒ Ⓓ Ⓔ

9 Julius and his family drove to New Orleans. On the way there, they drove 298 miles. They took a shorter route back and drove 286 miles. How many miles did they drive altogether?

F   384

G   484

H   584

J   12

K   NH

10 The tallest seventh-grade boy is $70\frac{3}{8}$ inches tall. What is his height rounded to the nearest half inch?

A   70 inches

B   71 inches

C $70\frac{1}{2}$ inches

D   80 inches

E   NH

11 Last month, Juanita ran the 100-meter dash in 12.56 seconds. Yesterday, she ran the 100-meter dash in 11.97 seconds. By how much did her time improve from last month?

F   0.59 seconds

G   0.65 seconds

H   0.69 seconds

J   0.75 seconds

K   NH

12 Lauren read 3 books last weekend. She made this table to show the time she spent reading.

Lauren's Weekend Reading			
Books	1	2	3
Hours	$4\frac{3}{4}$	$3\frac{1}{2}$	$1\frac{1}{4}$

How many hours did Lauren spend reading the 3 books?

A $8\frac{3}{4}$ hours

B $8\frac{1}{4}$ hours

C $7\frac{1}{4}$ hours

D $9\frac{1}{2}$ hours

E   NH

13 Tamiko and her class helped plant 120 saplings at local parks on Earth Day. If 30 of the saplings were maple trees, what percent of the trees were maple trees?

F   90%

G   75%

H   25%

J $33\frac{1}{3}$ %

K   NH

14 Molly bought 6 pounds of cornmeal at 39¢ per pound. How much did she spend on the cornmeal?

_____

_____

_____

_____

_____

STOP

Answers

9 Ⓕ Ⓖ Ⓗ Ⓙ Ⓚ   **11** Ⓕ Ⓖ Ⓗ Ⓙ Ⓚ   **13** Ⓕ Ⓖ Ⓗ Ⓙ Ⓚ

10 Ⓐ Ⓑ Ⓒ Ⓓ Ⓔ   **12** Ⓐ Ⓑ Ⓒ Ⓓ Ⓔ

Understanding Word Meanings

Directions: Darken the circle for the word or words that best complete the sentence you hear.

TRY THIS	Listen carefully to the sentence. Then look at the answer choices. Decide which words you know are wrong. Then look at the remaining words to make your choice.

Sample A

A fur   C teeth

B eyes   D bones

THINK IT THROUGH	The correct answer is <u>C</u>. Fangs are a kind of "teeth."

1 A confuse
   B miss
   C determine
   D report

2 F usual
   G unimportant
   H worthwhile
   J serious

3 A closed
   B unreliable
   C blameless
   D responsible

4 F calculate
   G know
   H grasp
   J estimate

5 A ratify
   B uphold
   C support
   D cancel

6 F lingering
   G hurrying
   H overtaking
   J running

7 A not serious
   B silly
   C not planned
   D deliberate

8 F vase
   G box
   H wreath
   J handful

9 A gather
   B collect
   C retain
   D distribute

Write your answer to the following question:

10 _____

_____

Answers

SA ⒶⒷⒸⒹ   2 ⒻⒼⒽⒿ   4 ⒻⒼⒽⒿ   6 ⒻⒼⒽⒿ   8 ⒻⒼⒽⒿ

1 ⒶⒷⒸⒹ   3 ⒶⒷⒸⒹ   5 ⒶⒷⒸⒹ   7 ⒶⒷⒸⒹ   9 ⒶⒷⒸⒹ

Building Listening Skills

Directions: Darken the circle for the word or words that best answer the question.

TRY THIS

Form a picture of the story in your mind. Listen carefully for the details given in the story.

Sample A

    A snow

    B rain

    C cold

    D heat

THINK IT THROUGH

The correct answer is <u>A</u>. The paragraph says that people in cold climates build houses with sloping roofs so the snow will slide off easily.

STOP

1
  A clothing
  B tents
  C paper
  D blankets

2
  F cattle
  G sheep
  H chickens
  J goats

3
  A the Pacific Northwest
  B the Southeast
  C the Northeast
  D the Southwest

4
  F The school had burned.
  G The school had been damaged by a hurricane.
  H The students were very poor.
  J School supplies were unavailable near the school.

5
  A on September 4
  B on September 22
  C in October
  D on September 15

6
  F individual classrooms
  G Jackson Junior High School
  H the school gym
  J the principal's office

7
  A the drive will not be successful
  B the principal may not approve the school-supply drive
  C the students will volunteer to adopt another school
  D Jackson Junior High School will rebuild and reopen soon

8
  F in a science book
  G in a teen magazine
  H in a newspaper
  J in a news magazine

9
  A make the goal specific
  B have as much time as possible
  C work on several goals at a time
  D try to achieve the goal without help

10
  F the time available to reach the goal
  G their interests, strengths, and values
  H who can help with achieving the goal
  J the reward for achieving the goal

STOP

Answers

SA Ⓐ Ⓑ Ⓒ Ⓓ   **3** Ⓐ Ⓑ Ⓒ Ⓓ   **6** Ⓕ Ⓖ Ⓗ Ⓙ   **9** Ⓐ Ⓑ Ⓒ Ⓓ

  1 Ⓐ Ⓑ Ⓒ Ⓓ   **4** Ⓕ Ⓖ Ⓗ Ⓙ   **7** Ⓐ Ⓑ Ⓒ Ⓓ   **10** Ⓕ Ⓖ Ⓗ Ⓙ

  2 Ⓕ Ⓖ Ⓗ Ⓙ   **5** Ⓐ Ⓑ Ⓒ Ⓓ   **8** Ⓕ Ⓖ Ⓗ Ⓙ

Test

Sample A

A reluctant
B cold
C friendly
D small

For questions 1–12, darken the circle for the word or words that best complete the sentence you hear.

1   A energetic
    B slow
    C precise
    D jerky

2   F cry
    G yelp
    H squirm
    J suffer

3   A harsh
    B kind
    C foolish
    D clever

4   F bring in
    G send away
    H accept
    J return

5   A gray
    B calm
    C silent
    D stormy

6   F scarce
    G large
    H meager
    J small

7   A wandering
    B settled
    C stationary
    D resident

8   F involved
    G biased
    H uninvolved
    J subjective

9   A worthwhile
    B useless
    C pointless
    D unprofitable

10 F bitter
    G tasteless
    H bland
    J delicious

11 A desire
    B skill
    C inability
    D job

12 F noticeable
    G invisible
    H insignificant
    J subtle

Write your answer to the following question:

13 _____
    _____
    _____
    _____
    _____

> GO ON

Answers

SA Ⓐ Ⓑ Ⓒ Ⓓ   3 Ⓐ Ⓑ Ⓒ Ⓓ   6 Ⓕ Ⓖ Ⓗ Ⓙ   9 Ⓐ Ⓑ Ⓒ Ⓓ   12 Ⓕ Ⓖ Ⓗ Ⓙ
1   Ⓐ Ⓑ Ⓒ Ⓓ   4 Ⓕ Ⓖ Ⓗ Ⓙ   7 Ⓐ Ⓑ Ⓒ Ⓓ   10 Ⓕ Ⓖ Ⓗ Ⓙ
2   Ⓕ Ⓖ Ⓗ Ⓙ   5 Ⓐ Ⓑ Ⓒ Ⓓ   8 Ⓕ Ⓖ Ⓗ Ⓙ   11 Ⓐ Ⓑ Ⓒ Ⓓ

Sample B

 A hobby magazine

 B history book

 C science magazine

 D psychology book

For questions 14–26, listen to the story. Then darken the circle for the word or words that best answer the question, or write in the answer.

14 **A** should exercise more

  B should take vitamin pills

  C need to learn about nutrition

  D buy more vitamins than other people

15 **F** "A Good Diet"

  G "Everyone Needs Vitamins"

  H "Why Take Vitamin Supplements?"

  J "Foods to Avoid"

16 **A** to inform

  B to persuade

  C to entertain

  D to inspire

17 **F** 1962

  G 1964

  H 1975

  J 1984

18 **A** set a new speed record

  B wrote newspaper articles

  C flew missions during World War II

  D flew missions during the Korean War

19 **F** put an American into space

  G help Glenn become a hero

  H train test pilots

  J win the Korean War

20 **A** an astronaut

  B a newspaper reporter

  C a test pilot

  D a Marine Corps pilot

21 **F** a squirrel

  G a dog

  H one of the friends

  J the writer's little brother

22 **A** to please their parents

  B to make money

  C to help their neighbors

  D to complete a school project

23 **F** mowing lawns

  G taking care of children

  H walking a dog

  J delivering newspapers

24 **A** Biff ran and pulled Alex with him.

  B Alex did not want people to see them.

  C They took pictures of Alex and Biff.

  D Biff was very shy.

25 **F** Janet's

  G Luis's

  H Joey's

  J Alex's

26 _____

   _____

Answers

SB Ⓐ Ⓑ Ⓒ Ⓓ **16** Ⓐ Ⓑ Ⓒ Ⓓ **19** Ⓕ Ⓖ Ⓗ Ⓙ **22** Ⓐ Ⓑ Ⓒ Ⓓ **25** Ⓕ Ⓖ Ⓗ Ⓙ

14 Ⓐ Ⓑ Ⓒ Ⓓ **17** Ⓕ Ⓖ Ⓗ Ⓙ **20** Ⓐ Ⓑ Ⓒ Ⓓ **23** Ⓕ Ⓖ Ⓗ Ⓙ

15 Ⓕ Ⓖ Ⓗ Ⓙ **18** Ⓐ Ⓑ Ⓒ Ⓓ **21** Ⓕ Ⓖ Ⓗ Ⓙ **24** Ⓐ Ⓑ Ⓒ Ⓓ

Prewriting, Composing, and Editing

Directions: Read each sentence carefully. Then darken the circle for the correct answer to each question.

TRY THIS

Pretend that you are writing each sentence. Use the rules that you have learned for capitalization, punctuation, word usage, and sentence structure to choose the correct answer.

A Vacation on a Working Ranch

Celina and her family want to spend their vacation at a working ranch. Celina is trying to find more information about working ranches. She decides to write a letter to one of the ranches.

Sample A

Dear Director,
  I am writing to ask you to send me information about vacationing at your working ranch. My family and I such a vacation. Please send the information as soon as possible. We are anxious to plan our vacation.

Which of these is *not* a complete sentence?

A I am writing to ask you to send me information about vacationing at your working ranch.

B My family and I such a vacation.

C Please send the information as soon as possible.

D We are anxious to plan our vacation.

THINK IT THROUGH

The correct answer is B. <u>My family and I such a vacation</u> is not a complete sentence.

STOP

Writing a Research Paper

Ken is studying coral reefs in geography class. He is interested in learning more about the Great Barrier Reef along the northeast coast of Australia. Ken decides to use the Great Barrier Reef as the subject of his research paper for geography class.

1 Once Ken decides what to include in his research paper, what can he do to organize his paper?

A plan a trip to the Great Barrier Reef

B ask people what they know about coral reefs

C make an outline or web of the information to include in the paper

D determine the length of the paper

GO ON

Answers
SA Ⓐ Ⓑ Ⓒ Ⓓ
1 Ⓐ Ⓑ Ⓒ Ⓓ

Ken found a book in the library on the Great Barrier Reef. Use the Table of Contents and Index from the book to answer questions 2–6.

Table of Contents

Index

2 Ken can find information in Chapter 1 about all of the following *except*—

F Australia

G cyclones

H colors of corals

J breakwater

3 Which pages would help Ken learn about Captain Cook's discovery of Australia?

A 13–17

B 48–49

C 57–61

D 21, 24

4 Which pages would have information about the types of coral found in the Great Barrier Reef?

F 1–6

G 21, 22

H 25

J 57–61

5 On which pages would Ken find information about caves found in the Great Barrier Reef?

A 18, 23, 35

B 21, 22

C 9, 11, 12

D 58–60

Write your answer for the following question:

6 Which chapter would have information about the kinds of fish that inhabit the Great Barrier Reef?

_____
_____
_____
_____
_____
_____

> GO ON

Answers

2 Ⓕ Ⓖ Ⓗ Ⓙ   3 Ⓐ Ⓑ Ⓒ Ⓓ   4 Ⓕ Ⓖ Ⓗ Ⓙ   5 Ⓐ Ⓑ Ⓒ Ⓓ

Here is a rough draft of the first part of Ken's paper. Read the rough draft carefully. Then answer questions 7–12.

The Great Barrier Reef

(1) The Great Barrier Reef forms the largest reef on earth. (2) It is 1,250 miles long and is made up of the hardened skeletons of millions of dead water animals called coral polyps. (3) The Great Barrier Reef located in the South Pacific Ocean. (4) It lies along the northeast coast of Australia. (5) The reef contains a system of deep channels, lagoons, shallow pools, underwater caves, and ledges. (6) The Great Barrier Reef forms a breakwater, or wall, against the ocean. (7) The reef is constantly battered by ocean waves.

(8) Billions of living coral polyps make their home on the reef. (9) Some of these sea creatures are as big as a dime others are as tiny as a pinhead. (10) Their brilliant colors include green, yellow, blue, red, and purple. (11) Coral takes calcium from the ocean, changes it into lime, and uses the lime to construct its home on top of the dead coral. (12) I was impressed with the quality and taste of the fish. (13) In this home the coral remains for life.

(14) In 1770, Captain James Cook was the first person to lead an expedition to explore the Great Barrier Reef. (15) He was the captain of the ship *Endeavor;* and, perhaps, he was its navigator. (16) This flat-bottomed wooden ship was 106 feet long and 29 feet wide. (17) Cook and his crew explored the coast of Australia.

GO ON

7 Which group of words is *not* a complete sentence?

    F 1

    G 2

    H 3

    J 4

8 Which is the topic sentence of the second paragraph?

    A 8

    B 9

    C 10

    D 11

9 Which sentence could be added after sentence 7?

    F Captain James Cook explored many islands in the Pacific Ocean.

    G The reef is sturdy, however, providing a home to thousands of sea creatures.

    H Barracuda can be seen hunting herring in the lagoons.

    J The colorful coral is harvested for jewelry.

10 Which sentence does not belong in Ken's paper?

    A 9

    B 10

    C 11

    D 12

11 In sentence 15, the word *perhaps* does not appropriately connect the ideas. Which word or words should be used instead?

    F however

    G then

    H thirdly

    J in addition

12 Rewrite sentence 13 making the idea clearer.

_____

_____

_____

_____

_____

_____

_____

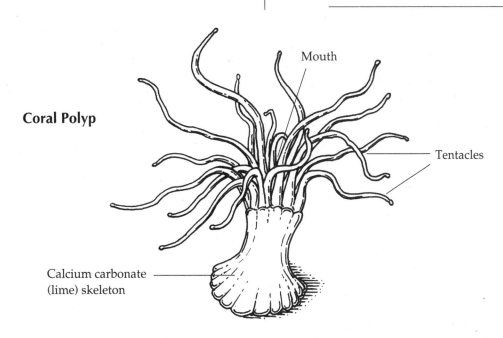

Coral Polyp

Mouth

Tentacles

Calcium carbonate (lime) skeleton

▶ **GO ON**

Answers

  7 Ⓕ Ⓖ Ⓗ Ⓙ   **8** Ⓐ Ⓑ Ⓒ Ⓓ   **9** Ⓕ Ⓖ Ⓗ Ⓙ   **10** Ⓐ Ⓑ Ⓒ Ⓓ   **11** Ⓕ Ⓖ Ⓗ Ⓙ

Here is the next part of Ken's rough draft for his paper. This part has certain words and phrases underlined. Read the draft carefully. Then answer questions 13–20.

Life is dangerous for the sea creatures of the Great Barrier Reef.
(18)

Most need protection from predators, or creatures that kill other
(19)

animals for food. Many animals are able to survived because their
(20)

colors or patterns camouflage them. For example, some brightly colored
(21)

fish live among the brightly colored corals and blend in with their

surroundings. Other fish change colors to match their surroundings.
(22)

Octopi are able to change their colors instantly. She can change quickly
(23)   (24)

from brown to blue to white to green to red to purple to stripes!

Lagoons, shallow ponds with no place to hide are dangerous places
(25)

for colorful fish. The bright colors of these fish would make it easy for
(26)

predators to see them. Therefore, fish that live in lagoons have dull
(27)

colors for protection.

The sea creatures of Australia's famous Reef have other ways of
(28)

protecting themselves from predators. For example, sea urchins have
(29)

long spines. They use these spines to prick or poison they predators. Sea
(30)   (31)

urchins also use the spines to secure their position in openings in coral.

A small sea slug, or nudibranch has no shell. It protects itself from
(32)   (33)

predators, by using poison. However, it doesn't produce its own poison.
(34)

Instead, this sea slug eats the poisonous parts of another sea creature,
(35)

the sea anemone. The sea slug can also sting predators with its tentacles.
(36)

GO ON

13 In sentence 18, <u>Life is dangerous</u> is best written—

    A Life was dangerous

    B Life are dangerous

    C Life were dangerous

    D As it is written.

14 In sentence 20, <u>survived</u> is best written—

    F has survived

    G survive

    H have survived

    J As it is written.

15 In sentence 24, <u>She can change</u> is best written—

    A They can change

    B He can change

    C We can change

    D As it is written.

16 Correctly rewrite sentence 25, <u>Lagoons, shallow ponds with no place to hide are dangerous places for colorful fish.</u>

    _____

    _____

    _____

    _____

    _____

17 In sentence 28, <u>Australia's famous Reef</u> is best written—

    F australia's famous reef

    G Australia's famous reef

    H Australia's Famous Reef

    J As it is written.

18 In sentence 30, <u>poison they predators</u> is best written—

    A poison our predators

    B poison his predators

    C poison their predators

    D As it is written.

19 In sentence 32, <u>small sea slug, or nudibranch</u> is best written—

    F small sea slug or nudibranch

    G small, sea, slug or nudibranch

    H small sea slug, or nudibranch,

    J As it is written.

20 Correctly rewrite sentence 33, <u>It protects itself from predators, by using poison.</u>

    _____

    _____

    _____

    _____

    _____

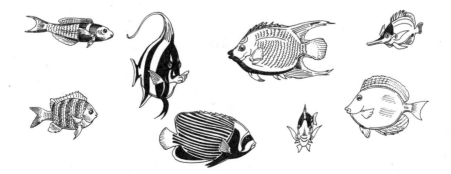

STOP

Answers

13 Ⓐ Ⓑ Ⓒ Ⓓ   **15** Ⓐ Ⓑ Ⓒ Ⓓ   **18** Ⓐ Ⓑ Ⓒ Ⓓ

14 Ⓕ Ⓖ Ⓗ Ⓙ   **17** Ⓕ Ⓖ Ⓗ Ⓙ   **19** Ⓕ Ⓖ Ⓗ Ⓙ

Identifying Misspelled Words

Directions: Read each sentence carefully. If one of the words is misspelled, darken the circle for that word. If all the words are spelled correctly, then darken the circle for *No mistake*.

TRY THIS	Read each sentence carefully. If you are not sure of an answer, first decide which answer choices are spelled correctly. Then see if you can recognize the misspelled word from your reading experience.

Sample A

We were <u>planning</u> to get <u>something</u> to eat at <u>intramission</u>. <u>No mistake</u>
        A   B   C   D

THINK IT THROUGH	The correct answer is <u>C</u>. The prefix should be <u>inter–</u>, not <u>intra–</u>. The correct spelling is i-n-t-e-r-m-i-s-s-i-o-n.

🛑 STOP

1   The two groups <u>reached</u> a <u>compromise</u> after a week of <u>discussion</u>. <u>No mistake</u>
                     A   B   C   D

2   Mr. McDonough will <u>announce</u> his <u>candidatcy</u> at a press <u>conference</u> next Friday. <u>No mistake</u>
                             F   G   H   J

3   We <u>purifyed</u> the water with an <u>iodine</u> <u>tablet</u>. <u>No mistake</u>
      A   B   C   D

4   Toshi's quick <u>reaction</u> <u>avertted</u> a potential <u>accident</u>. <u>No mistake</u>
                 F   G   H   J

5   I am <u>doutful</u> that we will <u>arrive</u> in time for <u>dinner</u>. <u>No mistake</u>
         A   B   C   D

6   The loud music <u>coming</u> from next door <u>intrafered</u> with my <u>concentration</u>. <u>No mistake</u>
                 F   G   H   J

7   The puppy was <u>wimpering</u> <u>outside</u> the door when she <u>arrived</u> home. <u>No mistake</u>
                A   B   C   D

8   The <u>souls</u> of my boots <u>need</u> to be <u>replaced</u>. <u>No mistake</u>
        F   G   H   J

🛑 STOP

Answers

SA Ⓐ Ⓑ ● Ⓓ   2 Ⓕ Ⓖ Ⓗ Ⓙ   4 Ⓕ Ⓖ Ⓗ Ⓙ   6 Ⓕ Ⓖ Ⓗ Ⓙ   8 Ⓕ Ⓖ Ⓗ Ⓙ

1 Ⓐ Ⓑ Ⓒ Ⓓ   3 Ⓐ Ⓑ Ⓒ Ⓓ   5 Ⓐ Ⓑ Ⓒ Ⓓ   7 Ⓐ Ⓑ Ⓒ Ⓓ

Test

Sample A

The world's first public railroad opened
(1)
in England in 1825. It operated between
(2)
the towns of Stockton and Darlington, a

distance of 20 miles.

By 1830 railways were operating in
(3)
France, Germany, Canada, Spain and,

Switzerland.

How is sentence 3 best written?

A   By 1830 railways were operating in France and Germany, Canada, Spain and Switzerland.

B   By 1830 railways were operating in, France, Germany, Canada, Spain, and Switzerland.

C   By 1830 railways were operating in France, Germany, Canada, Spain, and Switzerland.

D   As it is written.

STOP

The Olympic Games

Carl hopes to attend the next summer Olympic Games. Carl decides to write a letter to the United States Olympic Committee to learn more about the Olympics.

Carl used a dictionary to look up some words he wants to use in his letter to the United States Olympic Committee.

1   **Carl wants to find books about the history of the Olympic Games. Which kind of card catalog will best help him find a book about the Olympic Games?**

   A   Title

   B   Author

   C   Bibliography

   D   Subject

2   **Why is Carl writing a letter to the United States Olympic Committee?**

   _____

   _____

   _____

   _____

   _____

   _____

   _____

3   **What is the correct way to divide pentathlon into syllables?**

   F   pen ta thlon

   G   pen tath lon

   H   pent a thlon

   J   pent ath lon

4   **The "a" in pentathlon sounds most like the vowel sound in—**

   A   handkerchief

   B   negative

   C   partnership

   D   everyday

GO ON

Answers
SA Ⓐ Ⓑ Ⓒ Ⓓ   1 Ⓐ Ⓑ Ⓒ Ⓓ   3 Ⓕ Ⓖ Ⓗ Ⓙ   4 Ⓐ Ⓑ Ⓒ Ⓓ

91

Here is a rough draft of the first part of Carl's letter. Read the rough draft carefully. Then answer questions 5 and 6.

Dear U.S. Olympic Committee Members,

    I am an enthusiastic fan of the Olympic Games! I especially, the
    (1)   **(2)**

events in the Summer Games. I am writing for more information about
                              (3)

the Olympics.

    I know the Olympic Games consist of the Summer Games and the
    (4)

Winter Games. How is it decided where the games will be held? What
             (5)   **(6)**

events are held in the Summer Games, and what are held in the

Winter Games?

    I never miss the opening ceremonies of each Olympic Game. The
    (7)   **(8)**

lighting of the Olympic Flame is awesome! I've read that the lighted
                           (9)

torch is brought from the valley of Olympia, Greece, by cross-country

runners. My aunt lived in Greece for a year. What other traditions are
        (10)   **(11)**

practiced at the opening ceremonies of the Olympic Games?

---

5 **What is the best way to write sentence 2?**

  F I especially, enjoy the events in the Summer Games.

  G I, especially, enjoy the events in the summer games.

  H I especially enjoy the events in the Summer Games.

  J As it is written.

6 **Which sentence does *not* belong in this letter? Write the number.**

_____

_____

_____

_____

_____

_____

►GO ON►

Answers
  5 Ⓕ Ⓖ Ⓗ Ⓙ

Here is the next part of Carl's rough draft for his letter. This part has certain words and phrases underlined. Read the draft carefully. Then answer questions 7–12.

I have read that an Olympic athlete must be a citizen of the sponsor country.
(12)

Does an athlete actually have to live in the country they represent?
(13)

Starting with the 1988 Olympics professional athletes were allowed to compete.
(14)

National Olympic committees are allowed to pay our athletes while they train
(15)

for the Olympics. How much money does the United States Olympic Committee
(16)

pay athletes?

In "Modern Olympic Games the fifth chapter of *A History of the Olympics*, I
(17)

read that each country is allowed to use its own method for selecting athletes for

the Games. To be chosen from the United States, an athlete must finish high in
(18)

the competitions. Will this method of selection ever change?
(19)

How are Olympic events judged? I know that in diving, figure skating, and
(20)   (21)

gymnastics events, medalists are chosen by judges based on points awarded for

their performances. How are medalists chosen in swimming and track events?
(22)

I have one last question. Is it true that the Olympic Games were canceled
(23)   (24)

during world Wars I and II?

I look forward to receiving answers to my questions. I appreciate your time
(25)   (26)

and attention.

Sincerely yours,
Carl Hafner

7 In sentence 13, <u>they represent?</u> is best written—

    A he or she represents?

    B you represent?

    C we represent?

    D As it is written.

8 In sentence 14, <u>Starting with the 1988 Olympics</u> is best written—

    F Starting with the 1988, Olympics

    G Starting with the 1988 Olympics,

    H Starting, with the 1988 Olympics

    J As it is written.

9 What word should be substituted for "our" in sentence 15, <u>pay our athletes?</u>

    _____

    _____

    _____

    _____

    _____

10 Correctly rewrite sentence 17, "<u>Modern Olympic Games the fifth</u>—

    A "Modern Olympic Games," the fifth

    B Modern Olympic Games the fifth

    C "Modern Olympic" Games the fifth

    D As it is written.

11 In sentence 21, <u>in diving, figure skating, and gymnastics</u> is best written—

    F in diving, figure, skating, and gymnastics

    G in diving figure skating and gymnastics

    H in diving, figure skating and, gymnastics

    J As it is written.

12 In sentence 24, <u>world Wars I and II?</u> is best written—

    A world war one and two?

    B World war I and II?

    C World Wars I and II?

    D As it is written.

For questions 13–24, read each sentence carefully. If one of the words is misspelled, darken the circle for that word. If all the words are spelled correctly, then darken the circle for *No mistake.*

13   Dr. Rivera <u>treats</u> a number of <u>patience</u> at the West Side <u>Clinic</u>. <u>No mistake</u>
                    F   G   H   J

14   The <u>pressure</u> <u>intensifyed</u> as the gymnastics competition moved into the final <u>stages</u>. <u>No mistake</u>
                  A   B   C   D

15   The <u>winning</u> rose at the <u>annual</u> garden show has a <u>suttle</u> fragrance. <u>No mistake</u>
              F   G   H   J

16   The <u>manager</u> gave us <u>complementary</u> tickets to the next matinee. <u>No mistake</u>
              A   B   C   D

17   Mary <u>canceled</u> her <u>reservation</u> when she <u>herd</u> the news. <u>No mistake</u>
                F   G   H   J

18   Beautiful <u>frescoes</u> <u>adorned</u> the walls of the <u>ancient</u> temple. <u>No mistake</u>
                    A   B   C   D

19   <u>Literatcy</u> <u>continues</u> to be an important <u>issue</u> in our country. <u>No mistake</u>
        F   G   H   J

20   The United Nations is a <u>truly</u> <u>intranational</u> <u>organization</u>. <u>No mistake</u>
                                  A   B   C   D

21   The <u>seem</u> on my shirt <u>started</u> to <u>unravel</u>. <u>No mistake</u>
              F   G   H   J

22   The American team <u>prevailled</u> over the German team in the <u>volleyball</u> <u>match</u>. <u>No mistake</u>
                         A   B   C   D

23   Reynaldo was a <u>talented</u> <u>amateur</u> tennis <u>player</u>. <u>No mistake</u>
                      F   G   H   J

24   My <u>grandfather</u> liked to sit on the <u>porch</u> swing in the evening and <u>wittle</u>. <u>No mistake</u>
              A   B   C   D

Answers

13 Ⓕ Ⓖ Ⓗ Ⓙ	**16** Ⓐ Ⓑ Ⓒ Ⓓ	**19** Ⓕ Ⓖ Ⓗ Ⓙ	**22** Ⓐ Ⓑ Ⓒ Ⓓ	
14 Ⓐ Ⓑ Ⓒ Ⓓ	**17** Ⓕ Ⓖ Ⓗ Ⓙ	**20** Ⓐ Ⓑ Ⓒ Ⓓ	**23** Ⓕ Ⓖ Ⓗ Ⓙ	
15 Ⓕ Ⓖ Ⓗ Ⓙ	**18** Ⓐ Ⓑ Ⓒ Ⓓ	**21** Ⓕ Ⓖ Ⓗ Ⓙ	**24** Ⓐ Ⓑ Ⓒ Ⓓ	

Practice Test 1

Reading Comprehension

Sample A

Cliff Dwellings

Mesa Verde National Park is located in southwestern Colorado and has some of the most astounding cliff dwellings found in the United States. Approximately eight hundred years ago, the Anasazi people used stone blocks to construct apartment-like dwellings in the caves of the canyon walls.

Which of these is a *fact* stated in the selection?

  A The cliff dwellings have lasted because they were built well.

  B The cliff dwellings were never completed.

  C The Anasazi should have built with brick.

  D The Anasazi cliff dwellings were like apartments.

For questions 1–33, carefully read each selection and the questions that follow. Darken the circle for the correct answer, or write in your answer.

Chicago

Skyscrapers tower
along Lake Michigan
like building blocks.

They seem to lean
toward one another
as if for support.

In their glass sides we see
a reflection in primary colors
of sunset, water, and parks.

Unknowing, they take in
their surroundings and return them
to us as a dream.

1 **The poem compares the reflection from the skyscrapers' glass sides to—**

  A real life.

  B a dream.

  C a subconscious desire.

  D an artist's inspiration.

2 **This poem was probably written to describe—**

  F how Chicago's skyscrapers look.

  G how Chicago is not a dream.

  H a sunset on Lake Michigan.

  J buildings that look like they are dreaming.

3 **The buildings are compared to—**

  A sunsets.

  B blocks.

  C parks.

  D glass.

GO ON

Recycling Plastics

The best way to solve the problem of throw-away plastics is to find practical ways to reuse them. Many useful things are being made from recycled plastics. There are more than fifty types of plastics in use. They are made using a variety of chemicals, dyes, and processes. The different properties of plastics make them suitable for different types of recycled products. The chart below shows the types of plastic products used to recycle into new products. The six codes allow recyclers to separate plastics into groups of types that have the same properties.

PLASTICS RECYCLING CHART

Symbol	Uses	Recycled Products (made from recyclable plastics)
1 PETE	Plastic soft drink bottles, mouthwash jars, peanut butter and salad dressing bottles	Liquid soap bottles, strapping, fiberfill for winter coats, surfboards, paintbrushes, fuzz on tennis balls, soft drink bottles, film, egg cartons, skis, carpets, boats
2 HDPE	Milk, water, and juice containers; grocery bags; toys; liquid detergent bottles	Soft drink bottle base cups, flowerpots, drain pipes, signs, stadium seats, trash cans, recycling bins, traffic-barrier cones, golf bag liners, detergent bottles, toys
3 V	Clear food packaging, shampoo bottles	Floor mats, pipes, hose, mud flaps
4 LDPE	Bread bags, frozen food bags, grocery bags	Garbage bag liners, grocery bags, multipurpose bags
5 PP	Ketchup bottles, yogurt containers and margarine tubs, medicine bottles	Manhole steps, paint buckets, videocassette storage cases, ice scrapers, fast food trays, lawn mower wheels, automobile battery parts
6 PS	Videocassette cases, compact disk jackets, coffee cups, knives, spoons, forks, cafeteria trays, grocery meat trays, fast food sandwich containers	License plate holders, golf course and septic tank drainage systems, desktop accessories, hanging files, food service trays, flower pots, trash cans, videocassettes

GO ON

4 What is the code symbol for plastic products that can be recycled into hose?

F PP

G V

H HDPE

J PS

5 What is the correct code number for such products as bread bags and grocery bags?

A 1

B 3

C 4

D 5

6 What is the purpose of the symbols on plastic products?

F to make it easy for recyclers to sort plastics

G to indicate to consumers what new products will be made from the product

H to indicate to scientists the properties of the product

J to indicate to stores how much to charge for the product

7 Which of the following shows an original product and its recyclable product?

A peanut butter jars into mud flaps

B detergent bottles into grocery bags

C bread bags into surfboards

D medicine bottles into ice scrapers

8 List three recyclable products that can be made from videocassette cases and compact disk jackets.

_____

_____

_____

_____

_____

9 If you wanted to learn more about recycling plastics, which of the following articles would you choose to read?

F "Solving the Solid Waste Problem"

G "The History of Durable Goods"

H "Plastic Surgery Success Stories"

J "Manufacturing Plastics"

10 If the author added a sentence to the end of the introduction, which of these would best fit?

A Plastic "wood" never rots or splinters or gets termites.

B Then the plastics, grouped by code, can be shipped to companies that recycle plastics.

C Plastics are strong and used for thousands of purposes.

D Too many plastic products are disposed of immediately after using them just once.

11 Which code symbol is used for original plastic products that can be turned into recyclable plastic products such as skis, egg cartons, and film?

_____

_____

_____

_____

_____

GO ON

The Magic Tapestry: A Chinese Folktale

Long ago a widow lived in a cottage with her three sons. She supported the family by weaving tapestries. The tapestries were exquisite works of art that sold for much gold. One day the widow started a new tapestry. She wove into her fabric a magnificent mansion surrounded by brilliant flower gardens. Receding into the distance were rolling hills and towering mountains. Every day for months the widow worked on the tapestry. With *painstaking* care she added intricate details. She created a babbling brook with exotic fish, then wove a graceful footbridge.

Meanwhile Li Mo, her eldest son, and Li Tu, her middle son, began complaining. "When are you going to finish? We have no rice, and our clothes are ragged," Li Mo said. "Hurry and finish so that we can sell the tapestry," Li Tu demanded.

But their mother said nothing. She continued working at the loom from sunrise until late at night. Li Ju, her youngest son, became a woodcutter so that the family could eat.

One day after toiling for more than a year, the widow announced that the tapestry was almost complete. As Li Ju watched, she wove a resemblance of herself into the wall hanging. "This must be your dream," Li Ju said with conviction. The widow wove Li Ju's image into the work.

The other two brothers came in and tried to pry the tapestry off the loom. But their mother wouldn't let them touch it. She said, "This is a picture of everything I wish for and cherish. All my children should be in it, but I haven't had time to weave you in."

"What does it matter? Just give it to us so that we can sell it," Li Mo said. "Yes, all we care about is the gold," Li Tu added cruelly.

Just then a tremendous wind ripped the tapestry from the loom. The treasured work flew out the window and vanished into the eastern sky. The family raced outside but could not *retrieve* it. The widow was devastated. She called Li Mo and told him to travel east in search of the tapestry. "If you don't find it, I will surely die," she said.

Li Mo traveled east for a month; then he came to an old woman who lived in a stone hut. Outside the hut was a stone stallion. The woman told Li Mo that the fairies of Sun Mountain had stolen the tapestry. She said that Li Mo should pierce his finger and bleed on the stone horse. The stallion would take him to Sun Mountain. The old woman described the fiery mountains and icy seas he would have to cross on his journey. Li Mo shuddered at the thought of blood, fire, and ice. But when the old woman offered him a bag of gold, he gladly took it and journeyed to the big city, forgetting about the tapestry.

The widow was becoming weaker. When Li Mo did not return she sent Li Tu. But when Li Tu met the old woman in the hut he also accepted the gold and went to the big city. Li Ju pleaded with his mother to let him search for the tapestry. He knew that his mother was very ill.

When Li Ju reached the stone hut, he eagerly listened to the old woman's instructions. When she offered him a bag of gold, he refused. "I must find the tapestry or my mother will die," he said. Courageously he galloped through the fires and over the icy seas. At last he arrived at Sun Mountain. He was greeted by a beautiful fairy dressed in crimson. The fairy said that she would return the tapestry. The next morning she folded it and handed it to Li Ju. She bid him farewell, and Li Ju journeyed homeward. He hurried because he knew his mother must be near death. Finally he arrived and hung the tapestry on the wall so that his mother could see it. Magically the tapestry expanded until it became a giant landscape. Mother and son walked into the peaceful scene. Waiting for them at the door of the mansion was the fairy dressed in crimson. Li Ju married the fairy, and the three of them lived contentedly on the lovely estate.

One day two beggars who were really Li Mo and Li Tu knocked at the iron gate of the mansion. But a ferocious windstorm carried them away and deposited them on a desolate road. Each beggar held a tattered piece of tapestry in his hands.

GO ON

12 Where does this story take place?

F in Japan

G in China

H in India

J in Thailand

13 The widow supported her family by—

A cutting wood.

B selling weaving equipment.

C weaving beautiful tapestries.

D sewing clothes for rich people.

14 In this story, *painstaking* means—

F causing intense pain.

G great speed.

H over and over again.

J careful attention to detail.

15 By complaining about the time that their mother spent on the tapestry, Li Mo and Li Tu show that—

A they are worried about their mother's health.

B they are anxious to learn how to weave.

C they are concerned only about themselves.

D they dislike the tapestry.

16 Why did the widow work so long and hard on the new tapestry?

_____

_____

_____

_____

_____

_____

17 Li Mo and Li Tu were beggars because—

F they could not find steady work.

G they had been fired from their jobs.

H they were sick and could not find work.

J they had spent all their gold in the city and were too lazy to work.

18 In this story, the word *retrieve* means—

A sell.

B throw.

C get back.

D return.

19 Why were Li Mo and Li Tu swept by a ferocious windstorm?

F They were being punished.

G They were in the wrong place at the wrong time.

H It was the windy season.

J The fairy wanted them to go to Sun Mountain.

20 What lessons can be learned from this story?

_____

_____

_____

_____

_____

_____

_____

GO ON

A Great American Patriot

Paul Revere was made famous by the poet Henry Wadsworth Longfellow in the poem "Paul Revere's Ride." Other details of Revere's life are less well-known, but probably as important to the effort to free the American colonies from British rule.

Revere was born in 1735 in Boston, Massachusetts, and was of French descent. His father was a silversmith, which is why Revere learned that trade while he also studied at Boston's North Grammar School.

Revere's work as the leader of the Boston craftworkers fired his interest in freedom for the American colonies. He worked alongside Samuel Adams and John Hancock—two revolutionary leaders. Revere was a *co-conspirator* in the Boston Tea Party. He created engravings of political cartoons in support of American liberty. He often delivered special messages to Boston patriots.

During the Revolutionary War, Paul Revere commanded a unit at Castle William in Boston Harbor. He later led the artillery division in a failed attempt to recapture control of land in Maine. *Accusations* of cowardice and disobedience were filed against Revere in connection with this failed attempt. He was found not guilty at his court-martial and later left the service.

Revere's other contributions to the Revolutionary War effort included the manufacture of gunpowder for the Continental Army, the designing and printing of the Continental currency, and the creation of the state seal that is still used by Massachusetts. In addition, Revere's knowledge of metal working was helpful when he made bronze cannons for the army.

Revere's silversmithing trade continued after the war. His silver tea sets are prized possessions for those fortunate enough to own them. He also cast bronze bells that are still used in parts of New England today. His skill was put to good use when he made the copper fittings for the warship *U.S.S. Constitution*, also known as *Old Ironsides*.

GO ON

21 Why did Paul Revere learn the trade of silversmithing?

    A He learned the trade at Boston's North Grammar School.

    B He wanted to work with Samuel Adams.

    C His father was a silversmith.

    D He wanted to make copper fittings for warships.

22 What is the third paragraph *mainly* about?

    F Paul Revere's military career

    G Paul Revere's work in the American colonies' fight for freedom

    H Paul Revere's work as a silversmith

    J Paul Revere's education

23 In this selection, *co-conspirator* means—

    A one of many who were arrested.

    B a famous society person.

    C part owner.

    D one who secretly plots with others.

24 Which of Paul Revere's contributions to the Revolutionary War effort is the most famous?

    F the manufacture of gunpowder for the Continental Army

    G the design and printing of the Continental currency

    H his engravings of political cartoons

    J his ride to warn the American colonists that the British were coming

25 In this selection, the word *accusations* means—

    A formal charges.

    B proven lies.

    C military honors.

    D idle rumors.

26 There is enough information in this article to show that—

    F Paul Revere contributed in many ways to American freedom.

    G Paul Revere was the best soldier during the Revolutionary War.

    H Paul Revere was an excellent student at Boston's North Grammar School.

    J Paul Revere was a disappointing silversmith.

27 The web shows some ideas discussed in the selection.

```
                  Paul Revere
                 /           \
          Childhood           [          ]
          /      \            /         \
  born in   studied at   commanded   led an
  Boston    Boston's     a unit      artillery
            North                    division
            Grammar
            School
```

What word(s) would go in the empty box?

_____

_____

_____

_____

_____

_____

_____

_____

GO ON

SPEEDAWAY

The only name in bicycles. Our bicycles are the fastest ones on the road. That's why SPEEDAWAY is the bicycle brand you know and trust.

We make our bicycles with the customer in mind. Each bicycle is a SUPERIOR machine. You can't buy anything better. We guarantee that this bicycle will not be the CHEAPEST one you can buy. But we do guarantee that it is the best BRAND you can buy.

Our bicycles offer many special features. Here are some of them:

- 21-speeds

- Light-touch gear shifts for easy and accurate shifting

- Hand-pull caliper brakes

- 2-inch white side-wall tires

- Jelly-filled, cushioned seat

- 26-inch aluminum frame—This NEW and IMPROVED frame combines a reliably sturdy frame with the weight of a feather to produce a bicycle that literally flies down the road.

- 5-function electronic trip monitor that displays: speed, distance, average speed per mile, calories burned per mile, and length of time.

We truly believe in our bicycles. We are so sure you will like our bicycles that we will give you THREE FREE GIFTS—a safety helmet, a water bottle, and a pouch bag—when you purchase a SPEEDAWAY bicycle. If you are not satisfied with your bicycle, you may return it for your money back. BUT YOU GET TO KEEP THE FREE GIFTS!

Hurry on down to your local sporting goods store. If they don't have this bicycle, it's because they're sold out! Everyone carries our brand.

Buy SPEEDAWAY! You'll thank yourself for many years to come.

GO ON

28 Which of these is an *opinion* in the ad?

   A You can't buy anything better…

   B …electronic trip monitor that displays: speed, distance, …

   C …you may return it for your money back…

   D …you get to keep the free gifts…

29 All of these are features of the Speedaway bicycle *except*—

   F 2-inch white-wall tires.

   G a see-through plastic bug shield.

   H hand-pull caliper brakes.

   J a jelly-filled cushioned seat.

30 There is enough information in the ad to show that this product is—

   A made in the United States.

   B sold in most sporting goods stores.

   C the poorest-selling bicycle in the country.

   D used by most professional sports stars.

31 This ad was written mainly to tell about—

   F the many products made by the manufacturers of the Speedaway brand bicycle.

   G a new invention that is being sold.

   H the many features of a brand-name bicycle.

   J the stores where you can buy bicycles.

32 The ad tries to appeal to your desire to—

   A buy a brand-name bicycle.

   B have a bicycle like your best friend's bicycle.

   C spend less money.

   D look good.

33 The ad states that if you are not satisfied with the bicycle you may return it, get your money back, and keep the free gifts. Why do you think the company is making this offer?

   _____

   _____

   _____

   _____

   _____

   _____

   _____

   _____

STOP

Reading Vocabulary

Sample A

Something that is <u>desolate</u> is—

A happy

B bright

C bleak

D colorful

For questions 1–8, darken the circle for the word or group of words that has the same or almost the same meaning as the underlined word.

1 <u>Sequence</u> means—

A one at a time

B all at once

C in order

D as a group

2 <u>Puny</u> means—

F large

G significant

H tiny

J attractive

3 To <u>confirm</u> is to—

A believe

B contain

C choose

D prove

4 To <u>attain</u> something is to—

F lose it

G achieve it

H fail it

J confuse it

5 A <u>cunning</u> person is—

A popular

B sly

C educated

D well-known

6 Someone who is <u>fashionable</u> is—

F outdated

G clumsy

H crude

J stylish

7 A <u>smirk</u> is a kind of—

A smile

B cloth

C sound

D insult

8 Something that is <u>severe</u> is—

F weak

G harsh

H complete

J empty

▶ GO ON

Sample B

> Mom asked Tom to load the groceries into the car.

In which sentence does load have the same meaning as it does in the sentence above?

A   The mule carried a heavy load.

B   Her letter took a load off my mind.

C   Did you load the film into the camera?

D   We drove the load of potatoes to market.

For questions 9–13, darken the circle for the sentence in which the underlined word means the same as it does in the sentence in the box.

9
> The old prospector found a gold mine.

In which sentence does mine have the same meaning as it does in the sentence above?

A   The library is a mine of information.

B   Is this sweater yours or mine?

C   They own an agate mine.

D   Do they mine harbors with explosives?

10
> I lost my ring near the tennis net.

In which sentence does net have the same meaning as it does in the sentence above?

F   She will net the fish.

G   The net weight of the package is 9 ounces.

H   Grandma always wears a hair net to bed at night.

J   Will he net any profits from his investments?

11
> The meteorologists will track the hurricane.

In which sentence does track have the same meaning as it does in the sentence above?

A   What animal made this track?

B   Jimmy was about to track mud on the new carpet.

C   I was able to track the injured animal into the woods.

D   Dr. Lee knows he's on the right track with his research.

12
> The Mississippi River is a major waterway.

In which sentence does major have the same meaning as it does in the sentence above?

F   Is this symphony in a major key?

G   My uncle held the army rank of major.

H   I plan to major in science in college.

J   Suzanne spends the major part of her time studying.

13
> Louisa will begin first grade in the fall.

In which sentence does grade have the same meaning as it does in the sentence above?

A   What is the highest grade of beef?

B   Kareem is now in the sixth grade.

C   I will try to grade all your papers tonight.

D   Renee has taken a grade six government job.

▶ GO ON

106

Sample C

We tried to <u>procure</u> enough supplies to last for five days. <u>Procure</u> means—

A acquire

B pack

C find

D borrow

STOP

For questions 14–21, darken the circle for the word or words that give the meaning of the underlined word, or write in the answer.

14 My throat was <u>parched</u> after three hours in the sun. <u>Parched</u> means—

F sore

G red

H dry

J wet

15 The expert says that bowl is <u>authentic</u> Wedgwood china. <u>Authentic</u> means—

A ancient

B genuine

C false

D elegant

16 Janet did not care for his <u>brash</u> manner. <u>Brash</u> means—

F polite

G intelligent

H rude

J quiet

17 The <u>flaw</u> in the fabric made it unusable. <u>Flaw</u> means—

_____

_____

_____

_____

18 Many words are confusing because they have <u>multiple</u> meanings. <u>Multiple</u> means—

A individual

B few

C long

D several

19 The <u>horde</u> of aggressive reporters following the movie star was a big problem. <u>Horde</u> means—

F small group

G crowd

H few

J individual

20 Sandra said that she will <u>strive</u> to make the basketball team no matter how much work it takes. <u>Strive</u> means—

A try

B ask

C quit

D rest

21 Max was <u>flabbergasted</u> by the number of people who came to his birthday party. <u>Flabbergasted</u> means—

_____

_____

_____

_____

STOP

107

Part 1: Math Problem Solving

Sample A

Which fraction is greater than $\frac{5}{8}$?

A $\frac{2}{4}$ C $\frac{3}{4}$

B $\frac{2}{7}$ D $\frac{3}{5}$

 STOP

For questions 1–47, darken the circle for the correct answer, or write in the answer.

1 Which of the following decimals is greater than 0.273 and less than 0.291?

  A 0.279

  B 0.295

  C 0.259

  D 0.209

2 The number line shows 4 mice in a race. Which mouse is in the lead?

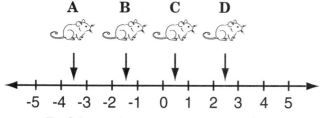

  F Mouse A

  G Mouse B

  H Mouse C

  J Mouse D

3 The temperature reading was –15°C at sunrise. By 3:00 P.M., the temperature had risen 20°. What was the temperature then?

_____

_____

4 At the candy store, 4 children each grabbed a handful of wrapped candy from the candy bin. The candy cost $1.49 per pound. The first child's handful of candy weighed $\frac{1}{3}$ pound. The second child's handful weighed $\frac{2}{5}$ pound, the third child's weighed $\frac{3}{10}$ pound, and the fourth's weighed $\frac{1}{4}$ pound. Which shows these amounts arranged in order from largest to smallest?

  A $\frac{2}{5}, \frac{1}{3}, \frac{3}{10}, \frac{1}{4}$

  B $\frac{3}{10}, \frac{1}{4}, \frac{2}{5}, \frac{1}{3}$

  C $\frac{1}{4}, \frac{2}{5}, \frac{3}{10}, \frac{1}{3}$

  D $\frac{1}{3}, \frac{2}{5}, \frac{1}{4}, \frac{3}{10}$

5 Which of these temperatures is colder than the temperature shown on the thermometer?

  F –6°

  G –2°

  H 3°

  J 0°

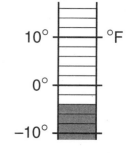

6 In the jet-engine racing car *Spirit of America*, a person can travel at 613.995 miles per hour. What is the value of the 5 in this number?

  A 5 ten-thousandths

  B 5 thousandths

  C 5 hundredths

  D 5 tenths

GO ON ▶

7 Madelynn lives 3 times as far from school as Liz does. If x is the number of blocks that Liz lives from school, which expression represents the distance Madelynn lives from school?

F $3x$

G $x - 3$

H $x + 3$

J $x/3$

8 Each ▱ represents 0.03.

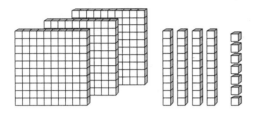

What decimal is shown by the figures above?

A 104

B 10.41

C 1.04

D 0.104

9 A special machine changes numbers according to a certain rule. The *out* number in the table shows the result when the rule is applied to the *in* number.

In	6	15	27
Out	2	5	9

What number will 24 be changed to ?

_____

_____

_____

_____

_____

10 Dexter does volunteer work at a local retirement village. He wants to take some of the residents to a movie. The tickets cost $4.00 each. Dexter figures that it will cost $6.00 to drive his van to and from the movie theater. Which expression can Dexter use to find C, the total cost of the outing?

F $C = 4 + 6 + n$

G $6n - 4 = C + 6$

H $C = 4n + 6$

J $6(4n) = C$

11 The Richter Scale measures the magnitude of earthquakes and ranks them on a scale of 1 to 10. Each number on the scale stands for 30 times the magnitude of the number just before it. For example, if a reading on the Richter Scale is 2 more than another quake, it is 30^2 times the magnitude. If an earthquake had a Richter Scale reading of 7, how would this be written to compare it to an earthquake with a Richter Scale reading of 2?

A 30^2

B 30^3

C 30^5

D 30^7

12 Look at the factor tree shown here.

Which numbers are missing from the factor tree?

F 2, 7

G 3, 6

H 4, 5

J 6, 9

13 When 30 students were surveyed, 6 stated that they watch $2\frac{1}{2}$ hours of television each day. If 450 students were surveyed, how many students could be expected to watch $2\frac{1}{2}$ hours of television each day?

A 5

B 20

C 90

D 420

14 Cybil was making a design for art class by gluing beads to posterboard. She had 2 beads in the first row, 5 beads in the second row, 8 beads in the third row, and 11 beads in the fourth row. If this pattern continues, how many beads will she use in each of the next 3 rows?

F 22, 25, 28

G 12, 15, 18

H 15, 19, 23

J 14, 17, 20

15 If digits cannot be repeated, how many 3-digit numbers can be made using only the digits 3, 5, 6, 8, and 9?

A 5

B 24

C 36

D 60

16 What is another way to write $(4 \times 6) + (4 \times 4)$?

_____

_____

_____

_____

_____

_____

_____

17 Howard used an air pump to launch a model rocket. The table shows the number of pumps required to launch the rocket to specific heights. If it continued to operate at this rate, how many pumps would be required to launch the rocket to a height of at least 100 feet?

Number of Pumps	Height in Feet
3	40
4	47.5
5	55
6	62.5
7	70

F 12

G 11

H 10

J 8

18 Angela has 6 nickels and 8 pennies in her coin purse. What is the probability that Angela will randomly pick a nickel out of her coin purse?

A $\frac{3}{7}$

B $\frac{1}{8}$

C $\frac{5}{5}$

D $\frac{1}{2}$

19 In how many different ways can the letters in the word *MATH* be arranged?

_____

_____

_____

_____

_____

_____

_____

▶ GO ON

Use the graph to answer questions 20–22.

Skate-Rite Monthly Sales

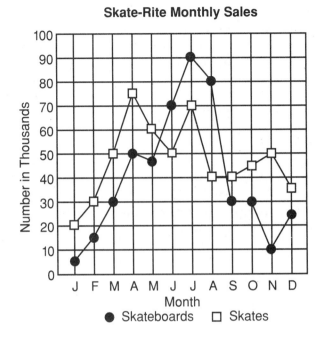

- ● Skateboards □ Skates

20 Which month on the graph shows the fewest sales of skateboards?

F January

G February

H September

J November

21 About how many more skates were sold in April than in November?

A 5,000

B 10,000

C 15,000

D 25,000

22 Describe the sale of skateboards between April and July.

_____

_____

_____

_____

In one week, a pet store made $1,000 in profits. The following graph shows the types of sales. Study the graph and answer questions 23 and 24.

PET STORE PROFITS

Total Profits = $1000

23 Which tally chart shows the data in the circle graph above?

F

Cats	ʖ ʖ ʖ ʖ
Dogs	ʖ ʖ ʖ
Fish	ʖ ʖ ʖ ʖ
Birds	ʖ ʖ ʖ
Other	ʖ ʖ

G

Cats	ʖ ʖ
Dogs	ʖ ʖ ʖ
Fish	ʖ ʖ ʖ ʖ IIII
Birds	ʖ ʖ ʖ I
Other	ʖ ʖ II

H

Cats	ʖ ʖ ʖ ʖ
Dogs	ʖ ʖ ʖ ʖ ʖ ʖ
Fish	ʖ ʖ ʖ ʖ IIII
Birds	ʖ ʖ ʖ ʖ
Other	ʖ

J

Cats	ʖ ʖ ʖ ʖ II
Dogs	ʖ ʖ ʖ II
Fish	ʖ ʖ ʖ ʖ ʖ I
Birds	ʖ ʖ ʖ III
Other	ʖ III

24 How much more did the store make from sales of dogs than sales of cats?

_____

_____

_____

GO ON

25 Which transformation moves the figure from position A to position B?

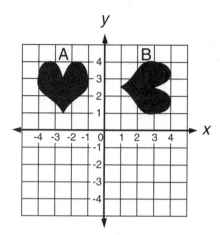

A   extension

B   rotation

C   reflection

D   translation

26 This bar graph shows Arnie's test scores in math class. What is his average (mean) score?

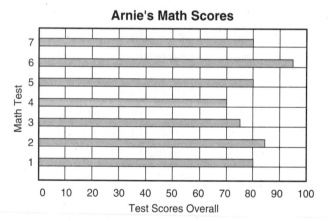

F   85

G   80

H   75

J   70

This table shows the prices and the number of shoes in stock in a shoe store. Study the table. Then answer questions 27 and 28.

Shoes in Stock		
Color	Number	Price per Pair
Red	54	$50
Brown	50	$35
Black	60	$36
Navy	46	$45

27 How many pairs of red shoes and navy shoes are in stock?

A   100

B   106

C   110

D   210

28 How much do 2 pairs of black shoes and 1 pair of navy shoes cost?

_____

_____

_____

_____

29 The diameter of circle J is represented by which line segment?

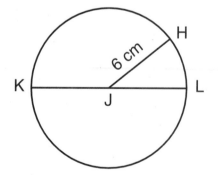

F $\overline{JH}$

G $\overline{JL}$

H $\overline{JK}$

J $\overline{KL}$

GO ON

30 Which coordinates best represent the location of Banner on the map?

A (4, 1)

B (3, 2)

C (2, 1)

D (2, 3)

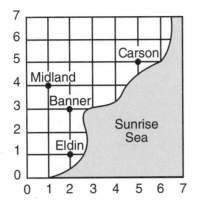

31 Which angle shown here is an acute angle?

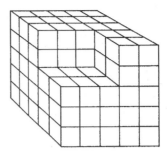

Use the two triangles shown here to answer question 32.

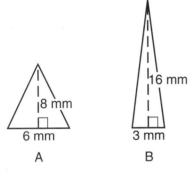

32 Which of the following statements about the two triangles is true?

A Triangle A is smaller in area than Triangle B.

B Both Triangle A and Triangle B have six angles that are right angles.

C The area of Triangle A is one-third larger than that of Triangle B.

D The area of Triangle A is equal to the area of Triangle B.

33 If each cube shown here represents 1 cubic unit, what is the volume of this figure?

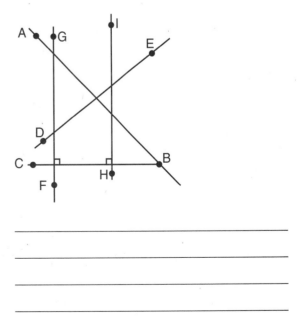

F 125 cubic units

G 113 cubic units

H 105 cubic units

J 25 cubic units

34 Each of the figures shown here can be folded to form a three-dimensional figure. Which can be folded to form a cube?

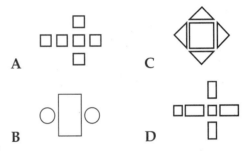

35 Which lines shown here are parallel?

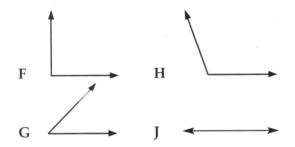

_____

_____

_____

_____

▶ **GO ON** ▶

113

36 What is the area of triangle DFG?
(Use $A = \frac{1}{2} bh$.)

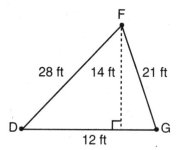

F 168 sq ft

G 84 sq ft

H 61 sq ft

J 49 sq ft

37 Larry wanted to bake granola bars for the club bake sale. Each batch took 1.5 cups of sugar. How many batches of granola bars could he make with a 3-quart container of sugar?

A 12

B 8

C 6

D 2

38 Which of the following metric units of measurement is best to use to measure the length of a room?

F meters

G liters

H centimeters

J kilograms

39 The picture shows that Toni is 10 yards from the tree. How many feet is that?

A 3 feet

B 30 feet

C 300 feet

D 3000 feet

40 For a history project, Jamie is making a scale drawing of the Washington Monument on a piece of posterboard that is $8\frac{1}{2}$ inches by 11 inches. If the monument is actually 555 feet high, what is a reasonable scale for her drawing?

F 1 in. represents 100 ft.

G 1 in. represents 10 ft.

H $\frac{1}{2}$ in. represents 1 ft.

J $\frac{1}{2}$ in. represents 10 ft.

41 The bus left the Dry Gulch Canyon bus station at 4:35 P.M. for a trip to Cherokee Flats that will take 2 hours and 50 minutes. At what time should the bus arrive at its destination?

_____

_____

_____

_____

_____

_____

▶ GO ON

42 The sum of the first two numerals in Max's apartment number is twice the sum of the last two numerals. Which of these could be Max's apartment number?

A 842

B 824

C 428

D 248

43 According to this table, about how much taller is the Sears Tower than the Empire State Building?

World's Tallest Skyscrapers	
Building	Height
Amoco	1,136 feet
Empire State Building	1,250 feet
John Hancock Center	1,127 feet
Sears Tower	1,454 feet
World Trade Center	1,350 feet

F 100 feet

G 150 feet

H 200 feet

J 300 feet

44 Which of the following units of measurement is best to use to describe the weight of a box of breakfast cereal?

A feet

B ounces

C liters

D inches

45 Marco took a box of popsicles to the park. He ate one and gave one to each of 5 friends. What do you need to know to find out how many popsicles Marco has left?

F how many friends chose grape popsicles

G how many popsicles altogether were in the box

H how many boxes of popsicles Marco ate at home

J how many orange popsicles were in the box

46 The cost of a pound of coffee is $3.69. The Martinez family buys 1.5 pounds of coffee each week. The Goldsmith family buys 2.5 pounds of coffee each week. Which question below cannot be answered using the data given above?

A What is the total weight of the coffee bought by the two families?

B What is the difference between the amount of coffee bought by the Martinez and Goldsmith families?

C How much coffee remains unused by each family at the end of the week?

D What would be the total cost of coffee bought by both families in one week?

47 Nora took swimming lessons before beginning piano lessons. She joined gymnastics class after beginning piano lessons. She began dance class before beginning swimming lessons. Which lessons did she begin first?

_____

_____

_____

_____

_____

_____

STOP

Sample A

Mr. Rafael uses his own truck at work. If he drove 128 miles last week, and 62 of those miles were for his personal use, how many miles did he drive on the job?

A 55 miles

B 58 miles

C 66 miles

D 190 miles

E NH

STOP

Sample B

196
× 9

F 954

G 1,764

H 1,954

J 9,764

K NH

STOP

For questions 1–14, darken the circle for the correct answer. If the correct answer is not given, darken the circle for *NH, Not Here*. If no choices are given, write in the answer.

1

208
× 14

A 2,812

B 2,912

C 2,922

D 3,912

E NH

2

$33\overline{)1746}$

F $22\frac{3}{11}$

G 52

H $52\frac{2}{11}$

J $52\frac{10}{11}$

K NH

3

706
× 80

A 56,480

B 56,408

C 56,068

D 5,648

E NH

4

$12\frac{1}{8}$
$+ 4\frac{1}{4}$

F $8\frac{1}{8}$

G $16\frac{1}{6}$

H $16\frac{3}{8}$

J $16\frac{3}{16}$

K NH

5

$1.758 \times 3.6 =$

A 0.63288

B 6.3288

C 63.288

D 632.88

E NH

6

$\frac{5}{6} \div \frac{2}{9} =$

F $3\frac{3}{4}$

G $4\frac{3}{4}$

H $\frac{5}{27}$

J $5\frac{2}{7}$

K NH

7

$8\frac{7}{8} - 3\frac{5}{6} =$

A $5\frac{1}{24}$

B $5\frac{1}{8}$

C $5\frac{3}{54}$

D $5\frac{3}{16}$

E NH

8

$0.9\overline{)0.72}$

F 8

G 0.8

H 0.08

J 0.008

K NH

GO ON

9 Tony brought a 132-ounce jug of a sports drink to football practice. If he wanted to share it equally with his 11 friends, how much would each person receive?

A 11 ounces

B 10 ounces

C 8 ounces

D 7 ounces

E NH

10 A paper company has two factories that produce cardboard boxes. Factory A produces $2\frac{3}{4}$ million boxes a year and Factory B produces $4\frac{2}{3}$ million boxes a year. What is the total cardboard box production for the company in one year?

F $7\frac{5}{12}$ million

G $7\frac{7}{12}$ million

H 8 million

J $8\frac{2}{3}$ million

K NH

11 Dominic bought 2 soccer balls for $39.45 each and a pair of soccer cleats for $44.99. Without including tax, how much did he spend altogether?

_____

_____

_____

_____

12 Danielle and 5 of her friends won 108 six-packs of juice drinks in a radio promotional contest. How many six-packs of drinks should Danielle receive as her $\frac{1}{6}$ share?

A 11

B 12

C 16

D 18

E NH

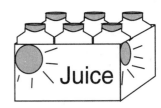

13 Marty tests water samples for the state park department. This morning he is preparing to test water from Lost Hollow Stream. How many $2\frac{1}{2}$-liter beakers can Marty fill with the 15 liters of water he has collected from the stream?

F 12

G 8

H 6

J 37.5

K NH

14 Diane's craft club raised money by raffling a quilt the members had made. They raised $986 by selling tickets. The quilt cost $135 to make. How much profit did the club make?

_____

_____

_____

_____

_____

STOP

Listening

Sample A

    A avoid

    B concentrate

    C mix

    D separate

 STOP

For questions 1–17, darken the circle for the word or words that best complete the sentence.

1   A completed

    B late

    C arrived

    D recent

2   F weak

    G ill

    H strong

    J lonely

3   A forgiven

    B encouraged

    C forbidden

    D taxed

4   F guard

    G servant

    H athlete

    J clerk

5   A speaker

    B carpenter

    C architect

    D governor

6   F an expert

    G a specialist

    H a veteran

    J a beginner

7   A welcome it

    B ignore it

    C follow it

    D include it

8   F following

    G next

    H previous

    J effective

9   A long

    B crumbling

    C winding

    D straight

10   F necessary

    G unimportant

    H optional

    J intelligent

11   A planning

    B strength

    C skill

    D frailty

12   F resist

    G welcome

    H deny

    J acknowledge

13   A soothed

    B comforted

    C bothered

    D relieved

14   F releasing

    G enlisting

    H rejecting

    J training

15   A false

    B humorous

    C truthful

    D complete

16   F different

    G famous

    H current

    J beautiful

17   A dread

    B peace

    C confidence

    D trust

▶ **GO ON**

Sample B

    A gases from burning fuels that mix with rain

    B heavy rainfall

    C rain that falls on forests

    D rain that falls over farms

For questions 18–30 darken the circle for the word or words that best answer the question.

18   **F** trees

    G stones

    H houses

    J calendars

19   **A** calendar

    B village

    C castle

    D school

20   **F** New York

    G England

    H Mexico

    J Holland

21   **A** "An Ancient Mystery"

    B "Fun Vacation Spots"

    C "Understanding Geology"

    D "The English Calendar"

22   **F** other countries

    G shopping malls

    H large cities

    J cold climates

23   **A** nacho

    B caramel

    C barbecue

    D butter

24   **F** pierce the skins

    G steam them first

    H microwave them

    J use a small amount of oil

25   **A** placing them in a steamer

    B baking them in an oven

    C cooking them quickly over high heat

    D microwaving them

26   **F** "A Well-Balanced Diet"

    G "Cooking Techniques for Vegetables"

    H "Steaming Vegetables"

    J "Vegetable Recipes"

27   **A** a biology book

    B a gardening book

    C a plant book

    D a cookbook

28   **F** refreshments

    G games

    H contests

    J music

29   **A** in the auditorium

    B in the school office

    C in your classroom

    D at a PTA meeting

30   **F** on May 30th

    G on the last day of school

    H in the morning

    J on April 30th

Language

Sample A

Shari is planning to write a letter to her community library to request that the library purchase books about hot-air balloons. Before she writes the letter, she wants to find the titles of some books on the subject. She is currently reading the book *Ballooning*. To help her find the titles of other books on ballooning, she should look in this book's—

A title page.

B bibliography.

C index.

D dictionary.

 STOP

For questions 1–4, darken the circle for the correct answer, or write in the answer.

In social studies class, Paul was assigned to write a report on some aspect of the history of transportation. He decided to research sailing ships and use this as the subject of his report.

1 What should Paul do before he writes his report?

A think of some famous sailing ships to include in his report

B reread his report for errors in sentence structure

C make a list of topics to include in his report

D check a dictionary for spellings of words to include in his report

2 What would Paul *not* want to include in his report?

F a chapter on ancient sailboats

G the development of steamships

H a discussion of the importance of the change from square to triangular sails

J a chapter on famous sailing ships

3 Where is the best place for Paul to find the most recent information about the design of modern sailing ships?

A a newspaper

B the *Readers' Guide to Periodical Literature*

C a telephone directory

D an encyclopedia

4 What method could Paul use to organize his thoughts before he writes his report?

_____

_____

_____

_____

_____

GO ON ▶

Here are the Table of Contents and the Index from a book Paul found on the history of sailing ships. Read them carefully. Then answer questions 5–9.

Table of Contents

Index

5 Which pages would have information on the voyages of the Golden Hind?

_____

_____

_____

6 Paul wanted to find information about explorers and the ships they used. All of these pages would be useful *except*—

F 40

G 42–45

H 55

J 28–30

7 Which chapter should Paul read to find the most information about the earliest kinds of sailing ships?

A Chapter 1

B Chapter 2

C Chapter 3

D Chapter 4

8 Which chapter should Paul read to find the most information about the ships used by Christopher Columbus when he landed in America?

F Chapter 3

G Chapter 4

H Chapter 5

J Chapter 6

9 Paul wanted to write a paragraph about a galleon used for fighting. On which pages could he probably find the most useful information on this topic?

_____

_____

_____

_____

_____

_____

_____

GO ON ▶

Here is a rough draft of the first part of Paul's report. Read the rough draft carefully. Then answer questions 10–16.

The History of Sailing Ships

The origin thousands of years ago, sailing ships date back to. Historians believe
(1)   (2)

that the earliest civilization to use sailing ships was that of the ancient Egyptians.

The shape of the sail on the earliest sailing ships was square. A square-shaped
(3)   (4)

sail moved the earliest sailing ships. The mast, designed like a flagpole, held up
(5)

the sail. Papyrus, a fibrous reedlike plant, grows plentifully along the Nile
(6)

River. Besides being used to make a writing material, mats, and sandals,
(7)

papyrus was used to make the earliest sails. Surprisingly, this early type of
(8)

sailing ship is still used along the Nile in Egypt today. In the 1700s, most navies
(9)

in the world were known as fleets.

As time passed, the Egyptians change in their sailing ships. They reworked
(10)   (11)

the mast so it was shaped like a long narrow A. The mast was secured to the
(12)

ship with ropes. The boats by the crewmen who paddled them.
(13)

GO ON

10 Correctly rewrite sentence 1.

_____

_____

_____

_____

_____

_____

_____

11 Which sentence needlessly repeats an idea?

A   2

B   3

C   4

D   5

12 Which of these sentences could be added after sentence 2?

F   The Egyptians used these ships to sail the Nile River.

G   The largest fighting ships, at this time, were made of iron.

H   By 1900 sailing ships were mostly used for pleasure or sport.

J   Why did people use sailing ships instead of steamboats?

13 Which sentence does *not* belong in paragraph 2? Write the number.

_____

_____

_____

_____

14 What is the best way to write sentence 10?

A   The Egyptians changed their sailing ships as time passed.

B   As time passed, the Egyptians changes in their sailing ships made.

C   As time passed, change in their sailing ships the Egyptians made.

D   As it is written.

15 Which of these sentences could be added after sentence 12?

F   Drawings of boats with sails have been found on early Egyptian pottery and on the walls of tombs.

G   Greek ships sailed everywhere in the Mediterranean world, from the Black Sea in the east to Spain in the west.

H   The ropes were lashed to the bow and to the stern of the ships.

J   The Egyptian ships were used to transport papyrus to the interior of Africa for trade.

16 Which group of words is *not* a complete sentence?

A   9

B   11

C   12

D   13

GO ON

Here is the next part of the rough draft of Paul's report. This part has certain words and phrases underlined. Read the draft carefully. Then answer questions 17–24.

The phoenician civilization was also known for its sailing ships. The powerful
(14)   (15)

Phoenicians were great sailors, traders navigators, and colonizers. They
(16)

controlled the trade on the Mediterranean Sea. They also had a large fleet of
(17)

sailing ships that were sturdy enough for the open seas of the Atlantic Ocean.

Phoenician ships had masts made from the timber of cedar trees and had
(18)

oars made of oak. In addition the boards for the hull were made from the timber
(19)

of fir trees. The hulls or frames of the sailing ships, were solidly built with ribs
(20)

for extra support. The front and back of the hull was sharp curved upward for
(21)

faster, smoother sailing. Linen cloth from Egypt was used for the sails.
(22)

Studying the construction of the earliest sailing ships makes people today
(23)

appreciate the skills of these early sailors. Anyone researching the history of
(24)

sailing ships were surprised at the seaworthiness of these early ships.

GO ON

17 In sentence 14, **The phoenician civilization is best written—**

F The Phoenician Civilization

G The Phoenician civilization

H the Phoenician civilization

J As it is written.

18 In sentence 15, **sailors, traders navigators, and colonizers is best written—**

A sailors, traders, navigators, and colonizers

B sailors and traders, navigators, and colonizers

C sailors and traders, and navigators and colonizers

D As it is written.

19 In sentence 17, **They also had is best written—**

F They also have

G We also had

H He and she also had

J As it is written.

20 In sentence 19, **In addition the boards is best written—**

A In addition the boards,

B In addition, the boards,

C In addition, the boards

D As it is written.

21 In sentence 20, **hulls or frames of the sailing ships, is best written—**

F hulls or frames of the sailing ships

G hulls, or frames of the sailing ships,

H hulls or frames, of the sailing ships

J As it is written.

22 In sentence 21, **was sharp curved upward is best written—**

A was sharp curve upward

B was sharpest curve upward

C were curved sharply upward

D As it is written.

23 In sentence 23, **makes people today is best written—**

F made people today

G gives people today

H has given people today

J As it is written.

24 In sentence 24, **were surprised is best written—**

A am surprised

B will be surprised

C will have been surprised

D As it is written.

GO ON

For questions 25–36, read each sentence carefully. If one of the words is misspelled, darken the circle for that word. If all the words are spelled correctly, then darken the circle for *No mistake*.

25   She was <u>horse</u> from <u>cheering</u> after the team's big <u>victory</u>. <u>No mistake</u>
                    F   G   H   J

26   I <u>dout</u> that the <u>package</u> will <u>arrive</u> today. <u>No mistake</u>
     A   B   C   D

27   Bill has <u>surffed</u> every <u>beach</u> on the northern <u>coast</u> of Hawaii. <u>No mistake</u>
               F   G   H   J

28   The actor's voice was <u>amplifyed</u> so he could be heard <u>throughout</u> the <u>theater</u>. <u>No mistake</u>
                      A   B   C   D

29   The Department of <u>Commerce</u> <u>imposed</u> a new <u>tariff</u> on certain foreign imports. <u>No mistake</u>
                  F   G   H   J

30   Her <u>house</u> is near the <u>intrasection</u> of Main Street and Willow <u>Avenue</u>. <u>No mistake</u>
      A   B   C   D

31   We have had very <u>unpleasant</u> <u>whether</u> <u>lately</u>. <u>No mistake</u>
               F   G   H   J

32   Muriel <u>wisked</u> the eggs well to make a <u>fluffy</u> <u>omelet</u>. <u>No mistake</u>
          A   B   C   D

33   Most <u>historians</u> consider Athens the <u>birthplace</u> of <u>democratcy</u>. <u>No mistake</u>
          F   G   H   J

34   The new budget <u>includes</u> a one-percent <u>increase</u> in sales <u>tacks</u>. <u>No mistake</u>
                 A   B   C   D

35   My <u>physics</u> teacher <u>illustrated</u> her point by using a <u>transparentcy</u>. <u>No mistake</u>
         F   G   H   J

36   Juanita <u>practices</u> the <u>piano</u> for two hours every <u>afternoon</u>. <u>No mistake</u>
          A   B   C   D

STOP

Answer Sheet

STUDENT'S NAME			SCHOOL:
LAST	FIRST	MI	TEACHER:

FEMALE ○   MALE ○

(Name grid columns with bubbles A–Z for each column)

BIRTH DATE

MONTH		DAY		YEAR	
Jan ○		⓪	⓪	⓪	⓪
Feb ○		①	①	①	①
Mar ○		②	②	②	②
Apr ○		③	③	③	③
May ○			④	④	④
Jun ○			⑤	⑤	⑤
Jul ○			⑥	⑥	⑥
Aug ○			⑦	⑦	⑦
Sep ○			⑧	⑧	⑧
Oct ○			⑨	⑨	⑨
Nov ○					
Dec ○					

GRADE ④ ⑤ ⑥ ⑦ ⑧

TEST BEST®
FOR TEST PREP

Fill in the circle for each multiple-choice answer. Write the answers to the open-ended questions on a separate sheet of paper.

STECK-VAUGHN
BERRENT
A Harcourt Company

TEST 1   Reading Comprehension

SA Ⓐ Ⓑ Ⓒ Ⓓ

1 Ⓐ Ⓑ Ⓒ Ⓓ	6 Ⓕ Ⓖ Ⓗ Ⓙ	12 Ⓕ Ⓖ Ⓗ Ⓙ	18 Ⓐ Ⓑ Ⓒ Ⓓ	24 Ⓕ Ⓖ Ⓗ Ⓙ	30 Ⓐ Ⓑ Ⓒ Ⓓ
2 Ⓕ Ⓖ Ⓗ Ⓙ	7 Ⓐ Ⓑ Ⓒ Ⓓ	13 Ⓐ Ⓑ Ⓒ Ⓓ	19 Ⓕ Ⓖ Ⓗ Ⓙ	25 Ⓐ Ⓑ Ⓒ Ⓓ	31 Ⓕ Ⓖ Ⓗ Ⓙ
3 Ⓐ Ⓑ Ⓒ Ⓓ	8 OPEN ENDED	14 Ⓕ Ⓖ Ⓗ Ⓙ	20 OPEN ENDED	26 Ⓕ Ⓖ Ⓗ Ⓙ	32 Ⓐ Ⓑ Ⓒ Ⓓ
4 Ⓕ Ⓖ Ⓗ Ⓙ	9 Ⓕ Ⓖ Ⓗ Ⓙ	15 Ⓐ Ⓑ Ⓒ Ⓓ	21 Ⓐ Ⓑ Ⓒ Ⓓ	27 OPEN ENDED	33 OPEN ENDED
5 Ⓐ Ⓑ Ⓒ Ⓓ	10 Ⓐ Ⓑ Ⓒ Ⓓ	16 OPEN ENDED	22 Ⓕ Ⓖ Ⓗ Ⓙ	28 Ⓐ Ⓑ Ⓒ Ⓓ	
	11 OPEN ENDED	17 Ⓕ Ⓖ Ⓗ Ⓙ	23 Ⓐ Ⓑ Ⓒ Ⓓ	29 Ⓕ Ⓖ Ⓗ Ⓙ	

TEST 2   Reading Vocabulary

SA Ⓐ Ⓑ Ⓒ Ⓓ

1 Ⓐ Ⓑ Ⓒ Ⓓ	4 Ⓕ Ⓖ Ⓗ Ⓙ	8 Ⓕ Ⓖ Ⓗ Ⓙ	11 Ⓐ Ⓑ Ⓒ Ⓓ	14 Ⓕ Ⓖ Ⓗ Ⓙ	18 Ⓐ Ⓑ Ⓒ Ⓓ
2 Ⓕ Ⓖ Ⓗ Ⓙ	5 Ⓐ Ⓑ Ⓒ Ⓓ	SB Ⓐ Ⓑ Ⓒ Ⓓ	12 Ⓕ Ⓖ Ⓗ Ⓙ	15 Ⓐ Ⓑ Ⓒ Ⓓ	19 Ⓕ Ⓖ Ⓗ Ⓙ
3 Ⓐ Ⓑ Ⓒ Ⓓ	6 Ⓕ Ⓖ Ⓗ Ⓙ	9 Ⓐ Ⓑ Ⓒ Ⓓ	13 Ⓐ Ⓑ Ⓒ Ⓓ	16 Ⓕ Ⓖ Ⓗ Ⓙ	20 Ⓐ Ⓑ Ⓒ Ⓓ
	7 Ⓐ Ⓑ Ⓒ Ⓓ	10 Ⓕ Ⓖ Ⓗ Ⓙ	SC Ⓐ Ⓑ Ⓒ Ⓓ	17 OPEN ENDED	21 OPEN ENDED

TEST 3   **Part 1: Math Problem Solving**

SA Ⓐ Ⓑ Ⓒ Ⓓ	**8** Ⓐ Ⓑ Ⓒ Ⓓ	**16** OPEN ENDED	**24** OPEN ENDED	**32** Ⓐ Ⓑ Ⓒ Ⓓ	**40** Ⓕ Ⓖ Ⓗ Ⓙ
1 Ⓐ Ⓑ Ⓒ Ⓓ	**9** OPEN ENDED	**17** Ⓕ Ⓖ Ⓗ Ⓙ	**25** Ⓐ Ⓑ Ⓒ Ⓓ	**33** Ⓕ Ⓖ Ⓗ Ⓙ	**41** OPEN ENDED
2 Ⓕ Ⓖ Ⓗ Ⓙ	**10** Ⓕ Ⓖ Ⓗ Ⓙ	**18** Ⓐ Ⓑ Ⓒ Ⓓ	**26** Ⓕ Ⓖ Ⓗ Ⓙ	**34** Ⓐ Ⓑ Ⓒ Ⓓ	**42** Ⓐ Ⓑ Ⓒ Ⓓ
3 OPEN ENDED	**11** Ⓐ Ⓑ Ⓒ Ⓓ	**19** OPEN ENDED	**27** Ⓐ Ⓑ Ⓒ Ⓓ	**35** OPEN ENDED	**43** Ⓕ Ⓖ Ⓗ Ⓙ
4 Ⓐ Ⓑ Ⓒ Ⓓ	**12** Ⓕ Ⓖ Ⓗ Ⓙ	**20** Ⓕ Ⓖ Ⓗ Ⓙ	**28** OPEN ENDED	**36** Ⓕ Ⓖ Ⓗ Ⓙ	**44** Ⓐ Ⓑ Ⓒ Ⓓ
5 Ⓕ Ⓖ Ⓗ Ⓙ	**13** Ⓐ Ⓑ Ⓒ Ⓓ	**21** Ⓐ Ⓑ Ⓒ Ⓓ	**29** Ⓕ Ⓖ Ⓗ Ⓙ	**37** Ⓐ Ⓑ Ⓒ Ⓓ	**45** Ⓕ Ⓖ Ⓗ Ⓙ
6 Ⓐ Ⓑ Ⓒ Ⓓ	**14** Ⓕ Ⓖ Ⓗ Ⓙ	**22** OPEN ENDED	**30** Ⓐ Ⓑ Ⓒ Ⓓ	**38** Ⓕ Ⓖ Ⓗ Ⓙ	**46** Ⓐ Ⓑ Ⓒ Ⓓ
7 Ⓕ Ⓖ Ⓗ Ⓙ	**15** Ⓐ Ⓑ Ⓒ Ⓓ	**23** Ⓕ Ⓖ Ⓗ Ⓙ	**31** Ⓕ Ⓖ Ⓗ Ⓙ	**39** Ⓐ Ⓑ Ⓒ Ⓓ	**47** OPEN ENDED

Part 2: Math Procedures

SA Ⓐ Ⓑ Ⓒ Ⓓ Ⓔ	**2** Ⓕ Ⓖ Ⓗ Ⓙ Ⓚ	**5** Ⓐ Ⓑ Ⓒ Ⓓ Ⓔ	**8** Ⓕ Ⓖ Ⓗ Ⓙ Ⓚ	**11** OPEN ENDED	**14** OPEN ENDED
SB Ⓕ Ⓖ Ⓗ Ⓙ Ⓚ	**3** Ⓐ Ⓑ Ⓒ Ⓓ Ⓔ	**6** Ⓕ Ⓖ Ⓗ Ⓙ Ⓚ	**9** Ⓐ Ⓑ Ⓒ Ⓓ Ⓔ	**12** Ⓐ Ⓑ Ⓒ Ⓓ Ⓔ	
1 Ⓐ Ⓑ Ⓒ Ⓓ Ⓔ	**4** Ⓕ Ⓖ Ⓗ Ⓙ Ⓚ	**7** Ⓐ Ⓑ Ⓒ Ⓓ Ⓔ	**10** Ⓕ Ⓖ Ⓗ Ⓙ Ⓚ	**13** Ⓕ Ⓖ Ⓗ Ⓙ Ⓚ	

TEST 4   **Listening**

SA Ⓐ Ⓑ Ⓒ Ⓓ	**6** Ⓕ Ⓖ Ⓗ Ⓙ	**12** Ⓕ Ⓖ Ⓗ Ⓙ	**18** Ⓕ Ⓖ Ⓗ Ⓙ	**24** Ⓕ Ⓖ Ⓗ Ⓙ	**30** Ⓕ Ⓖ Ⓗ Ⓙ
1 Ⓐ Ⓑ Ⓒ Ⓓ	**7** Ⓐ Ⓑ Ⓒ Ⓓ	**13** Ⓐ Ⓑ Ⓒ Ⓓ	**19** Ⓐ Ⓑ Ⓒ Ⓓ	**25** Ⓐ Ⓑ Ⓒ Ⓓ	
2 Ⓕ Ⓖ Ⓗ Ⓙ	**8** Ⓕ Ⓖ Ⓗ Ⓙ	**14** Ⓕ Ⓖ Ⓗ Ⓙ	**20** Ⓕ Ⓖ Ⓗ Ⓙ	**26** Ⓕ Ⓖ Ⓗ Ⓙ	
3 Ⓐ Ⓑ Ⓒ Ⓓ	**9** Ⓐ Ⓑ Ⓒ Ⓓ	**15** Ⓐ Ⓑ Ⓒ Ⓓ	**21** Ⓐ Ⓑ Ⓒ Ⓓ	**27** Ⓐ Ⓑ Ⓒ Ⓓ	
4 Ⓕ Ⓖ Ⓗ Ⓙ	**10** Ⓕ Ⓖ Ⓗ Ⓙ	**16** Ⓕ Ⓖ Ⓗ Ⓙ	**22** Ⓕ Ⓖ Ⓗ Ⓙ	**28** Ⓕ Ⓖ Ⓗ Ⓙ	
5 Ⓐ Ⓑ Ⓒ Ⓓ	**11** Ⓐ Ⓑ Ⓒ Ⓓ	**17** Ⓐ Ⓑ Ⓒ Ⓓ	**23** Ⓐ Ⓑ Ⓒ Ⓓ	**29** Ⓐ Ⓑ Ⓒ Ⓓ	

TEST 5   **Language**

SA Ⓐ Ⓑ Ⓒ Ⓓ	**8** Ⓕ Ⓖ Ⓗ Ⓙ	**16** Ⓐ Ⓑ Ⓒ Ⓓ	**24** Ⓐ Ⓑ Ⓒ Ⓓ	**32** Ⓐ Ⓑ Ⓒ Ⓓ
1 Ⓐ Ⓑ Ⓒ Ⓓ	**9** OPEN ENDED	**17** Ⓕ Ⓖ Ⓗ Ⓙ	**25** Ⓕ Ⓖ Ⓗ Ⓙ	**33** Ⓕ Ⓖ Ⓗ Ⓙ
2 Ⓕ Ⓖ Ⓗ Ⓙ	**10** OPEN ENDED	**18** Ⓐ Ⓑ Ⓒ Ⓓ	**26** Ⓐ Ⓑ Ⓒ Ⓓ	**34** Ⓐ Ⓑ Ⓒ Ⓓ
3 Ⓐ Ⓑ Ⓒ Ⓓ	**11** Ⓐ Ⓑ Ⓒ Ⓓ	**19** Ⓕ Ⓖ Ⓗ Ⓙ	**27** Ⓕ Ⓖ Ⓗ Ⓙ	**35** Ⓕ Ⓖ Ⓗ Ⓙ
4 OPEN ENDED	**12** Ⓕ Ⓖ Ⓗ Ⓙ	**20** Ⓐ Ⓑ Ⓒ Ⓓ	**28** Ⓐ Ⓑ Ⓒ Ⓓ	**36** Ⓐ Ⓑ Ⓒ Ⓓ
5 OPEN ENDED	**13** OPEN ENDED	**21** Ⓕ Ⓖ Ⓗ Ⓙ	**29** Ⓕ Ⓖ Ⓗ Ⓙ	
6 Ⓕ Ⓖ Ⓗ Ⓙ	**14** Ⓐ Ⓑ Ⓒ Ⓓ	**22** Ⓐ Ⓑ Ⓒ Ⓓ	**30** Ⓐ Ⓑ Ⓒ Ⓓ	
7 Ⓐ Ⓑ Ⓒ Ⓓ	**15** Ⓕ Ⓖ Ⓗ Ⓙ	**23** Ⓕ Ⓖ Ⓗ Ⓙ	**31** Ⓕ Ⓖ Ⓗ Ⓙ	

CUT HERE